More Than 100 Easy Recipes
for Pure Food When You
Can't Buy 100% Organic

FRESH
CHOICES

Thanks for your effort in support of student health.
Rochelle
Feb 2013

David Joachim
and Rochelle Davis, Executive Director, Generation Green
Foreword by Peter Hoffman, Chef/Owner of Savoy
and Chair of Chefs Collaborative

The recipes for Guacamole with Fresh Tortilla Chips, Chunky Tomato Salsa, Watermelon Gazpacho, and Chile Rellenos Gratin first appeared in slightly different form in *Cooking Light*, May 2003. The recipes for Orange Banana Smoothie, Tofu Bites, Peanut Butter Banana Spirals, Creamy Tomato Rice Soup, and Tortellini with Broccoli and Chickpeas first appeared in slightly different form in *Cooking Light*, September 2003. The recipes for Jesse Cool's Steak with Fruit Sauce and Chicken with Dried Cherries, Olives, and Chiles are adapted from *Your Organic Kitchen* (Rodale, 2000) with permission from Jesse Cool and Rodale Inc.

Printed in the United States of America

Rodale Inc. makes every effort to use acid-free ∞ , recycled paper ♻ .

Cover design by Carol Angstadt
Cover photo by Mitch Mandel (hardcover) or John Wilkes (paperback)
Interior book design by Joanna Williams

Library of Congress Cataloging-in-Publication Data

Joachim, David.
    Fresh choices : more than 100 easy recipes for pure food when you
can't buy 100% organic / David Joachim and Rochelle Davis ; foreword by Peter Hoffman.
      p.   cm.
    Includes bibliographical references and index.
    ISBN 0–87596–895–3 hardcover
    ISBN 0–87596–896–1 paperback
    1. Cookery, American. 2. Cookery (Natural foods) I. Davis, Rochelle, date.
  II. Title.
TX715.J59 2004
641.5'63—dc22   2003025695

Distributed to the book trade by St. Martin's Press

2 4 6 8 10 9 7 5 3 1 hardcover

2 4 6 8 10 9 7 5 3 1 paperback

RODALE

WE **INSPIRE** AND **ENABLE** PEOPLE TO IMPROVE
THEIR LIVES AND THE WORLD AROUND THEM

FOR MORE OF OUR PRODUCTS
WWW.RODALESTORE.COM
(800) 848-4735

For Ronald Joachim (1945–2003),
who loved the earth and enjoyed its gifts

Contents

Foreword

Every Monday morning, after I drop my kids off at school, my workweek begins with a trip to the farmers' market in Union Square in New York City. I usually ride my bicycle to the market in search of the best locally grown fruits and vegetables for my restaurant, Savoy. As a chef, I spend more time foraging for my restaurant's food than actually cooking it. This might seem strange to those who think that a chef belongs behind the stove. For me, ensuring quality for my customers starts with knowing as much as I can about where my ingredients come from.

To put it simply, choosing good food is the first step toward good cooking. I teach my children this principle by taking the whole family to shop at farmers' markets. We also visit real farms at least twice a year. The tactile experience of seeing firsthand what broccoli looks like on the whole plant and searching for ripe strawberries among the plant's green leaves teaches my kids more about taste and choosing good food than I could ever explain to them. My kids know what thriving plants look like and recognize the beauty of unprocessed, local food that doesn't come wrapped in plastic from the supermarket.

I read the classic children's story *The Farm* by Lois Lenski to my kids. With beautiful illustrations, it depicts a thriving farm where horses, cows, pigs, chickens, and rabbits are raised amid vivid fields and orchards of corn, wheat, apples, and cherries. The book helps to remind us that all food comes from living organisms. Food is real and alive. It doesn't spring into existence shrink-wrapped in plastic any more than money grows on trees.

The Farm, along with endless recitations of "Old MacDonald Had a Farm," reinforces for us the vital image of a farm as a diverse and humane microcosm, fecund, and supportive of life. Sadly, this image of the farm is largely false, at least by today's commercial food-production standards. This way of life is rapidly disappearing from the American landscape. But it's not too late. We can still have *The Farm* and carefully produced, good-quality food. By visiting farms and showing that we really do care how our food is raised, by shopping at farmers' markets and supporting local farmers, and by teaching our children what good food is and should be, we can keep *The Farm* alive.

Most Americans are so busy with other things these days, we've nearly lost the basic ability to choose good food. Many people haven't the faintest idea how food is produced and what good-quality raw ingredients should look like—let alone how to prepare them well. In many households today, preparing meals with parents or grandparents has been replaced by watching food channels of distant chefs performing on-camera wizardry that bears little relation to home cooking.

We've also lost some of the community and social comfort provided by time spent in a warm kitchen cooking food together. The ever-present availability of ready-made meals has certainly made modern life more convenient—but not necessarily any better. The fact is, when we make even the smallest effort to cook for friends and family, we're providing more than just food on the table. We're nourishing our loved ones with the time, energy, and good ingredients that pass from our hands to their bodies.

My goal in the kitchen is to provide great meals by enhancing the natural taste, vibrancy, and beauty of the foods I choose. That means starting with the best raw materials I can find. As a chef, I spend a lot of time looking for clear information and learning about the products I use. Because I spend so much time researching ingredients, I'm constantly asked by customers and friends, What should I be buying? What should I know?

The best answer I can give is this: Find out as much as you can about your food before buying it. It's not as simple as saying "buy organic" or "buy in season." These answers don't address all the complexities of modern food production. Today, you can buy an organic frozen TV dinner. But that food choice, while organic, still gives you a heavily processed, low-quality meal. Similarly, shoppers in New York can buy shiny red apples from Washington State throughout the fall. But buying seasonally makes little sense if your seasonal fruit traveled 3,000 miles across the country to get to you. The point of buying seasonally is to buy what's available *in your area* at any given time of the year.

Regardless of where you live or what your food concerns are, the one thing that you can do to get better food on your table is to learn about how your food is produced. That's why this book is so invaluable. It shows you how different foods are produced and explains the value of buying locally. Knowing these things can help you choose better food and, ultimately, be a better cook. While good cooking is more than the sum of the raw materials, it certainly begins there.

—Peter Hoffman, *chef/owner of Savoy and chair of Chefs Collaborative*

Acknowledgments

Writing this cookbook has been like growing a garden. We planted a few seeds, they sprouted, and then they grew . . . and grew . . . and grew! But the book wouldn't have had a fighting chance in its environment without all the people who helped out during the growing season.

Hugs and a thousand thank-yous to Lisa Ekus, a swift agent who, like the wind, scattered the seed of this book to many publishers before it found its home in Rodale soil.

And a toast to Margot Schupf, who gently covered the seed and allowed it to take root and grow.

For infinite rays of sunshine, we owe a debt of thanks to Jeffrey Bouley, a skilled researcher and writer who helped make several plots thrive.

Many thanks to the rest of the staff at Generation Green, especially Cheryl Bondy Kaplan and Gail Siegel, for making sure our rows were straight and our tomato plants were staked.

Inspiration and information came from people at numerous environmental, health, and food organizations. We are indebted to these folks and their organizations for generously sharing their time and expertise: the American Egg Board, American Pastured Poultry Producers Association, Living Oceans Program at the National Audubon Society (especially Dr. Carl Safina), National Marine Fisheries Service, Marine Fish Conservation Network, Marine Stewardship Council, Monterey Bay Aquarium, Seafood Choices Alliance, Pew Oceans Commission, Chefs Collaborative (particularly Peter Hoffman), Organic Trade Association, International Federation of Organic Movements, Organic Consumers Association, Worldwatch Institute, Center for Children's Health and the Environment at Mount Sinai School of Medicine (especially Dr. Phil Landrigan), Institute for Agriculture and

Trade Policy (thank you, David Wallinga!), Consumer's Union, Union of Concerned Scientists, Natural Resources Defense Council, Environmental Working Group (thanks, Kai Roberts!), Environmental Defense, Center for Science in the Public Interest (especially Dr. Michael Jacobson), and Pesticide Action Network North America.

We are especially grateful to the members of our scientific advisory board for their careful weeding and replanting and for their bird's-eye view of the garden during its final weeks before harvest.

Thanks also to Adam Goldberg for some insightful criticism.

To Alisa Bauman, we can't thank you enough for providing a lead on where to grow this garden. And a big thank-you to Mark Bowman for recipe testing during the dog days of summer.

Cheers to all the recipe testers and tasters who sampled the fruits of our labor and offered good advice, especially Chris and Lisa Neyen, Selene Yeager, Dave Pryor, Tom Aczel, Michele Raes, Josh and Stacie Lampe, Andrew and Kim Brubaker, and Beth and Bill Strickland.

To our best friends in food, Sharon Sanders, Raghavan Iyer, and Normand LeClair, thank you for your warm companionship, great table talk, and inspiration.

Huge thanks to Shea Zukowski, a dream editor who weeded, watered, and nurtured this book into a full-grown garden of earthly delights.

To Jean Rogers, you have an eagle eye for correctness on the printed page. Thanks for turning that eye our way.

For yet another brilliant design, we humbly bow to designers Carol Angstadt and Joanna Williams.

Reams of gratitude to Cathy Gruhn, Dana Bacher, and the rest of the publicity staff at Rodale for your tireless enthusiasm and marketing savvy.

To Jackie Kendall and Jan Schakowsky, pioneers in organizing for better food labeling, thank you for decades of inspiration, friendship, and leadership.

Thanks to Brian and Emily Rolling for ferreting out just the right pop stars, for eating waffles in the morning and fruits and vegetables in the afternoon, and for helping to make the world a better place. Yes, you really can be anything you want after college!

And to Ken Rolling, what can be said? We started our journey long ago and who knew we would come this far? Deepest love and gratitude for helping with Generation Green and standing by all our work for more than 20 years.

A special, teary-eyed thank-you to Ron Joachim, who embraced an organic lifestyle for 57 years and died suddenly in a car accident during the writing of this book. Warm hugs and love to Bonnie Joachim, whose strength and love continues to light the path they took together.

To August and Maddox Joachim, thanks for being willing guinea pigs and fun kitchen helpers. And to Christine Bucher, eternal kisses and gratefulness: Without your steady support and love, this book would have never been written.

Advisory Board

Lynn R. Goldman, M.D., M.P.H., professor, Johns Hopkins University, Bloomberg School of Public Health, chair, Children's Environmental Health Network

Kai Robertson, director of Private Sector Initiatives, Environmental Working Group

David Wallinga, M.D., M.P.H., Antibiotic Resistance Project director, Institute for Agriculture and Trade Policy

Susan West, M.P.H., Environmental Health Education and Outreach for Physicians for Social Responsibility

Andy Igrejas, Environmental Health Campaign director, National Environmental Trust

Rabbi Daniel Swartz, executive director, Children's Environmental Health Network

Photo Credits

Rick Bayless (page 114): © Tim Turner

Raffi Cavorkian (page 89): © Carrie Nuttall

Nancy and Jim Chuda (page 235): © Wendy Merriman

Jesse Cool (page 138): © Elizabeth Fenwick

Lynn Goldman, M.D., M.P.H. (page 273): © Howard Korn

Greg Higgins (page 50): © 2003 Basil Childers

Gary Hirshberg (page 202): Courtesy of Stonyfield Farm

Michael Jacobson (page 232): Courtesy of Michael Jacobson

Phil Landrigan, M.D., M.S.C. (page 5): Courtesy of Phil Landrigan, M.D., M.S.C.

Nell Newman (page 84): © Luciana Pampalone

John Peterson (page 265): Courtesy of John Peterson

Kelly Preston (page 204): © Rod Spicer

LaDonna Redmond (page 74): © Jolesch Photography

Jan Schakowsky (page 177): © Dean La Prairie

Jane Seymour (page 146): © Charles Bush

Peggy Shepard (page 118): Courtesy of WE ACT

Sandra Steingraber (page 22): © Carrie Branovan for Organic Valley 2004

Rodney Taylor (page 40): Courtesy of Rodney Taylor

Organic and Beyond

I recently stopped by my local grocery store to pick up some fresh strawberries for a recipe I was developing: Strawberry-Stuffed French Toast. But my store only had conventionally grown strawberries. According to federal pesticide data, they are one of the foods highest in pesticide residues, so I really wanted organic strawberries. I believe that's the right choice for my family's health and for the environment. What was I to do? Buy the conventional strawberries and admit defeat? No! Why would I when a better alternative was in plain sight? Instead, I chose to buy blueberries—a terrific substitute for strawberries and one of the fruits lowest in pesticide residues. I ended up making blueberry-stuffed french toast, and it was absolutely delicious. (See the final recipe, which also includes cranberries, on page 200.)

The concept of such choices is at the heart of this book. Of course, organic foods are usually the first choice for those concerned with their health and the health of our planet. But organic food isn't always available to everyone. What's more, organic food seems too expensive to many consumers. And the real fact is, sticking to environmental and health principles isn't always simply a matter of buying organic. There *are* healthy alternatives to organic foods—it's a matter of knowing which ones make the best choice in a tough situation.

In this book, my coauthor, Rochelle Davis, and I help you navigate such decisions. We show you which conventionally grown fruits and vegetables are lowest in pesticides and provide great-tasting recipes using those foods. We also show you which foods are highest in pesticide residues and point out viable alternatives, such as blueberries instead of strawberries. And we steer you in the direction of the purest and safest meats, poultry, seafood, and dairy products. Options like pasture-raised chicken, grass-fed beef, and rBGH-free milk are increasingly available in local food markets.

These are the foods used throughout the recipes in this book. If you follow the recipes and use the ingredients as written, rest assured your diet will be good for you and for the planet—without having to buy organic every time you shop.

Some recipes, like Frozen Chocolate Pudding Pops (page 210), are a surefire hit with kids. Others, like Lemon Herb Cornmeal Cake with Macerated Berries (page 274), are perfect for entertaining and showcase the fabulous flavors of naturally healthy foods. Plus, you'll find a mix of dishes for everyday meals as well as for special occasions. For instance, Sautéed Chicken with Sage and Gingered Plums (page 135) brings together fruit, herbs, and poultry in a simple yet full-flavored entrée that gets to the table in less than 30 minutes. All of the recipes were tested in a home kitchen, and while these recipes keep one sharp eye on health, the other is squarely focused on flavor.

In addition to the recipes, you'll notice profiles of key people throughout the book. They are people like Jan Schakowsky, a congresswoman fighting for safer consumer protection laws; John Peterson, a farmer who runs one of the country's largest community-supported farms; Jesse Cool, a chef who uses local, organic foods in her California restaurants; and Raffi, an entertainer who has helped spread the message of respecting our children's health to millions of people. Many of these people have generously shared their favorite recipes in the book.

The book also explains how government policies affect your ability to make good food choices. Current policies are given in every chapter, but these laws are constantly changing. To get the latest updates, see our free newsletter *Fresh Choices Quarterly,* available from freshchoices@generationgreen.org or by calling 800-652-0827.

We hope that the recipes, stories, and food-choosing tips in these pages will help to keep you and your family healthy and fully satisfied by what you eat. These days, choosing the best food has become something of a minefield, a series of necessary questions that don't always have easy answers. Our goal is to provide you with a road map that leads to a more picturesque landscape. In this landscape, food is grown with your health and the planet's health in mind so that the foods you eat are a source of pure enjoyment without hesitation.

Chapter 1

From Farm to Fork: Good Reasons to Choose Pure Food

When I was growing up in northeast New Jersey, I witnessed more and more of our 2-acre lawn disappear. My parents were avid gardeners who gradually replaced our semirural grass with purple coneflower, plump red tomatoes, and frilly baby lettuce greens. This was my introduction to organic farming. My mom and dad worked hard to build and enrich the local soil rather than relying on synthetic chemicals to help their plants grow.

In 1993, my parents ripped up what little lawn we had left and fully committed themselves to small-scale organic farming. That year, they opened a farmer's market called Homegrown Naturally and began selling organic vegetables, fruits, and flowers to local residents, restaurants, and grocery stores. The business took off, as did many similar organic enterprises.

In general, the mid 1990s saw explosive growth of the organic food industry. Since 1992, U.S. organic food sales have increased by 23 percent every year, according to Organic Trade Association figures. That growth was about five times faster than food sales in general. And sales of organic food continue to grow today for a variety of reasons.

Some people choose organic food for health purposes. Some buy it because they like the taste better. Others want to support farming methods that don't do unnecessary damage to the environment. Whatever their reasons, more and more people are choosing to eat organic food. And while mounting evidence confirms that organic foods are usually the best choice for human health and the environment, it also reveals that our options are hardly so black and white. There is a wide and wonderful range of fresh choices to consider among foods that don't carry an organic label—and that group includes some conventionally grown foods, too.

For instance, laboratory analysis shows that some conventionally grown fruits and vegetables (such as strawberries and spinach) typically contain enough pesticide residues that they may be harmful, especially to children. So presented with a choice, it makes good sense to buy organic strawberries and spinach. But you can also choose conventionally grown alternatives that are low in pesticide residues, such as blueberries and chard. Likewise, some fish varieties (like tuna and swordfish) have tested high enough in environmental contaminants such as mercury that the Food and Drug Administration warns pregnant women to limit or avoid eating these varieties. So if you're in a similar situation, it might help to know that wild Pacific and Alaskan salmon are good alternatives to tuna and swordfish.

You might wonder why nutritious foods like fish, vegetables, and fruits suddenly pose so many health concerns. Well, keep in mind that the foods themselves still offer quite a few health benefits, and in general most people should still eat them. But because of the way they are grown and processed, it may help your health in the long run to choose certain foods rather than others. To find out why, let's take a quick look at how our food is produced.

The Age of Industrial Food Production

Agriculture has been developing ever since humans first domesticated plants such as corn more than 6,000 years ago. In the United States, some of the most significant developments occurred during the 1940s and 1950s, when food production became increasingly industrialized. Before then, many farmers grew a variety of crops every year and rotated their plantings to complement the strengths of certain crops and compensate for the weaknesses of others. Crop rotation helped to minimize damage caused by pests as well as to reinvigorate the soil. Most agricultural farmers also raised animals and periodically rotated their cattle, sheep, hogs, and chickens on different pastures so that their manure would be dispersed over a large area of farmland. This practice, known as rotational grazing, naturally fertilized the soil, which helped to raise high-quality plants that, in turn, made it easier to grow healthy animals.

Farmers approached the farm as a total system linking plants, animals, food, and humans together in a dynamic cycle of production and consumption. Farming was fairly labor-intensive, but nothing was wasted. Today, this sort of farming might be called "organic" or "sustainable." Back then, it was just the best way to run a farm.

As our nation grew, its food needs changed, and within a few short decades, the business of producing food had become highly competitive. Farmers had to cut costs, boost production, and increase profits to survive. To do so, many farmers isolated agriculture from livestock farming to focus production on just one type of food.

The Rise of Intensive Agriculture

In the 1940s, mechanical inventions such as the self-propelled combine reduced manual labor needs and sped up production of grain commodities. As competition for profits increased, agricultural farmers began to concentrate on growing the most profitable crops such as corn, soy, and wheat. This new approach, often referred to as monocropping or monoculture, streamlined the farm system and boosted profits. But it eliminated (or at least weakened) the soil-enriching practices of crop rotation and livestock grazing, making farmers more dependent upon synthetic or petroleum-based fertilizers in place of natural manure for strengthening the soil.

Around the same time, pharmaceutical companies also helped to reduce the labor costs of farming and increase crop yields by developing chemical formulations that could kill pests. While some arsenic- and lead-based pesticides had been used widely since the late 1800s, several new formulations came on the market and saw widespread use during the mid-century agriculture boom. Methyl bromide, a fumigant once widely applied to soil and crops to kill insects and weeds, was first approved for sale in 1947. The herbicide atrazine was approved in 1959 and has since become the most heavily used pesticide in U.S. history, with some 60 million pounds applied annually.

Dr. Phil Landrigan
Children Are Our Common Responsibility

Early in his career, pediatrician Phil Landrigan, M.D., joined the Centers for Disease Control as an epidemiologist. His job? Chasing down epidemics that affected children. In the mid 1970s, he studied lead poisoning outbreaks near smelters in El Paso, Texas, and Kellogg, Idaho. These were the first systematically analyzed epidemics linked to toxic exposure. Ultimately, Landrigan's work shut down one smelter and cleaned up others, prompting his lifelong commitment to reducing children's exposure to toxic substances.

Landrigan zeroed in on food in 1988, when he chaired the National Academy of Sciences Committee on Pesticides in the Diets of Infants and Children. The Committee determined that children were being exposed to toxic levels of pesticides due to their unique vulnerability to toxins coupled with inadequate protective policies. Legislators responded in 1996 by passing the Food Quality Protection Act. "Some progress has been made," notes Landrigan. "The EPA has pulled several pesticides off the market." But, he says, much more work needs to be done.

Landrigan currently works on legislative and regulatory reform as chair of the department of community and preventive medicine as well as director of the Center for Children's Health and the Environment at the Mount Sinai School of Medicine in New York City. He is also responsible for helping to establish the Office of Children's Health Protection at the EPA. Landrigan advocates for children's rights on both sides of the political corridor. "Children are not a partisan issue," he says. "All political factions have a common responsibility to protect children from harm."

As a politically aware pediatrician, Landrigan recommends getting organized and getting active to protect children. That could be as simple as urging your local grocery store produce manager to stock more organic produce. On the homefront, he advises parents to offer children more fruits and vegetables and fewer sweets and red meats. Buy in season and organic, if possible. Or visit farmers' markets for local produce treated with fewer pesticides. To prevent toxic buildup in the body, he suggests eating a variety of fruits and vegetables throughout the week. For more tips, see Landrigan's book *Raising Healthy Children in a Toxic World*.

Chlorpyrifos, another widely used agricultural insecticide, was approved in 1965. Since the mid 1960s, total pesticide use in America has more than tripled. Today, more than 1 billion pounds of agricultural pesticides are purchased each year in the United States.

These synthetic chemicals have dramatically increased crop yields for farmers, who have become dependent upon them to make their crops profitable. But pesticides have also been harmful to our health and environment. Many pesticides in current use have been shown to cause brain and nervous system damage, birth defects, developmental abnormalities, reproductive system damage, endocrine (hormone) and immune system dysfunction, and certain cancers. These health risks are strongest for children because their sensitive bodies are still developing, but adults may be affected, too.

The Concentration of Meat, Poultry, and Fish Production

As American agriculture became more efficient, streamlined, and industrialized throughout the latter half of the 1900s, so did livestock production. In fact, so much grain was produced in agriculture that surplus grain was fed to livestock. And because grains such as corn are higher in calories than grass or pasture, the new diet brought livestock up to slaughter weight much sooner than the previous pasture-based diet. As a result, meat production increased, and with improvements in meatpacking, refrigeration, and shipping, meat became more widely available around the country and around the world.

To stay competitive, many livestock producers began to focus on the most profitable food animals: cattle, hogs, chickens, and turkeys. Producers also found new ways to reduce their labor costs and simplify the production process by relying on smaller, more confined housing arrangements. Today, the technical term for the place where most livestock animals are raised is a "concentrated animal feeding operation," or CAFO. The typical CAFO confines about 75,000 cows or 100,000 chickens in an enclosed feedlot. According to the U.S. Environmental Protection Agency (EPA), nearly a quarter million such operations produce the majority of the meat and poultry sold in U.S. supermarkets and restaurants.

Modern fish farming, also known as aquaculture, took its cues from the same intensive production model and has yielded similar results. Atlantic salmon makes a particularly good example of aquaculture's rise and subsequent effect on marine environments. Due to weak regulation and overfishing, Atlantic salmon was put on the endangered species list in 2000. As a result, aquaculture operations flourished, and now more than 70 percent of the fresh salmon we eat comes from fish farms. The typical salmon farm confines about 250,000 fish in a metal or open-mesh net pen in coastal waters. Such farms produce about 2 metric tons of waste a day—about the same amount that humans produce in a small city. Because the net pens float in the ocean, any mismanaged waste, pollution, disease, or escaped fish from these farms directly affect the surrounding marine ecosystems. Today, the growth of aquaculture annually outpaces that of all other animal food production, according to the United Nations' Food and Agriculture Organization (FAO).

Both on land and in the sea, intensive animal feeding operations have dramatically sped up the process of producing the meat, poultry, and fish we eat. But they have also increased the spread of disease among wildlife and humans. In most CAFOs, overcrowding and growth-promoting feed create an unnatural amount of stress that invites poor health. Parasites and diseases tend to spread rapidly, and huge amounts of contaminated waste are released into the surrounding soil and water, which leads to excessive and damaging pollution. These environmental problems eventually become human health problems because pollutants make their way up the food chain, ending up in the food we eat and consequently in our bodies. Research continues to link human illnesses and diseases to environmental contaminants released as by-products of modern food production.

Healthy and Sustainable Food Production

Despite their environmental and human health impact, our current food systems aren't all bad. Industrial agriculture, aquaculture, and factory farming of animals have benefited us in multiple ways. They have increased profits for food producers

What Is Organic?

It may be hard to believe, but not too long ago organic food was the *only* choice when you went to market. The term "organic" has only surfaced in the wake of agriculture's intensive industrialization in the late 1940s when agricultural chemical use skyrocketed.

By the 1950s, though, some people were already raising red flags. One of them was British scientist Norman Moore, the first to suggest that declining eagle populations resulted from the overuse of DDT, a very popular insecticide at the time. Rachel Carson's 1962 book, *Silent Spring*, popularized Moore's theory that using chemicals to grow food might carry a hefty price tag. The "back-to-the land" movement of the late 1960s and early 1970s followed from this increased awareness and focused on growing food naturally without synthetic chemical inputs.

The only problem with this initial return to organic agriculture was the lack of standards. What one farm called organic might not be practiced on another farm. California, one of the nation's key agricultural states, took the first steps to establish some parameters when 50 California farmers created the California Certified Organic Farmers (CCOF) guidelines in 1973.

The CCOF guidelines introduced the idea of standardized production techniques certified by neutral third-party inspectors. The standards also formed the basis for the California Organic Foods Act, which became law in 1990.

Around the same time, activity at the federal level began to take shape. In the late 1980s, the organic industry petitioned Congress to draft the Organic Foods Production Act (OFPA) to define the term organic. The OFPA was passed, but it was only the first step, mostly requiring the United States Department of Agriculture (USDA) to write a regulation that explained what organic was. It took more than a decade of further debate to establish clear-cut national organic standards. The USDA's standards for production of organic foods finally became law in December 2000 and went into effect on October 21, 2002.

The organic standards encompass pages and pages of detailed requirements (to read them, visit the USDA Web site at www.ams.usda.gov/nop). The basic rules are that organic food is produced without using most conventional synthetic pesticides, petroleum- or sewage-sludge-based fertilizers, bioengineering, or ionizing radiation. Organic meat, poultry, eggs, and dairy products must come from animals fed 100 percent organic feed and no antibiotics or growth hormones. Before a product can be labeled "organic," an inspector visits the farm where the food is produced to make sure the farm meets USDA standards. As for the labels you might see on foods, here's what they mean.

100 Percent Organic. Must contain 100 percent organically produced ingredients, not counting added water and salt.

Organic. Must contain at least 95 percent organic ingredients, not counting added water and salt, and cannot contain added sulfites.

Made with Organic Ingredients. Must contain at least 70 percent organic ingredients, not counting added water and salt. Cannot contain added sulfites, with the exception of wine, which may contain a certain level of added sulfur dioxide.

and strengthened our national economy in the global marketplace. Combined with federal agricultural subsidies, modern food systems have made food more plentiful and less expensive for Americans than ever before. We currently spend less money on food than any other nation in the world—about 10 percent of our annual income.

But the quality of low-cost, mass-produced food is sometimes less than desirable: fruits and vegetables with limp textures, lackluster colors, weak flavors, and fewer nutrients; runny eggs with pale-colored yolks; and uniform-tasting meats lacking complex, interesting flavors. If the ultimate goal of a food system is to produce nourishing food that satisfies and tastes great, preventing disease and improving the quality of life, then industrial food production is not ideal. Many scientists say that current intensive food production systems will not be sustainable over the long haul.

Since the mid 1960s, concerns over our health and the vitality of our environment have helped organic and sustainable methods of food production to flourish. Many small farms have abandoned the industrial view of agriculture and focused on producing high-quality food while protecting and improving the quality of soil and water, reducing dependence on nonrenewable resources such as synthetic pesticides and petroleum-based fertilizers, and enriching the ecosystems in which food is produced.

According to a 2003 report from the International Federation of Organic Agriculture Movements (IFOAM), more than 56 million acres are now under organic management worldwide. The Organic Trade Association reports that 39 percent of Americans now regularly use organic products, and total U.S. retail sales are expected to reach $20 billion by 2005.

We now have two general systems of food production competing in the national and global marketplace. On the one hand, there is industrial agriculture, aquaculture, and factory farming of animals. This production system approaches the farm as a factory with inputs (such as pesticides, feed, and fertilizers) and outputs (such as corn, beef, and fish). The goal of industrial food farming is to increase profits by producing the most possible output of food for the least possible input of money.

On the other hand, there is organic and sustainable agriculture, along with environmentally responsible fishing, aquaculture, and animal husbandry. This food production system approaches the farm as an ecosystem that thrives through the careful management of natural resources such as soil, water, and surrounding wildlife. The goal of organic and sustainable food production is to increase profits by producing healthy, high-quality food while reducing the use of synthetic chemical inputs and maintaining the environment's biodiversity, productivity, and natural ecological processes. While relatively new, the organic food system has been steadily building throughout the United States and other developed nations for the past 50 years.

Why Buy Locally?

Food in the United States travels an average of 1,300 miles from the farm to the market shelf. While many states are prolific agricultural producers, almost every state in the country buys 85 to 90 percent of its food from someplace else. This food importing can sometimes weaken local and state economies. In Massachusetts, for example, the food import imbalance causes $4 billion in annual losses to the state economy, according to University of Massachusetts researchers. Analysts say that with some adjustments, Massachusetts could produce closer to 35 percent of the statewide food supply and thereby contribute $1 billion annually to the state economy.

Our current long-distance food system also takes a toll on the environment. According to a 2002 study from the Washington, D.C.-based Worldwatch Institute, the value of international food trade has tripled over the last 40 years, and the tonnage of food shipped between nations has grown fourfold, while population has only doubled. The study concluded that a basic diet (including a variety of meats, grains, fruits, and vegetables) using imported ingredients burns up four times more energy and generates four times the greenhouse gas emissions of an equivalent diet with ingredients from domestic sources.

In contrast, buying locally uses relatively few resources and generates an insignificant amount of greenhouse gases. Buying food from local farmers strengthens regional and state economies by giving money directly to farmers rather than food traders, distributors, brokers, and other middlemen. In many cases, it also helps to support small family farms and helps consumers get to know the people who grow and produce their food.

More Good Reasons to Choose Organic and Sustainably Produced Food

If you haven't recently compared organic food with conventionally grown food, conduct a side-by-side taste test at home. Buy organic carrots and conventionally grown carrots. Eat both of them raw and taste for yourself. Organic carrots are almost always juicier, sweeter, and fuller in flavor. Or grill up two fillets of salmon: one farmed and one wild. There's an extremely good chance that the wild salmon will taste better.

While organic food of the 1970s sometimes looked less appealing, most of today's organic and sustainably harvested food appears more vibrant and tastes richer and more complex than conventionally grown food. An increasing body of studies also shows that organic and sustainably produced food tends to be higher in key nutrients and lower in harmful environmental contaminants. Better taste, higher nutrient content, and fewer harmful chemicals are all pretty good reasons to choose organic or sustainably produced food when you can. Here are details on the most convincing reasons.

Get More Nutritious Food

Recent studies have finally confirmed what organic farmers have suspected all along: If you grow plants in well-nourished soil, those plants will be healthier than plants grown in depleted soil. Similarly, if you feed nutrient-rich plants to animals, those animals will be healthier than those fed a nutrient-poor diet.

In 2001, Johns Hopkins University researcher Virginia Worthington analyzed the nutrient composition data of various types of produce from 41 studies published between 1947 and 1997. She found that organic fruits and vegetables contained an average of 27 percent more vitamin C, 21 percent more iron, 29 percent more magnesium, 14 percent more phosphorus, and 15 percent fewer harmful nitrates than conventionally grown produce.

A 2002 study from scientists at the University of Strathclyde in Scotland also found more salicylic acid in commercial organic vegetable soup than in nonorganic soup.

Plants produce salicylic acid as a defense against stress and disease. This natural substance is also the anti-inflammatory agent in aspirin and has been shown to combat hardening of the arteries and bowel cancer. So more of it in our food is a good thing.

Most recently, in 2003, researchers at the University of California found that organic produce is higher in cancer-fighting phenolics than conventionally grown plants. Phenolics are antioxidants also produced by plants as natural defenses against pests. The study suggests that synthetic pesticides actually suppress the production of phenolics in plants, while natural fertilizers boost plant levels of these anticancer compounds. And more antioxidants in your food is a good thing, because antioxidants help prevent the free-radical damage that naturally occurs at the cellular level in our own bodies.

Organic and sustainably produced meat, poultry, eggs, and milk have also tested higher in key nutrients. Animals raised on pasture or grass (rather than growth-promoting grain) simply take in more beneficial nutrients like omega-3 fatty acids and conjugated linoleic acid (CLA). While omega-3 fats are best known as heart-protecting compounds found in certain fish, all omega-3s originate in plant foods like grass and algae. About 60 percent of the fatty acids in grass are omega-3s, created during photosynthesis. As a result of grazing on pasture, grass-fed beef can contain as much as 6 times more beneficial omega-3 fats than feedlot beef. Similarly, eggs from pasture-raised hens have up to 20 times more omega-3s than eggs from hens raised in confinement, according to laboratory analysis.

CLA, another type of fatty acid, has recently been shown to help prevent excess weight gain, heart disease, and cancer—particularly breast cancer. Several recent studies indicate that milk, butter, cheese, yogurt, and other dairy products from grass-fed cows are higher in CLA than dairy products from conventionally farmed dairy cows. Pasture-raised meat, poultry, eggs, and dairy products have also tested higher in vitamin E and vitamin A.

The evidence is mounting that organic and sustainably produced food contains higher concentrations of key nutrients. Grown from nutrient-rich soil, water, and grass, these types of food may actually give you a leg up on preventing disease and healing illness.

Enjoy Better-Tasting Food

As if the higher nutrient content of organic food isn't compelling enough, the better taste of most organic food is what wins many people over.

Great chefs have long sought out organic and carefully produced fruits, vegetables, fish, meat, poultry, and dairy products to use in their restaurants. These foods almost always taste better than the mass-produced, "factory-farmed" food sold in supermarkets. Chefs know that great-tasting food begins with clean, unpolluted water, land, and air, which is the goal of environmentally sustainable farming and fishing. Some recent taste tests provide evidence that chefs know what they're talking about.

Food critics for the *New York Times* and *Washingtonian* magazine recently published taste tests of poultry and found organic chickens and turkeys to be superior to conventionally farmed poultry in taste, texture, and color. If you've never tasted the difference between a supermarket chicken and an organic one, try organic and taste for yourself.

A pair of recent studies on apples also found that organic methods produce higher-quality, better-tasting fruit. Researchers at Washington State University farmed three plots of Golden Delicious apples over a 6-year period using organic, conventional, and integrated pest management (a combination of organic and conventional methods) techniques. The organic apples ranked first for taste and texture. Plus, the organic orchard ranked number one for environmental sustainability, profitability, and energy efficiency.

Another recent comparative study, from Swiss researchers at the Research Institute of Organic Agriculture, found that organically grown apples are higher in overall quality than conventionally grown apples. This study concluded that organic apples were firmer, higher in fiber and phenolic compounds, and more complex in flavor than conventional apples.

Reduce Your Body's Chemical Burden

All pesticides and mismanaged animal waste contribute to soil and water pollution and indirectly affect our health. But several environmental contaminants make their way directly into our food. Many of these chemicals are produced by the plastics and power-generating industries and persist in the environment for decades, accumulating in the tissues of animals and plants. These include PCBs (polychlorinated biphenyls), dioxins, furans, phthalates, and metals like lead and mercury. As these contaminants make their way up the food chain, they become more concentrated in the foods that we eat.

For instance, PCBs are synthetic chemicals that don't burn easily, so they were once used as coolants and lubricants in transformers, capacitors, and other electrical equipment. PCBs were banned in 1976 because it became apparent that they accumulate in the environment and our bodies, causing health problems such as nervous system damage and certain cancers. However, due to their persistence and bioaccumulation, PCBs continue to contaminate our food supply and can even be found in human bodies. Intensively farmed salmon are especially high in PCBs because they are fed concentrated pellets of fish oil derived from fatty fish parts, the very parts in which PCBs tend to accumulate over time. A 2003 report from the Environmental Working Group tested salmon samples from around the United States and concluded that farmed salmon are likely the most PCB-contaminated protein source in our food supply.

However, if you choose wild salmon instead of farmed when you can, you'll help to lower your body's overall chemical burden. Wild salmon feed on krill and shrimp rather than PCB-laden fish pellets. If wild salmon isn't available, look for other responsibly farmed and sustainably harvested fish types; see the chapter on fish, beginning on page 91.

This particular example is one of the more dramatic illustrations of why buying organic and sustainably produced food helps to lower your exposure to chemical residues. But looking at the bigger picture, buying any organic food when you can makes sense for the same reasons.

Protect Future Generations

Children are especially vulnerable to pesticides' effects because, pound for pound, children eat more food, drink more water, and breathe more air than adults. For example, infants under age 1 consume 15 times more apple products relative to their body weight than the national average, yet apples have the highest pesticide residues of any fruit. Children's immature metabolic systems are also less able to detoxify and excrete many chemical toxins. Plus, children have greater relative exposure to harmful substances because they crawl, play outside, and put things in their mouths more than adults do. In studying eight different pesticides, the National Resources Defense Council found that, on average, preschoolers received four times greater exposure to harmful pesticides than adults.

That's why it makes good sense to be cautious with food, one of the primary sources of exposure to pesticides for most children. Apples, pears, peaches, and grapes are among the most common sources of exposure for American children age 5 and under, according to a recent analysis of federal data by the Environmental Working Group (EWG). For healthy alternatives to these high-pesticide foods, see the chapter on fruit, beginning on page 27.

While no food will ever be completely pesticide-free due to the environmental persistence of these chemicals, choosing organic food can dramatically reduce a child's exposure. In 2002, the first scientific comparison of organic and conventionally grown produce found that organic fruits and vegetables do indeed contain fewer pesticide residues than conventionally grown fruits and vegetables—about one-third fewer residues overall. A 2003 study from the University of Washington also found that preschool children who ate organic food had one-sixth the concentration of pesticides in their bodies as did children who ate conventionally grown food. In the study, children who ate organic food had pesticide exposure levels below EPA safety standards, while the children on conventional diets tested above those standards.

Even if you can't get organic fruits and vegetables, you can still reduce pesticide exposure. Certain conventionally grown fruits and vegetables such as blueberries and broccoli are naturally lower in pesticide residues than other conventionally grown produce. Check out the fruit chapter (page 27) and the vegetable chapter (page 57) to find out more about conventionally grown produce that you can buy with confidence when organic isn't an option.

Pesticide Toxicity and Children

Pesticides are often studied for acute and obvious toxicity. However, recent research shows that many children experience a type of continuous exposure to low doses of pesticides that may cause health problems over time. One theory: Their developing bodies have more time to accumulate toxins and experience the compounded effect of toxic buildup.

For example, roughly 12 million children in America suffer from developmental disabilities. About 25 percent of these disorders are attributable (in part) to environmental toxins such as pesticides, according to an expert committee of the National Academy of Sciences convened in July 2000. Three recent animal studies provide evidence that constant exposure to low doses of chlorpyrifos (marketed as Dursban or Lorsban), a widely used organophosphate pesticide, can cause developmental disabilities. In 2003, the Centers for Disease Control and Prevention (CDC) released a report that found chlorpyrifos levels in American children to be about twice as high as those found in adults, showing that childhood behaviors do indeed result in more pesticides getting into children's bodies.

Other types of pesticides may also pose health risks for children. Some organochlorine pesticides are suspected of causing hormonal problems (or "endocrine disruption") in children. Studies have shown that organochlorines such as endosulfans and dieldrin may disturb the effects of hormones on human cells. Although research is preliminary, scientists suspect that recent increases in testicular cancer among boys and early onset of puberty in girls may be attributed to hormone-disrupting substances in the environment, including pesticides.

Despite the vulnerability of children to pesticide exposure, only 43 percent of the synthetic chemicals produced in high-volume quantities have been tested for potential human toxicity, and only 7 percent have been studied for possible developmental effects among children, according to research from the Center for Children's Health and the Environment at Mount Sinai School of Medicine in New York City.

In the absence of adequate federal testing, scientists have worked backward to observe the effects of chemical use on animals and humans. As a result, many pesticides have now been linked to brain and nervous system damage, certain cancers, immune disorders, and hormone dysfunction. Organophosphate insecticides are among the environmental contaminants that play a role in some of the major chronic illnesses and diseases afflicting American children, such as leukemia and other cancers, birth defects, learning disorders, and certain developmental or behavioral disorders.

Fortunately, new research into children's environmental health is beginning to get funding. The CDC, EPA, and some key child health organizations are funding a prospective study that will follow nearly 100,000 children from fetal development during pregnancy to age 21 and examine the effects of early environmental exposures on child health and development.

Improve Soil Quality

Protecting your health and the health of future generations is perhaps the most important reason to choose organic and sustainably produced food. And improving soil quality actually helps to achieve that goal. Soil fertility is typically viewed only as an environmental benefit of sustainable agriculture, but healthy soil eventually translates into healthy people. That's because nutrient-rich, living soil produces the most nutrient-rich foods. And when humans eat healthier, high-quality food, it helps to heal our illnesses and prevent life-threatening disease.

It's no secret that organic and sustainable methods of food production are much better for ensuring the long-term fertility of our soil than conventional, industrial agriculture. That's one reason why these modes of production have steadily grown since the 1960s. Every year, 3 billion tons of topsoil erode from cropland in the United States. Much of that soil erosion results from industrial farming practices. The intensive farming of single crops (monocropping) year after year depletes the soil and increases the need for synthetic fertilizers. Likewise, the industrial approach of concentrated animal-feeding operations requires enormous quantities of grain feed and produces animal waste that can contaminate nearby soil and water with excessive pollution from farm runoff. Globally, the concentrated production of beef and pork has had more impact on the world's soil than any other type of food production.

On the other hand, organic and sustainable food production treats soil as the foundation of a healthy food chain. Organic farmers work hard to protect and build healthy soil by rotating crops, cover-cropping, and composting. These agricultural methods produce richer soil due to the diversified plant life being grown. In rotations, farmers can plant crops like legumes that replenish plant nutrients and reduce the need for chemical fertilizers. A good example is soybeans, a valuable crop that converts nitrogen into a biologically useful form. Corn grown in a field previously planted with soybeans typically needs fewer nitrogen inputs to produce high yields.

Cover-cropping also helps to prevent soil erosion, suppress weeds, and improve soil quality. Rather than leave the ground bare or overtax it with another season of the same crop, organic and sustainable farmers often plant cover crops like hairy vetch,

Beyond the Supermarket

Sometimes, you have to look past the grocery store to get good-quality food. Knowing where your food comes from and how it is produced can also give you great peace of mind. Here are some alternative ways to buy food in your community.

Buy food at farmers' markets. According to the United States Department of Agriculture's (USDA) Agricultural Marketing Service, the number of farmers' markets in the United States jumped from 1,755 in 1994 to 2,863 in 2000. The number of farmers and consumers frequenting these markets tripled in the same period to 66,700 farmers serving 2.7 million American consumers in 2000. At a farmers' market or roadside stand, you can talk directly to farmers about how they grow or raise the food you're buying. Farmers learn about what customers want, too. These markets are one of the best ways for food producers and consumers to forge a direct relationship. To help find a farmers' market near you, go to www.localharvest.org or the USDA's farmers' market Web site at www.ams.usda.gov/farmersmarkets.

Visit a U-Pick farm. Many fruit farms open the orchards to customers who like to pick their own fruit. You may be able to pick apples, pears, blueberries, raspberries, or other fruits grown on the farm. Picking fruit yourself can be fun and a great way to directly support farmers. Keep in mind that fruit on U-Pick farms may be heavily sprayed with pesticides. Find out how the fruit is grown before you pick.

Join a CSA. Many farmers sell directly to customers through a system known as community supported agriculture (CSA). Customers, or "shareholders," pay for food at the beginning of the farmer's growing season to cover production costs. Then they receive a weekly box or bag of fruits, vegetables, eggs, cheese, meat, flowers, or whatever else the farmer grows and sells. More often than not, CSAs offer organically grown produce and meat, poultry, eggs, and dairy products from pasture-raised animals. Many CSAs allow you to choose what you want in your box each week; others give you a grab bag of goodies, including rare heirloom varieties of produce you would never find in a grocery store. CSAs are perhaps the easiest and best way to support smaller farmers, buy locally, and buy seasonally. More than 1,000 CSAs operate around the country. To find one in your area, visit www.localharvest.org.

Join a community garden. You may find that growing food yourself is the most rewarding way to get food on your table. Gardening can be a lot of fun. Children especially love to plant seeds in spring, watch the plants grow through the summer, and finally eat the fruits of their labor through the summer and fall. If you don't have land around your home to grow a garden, try growing herbs, tomatoes, and other vegetables in pots. Or join a community garden. Many communities, particularly in urban areas, are converting large vacant spaces into community farms. These farms help to provide access to healthy food and build upon the strengths of various community members. To find community farms in your area, visit www.communityharvestdc.org.

clover, or oats. These may not always be harvested for sale but are cost effective by reducing the need for chemical inputs such as herbicides, insecticides, and fertilizers.

Organic farmers further enrich and invigorate the soil by composting, the practice of incorporating manure and plant debris into the soil. All of these basic sustainable agriculture methods help to build healthy soil and improve yields by producing robust crops that are less vulnerable to pests.

Organic or pasture-raised meat and poultry can improve soil quality, too. Half of the world's total harvest of industrially produced grain goes to feeding livestock. Organically raised animals, however, are fed only grains grown with soil-enriching organic methods. Likewise, pasture-raised animals primarily eat a diet of easy-to-grow grass with only supplemental grain. Grass-fed animals fertilize the soil with manure as they graze on various pasturelands through the practice of rotational grazing.

Rest assured that when you buy organic and sustainably produced food, you are doing our soil a big favor.

Improve Water Quality

Of the more than 600 active pesticide ingredients registered for use in the United States, organophosphate insecticides account for approximately half of all insecticides used. A 2002 report from the Centers for Disease Control and Prevention (CDC) estimates that 60 million pounds of organophosphate pesticides are applied to about 60 million acres of U.S. agricultural crops annually, and an additional 17 million pounds are used per year in household pest control products and in lawn and garden sprays. These and other pesticides run off from farm fields and lawns into nearby water systems, where they pollute drinking water and lead to damaging algae overgrowth. The EPA itself estimates that pesticides pollute the primary source of drinking water for more than half of the country's population.

Intensive livestock farming also contributes to declining water quality. The nearly two trillion pounds of animal waste from livestock generated every year in the United States is typically transferred from the animal confinement area to giant storage "lagoons" until it can be liquefied and sprayed onto fields as fertilizer. The problem is that storage lagoons are prone to leaking, spills, and excessive runoff, which have caused widespread nitrogen pollution in our water. North Carolina, one of the country's largest pork producers, witnessed the most devastating manure spill on record in 1995. Twenty-five million gallons of hog manure spilled from a concentrated storage lagoon, killing about 10 million fish and closing more than 350,000 acres of coastal wetlands to shell fishing.

Living near such concentrated amounts of waste can be hazardous to local residents. According to a 2003 report from the EPA, the drinking water wells of more than 4.5 million Americans have been exposed to elevated levels of nitrates (the most widespread agricultural contaminant). High nitrate levels have been linked to gastrointestinal problems, miscarriages, and some types of cancers.

Less intensive and more sustainable methods of raising livestock help to minimize water pollution. When animals are raised on pasture and rotationally grazed rather than confined to feedlots, manure is deposited over a large area of grassland, where it naturally fertilizes the soil and doesn't adversely affect groundwater and drinking water.

Organic meat, while not necessarily grass-fed, also helps to improve water quality. Organically raised animals are fed only 100 percent organic feed. Growing that animal feed organically helps to keep massive amounts of unnecessary pesticides out of our drinking water supplies. The same goes for other organic or sustainably produced foods such as fruits, vegetables, and grains. These are grown without harmful chemicals and nitrogen fertilizers, which helps to conserve water resources and clean up our water supply over time.

Protect Farm Worker Health

Due to their proximity and constant exposure to agricultural chemicals and feedlot pollutants, farm workers and farm families carry a greater risk of developing health problems related to environmental contaminants. In fact, about 300,000 farm workers are poisoned every year by pesticides, according to the Office of Technology Assessment.

Farmers are also more likely to become infected by bacteria such as campylobacter and salmonella that flourish in the crowded, unsanitary conditions of concentrated animal feeding operations. And traditional antibiotics might not help to heal their illnesses. In most of these operations, antibiotics are routinely fed to livestock to compensate for the health risks of confinement. Widespread antibiotic use has accelerated the problem of bacteria becoming resistant to these antibiotics. As a result, once-reliable antibiotics have become less effective in treating human illness in all of us—but particularly among farm workers who are more directly exposed to antibiotic-resistant bacteria. The World Health Organization now considers antibiotic resistance one of the top three threats to public health and recommends banning all antibiotics in animal feed.

Animal waste creates additional problems for animal farm workers. Research shows that more than half of hog farm workers suffer from impaired breathing because they inhale noxious gases that accumulate inside confined hog facilities overloaded with decomposing manure.

Choosing responsibly raised beef, pork, chicken, and turkey can help to protect the health of farm workers. Producers on such farms avoid crowded growing conditions, manage waste better, and raise their livestock without antibiotics. Likewise, choosing fruits, vegetables, and other plant foods that are grown without synthetic pesticides can help to reduce farm workers' exposure to these harmful chemicals.

Help Small Family Farmers

Although more and more large-scale farms are making the conversion to organic practices, most organic farms are small, independently owned and operated family farms. Since the 1930s, the number of these farms has steadily declined from about 6 million to less than 2 million farms today. At the same time, the size of some farm operations has increased dramatically, indicating that the business of agriculture has become concentrated into the hands of just a few. In 1997, half of U.S. farm production came from only 2 percent of farms, according to the United States

SANDRA STEINGRABER
Taking Care of Internal and External Environments

For some people, the body is a temple. Others think of it more like a battlefield. But Sandra Steingraber, Ph.D., takes a wider view of the body as an entire environment—a world that needs to be nourished, cultivated, protected, and maintained to help protect future generations.

"The dangers in utero are unique because our children are at specific points of development they'll never be at again," says Steingraber, a biologist and author of the widely read books *Living Downstream: An Ecologist Looks at Cancer and the Environment* and *Having Faith: An Ecologist's Journey to Motherhood*. "We need to take pregnancy and motherhood out of its current cultural position and bring it into the world of policy and public health and decision making," she argues.

Steingraber's scientific work has shown that the womb is not an inherently safe haven like a space-craft protecting astronauts. Rather, it is an "open doorway" for the outside environment. "When pregnant, a woman is eating more and breathing more," Steingraber explains. "She is taking in more molecules of air, food, and water—and whatever toxic chemicals are present in the air, food, and water. My argument is that air pollution is a prenatal issue and that organic agriculture is part of prenatal care."

Even while Steingraber extols breast milk as the best food for human infants—providing strong immune systems, better IQs, and other developmental benefits—she notes that it could be so much better if the environment around us were less toxic. "Breast milk is the most polluted human food," she says. "One way of taking action and getting pesticides and other toxic chemicals out is to support organic agriculture. Eating organic may not have much effect on the purity of your own breast milk, but your daughters will have cleaner milk."

Steingraber, whose books take an intensely personal, emotional, and scientific view of environmental exposure to toxins, sees herself more as a messenger than as a direct agent of change. "Writing books and giving lectures is my way of planting seeds," she offers. "I don't always know what happens after I leave."

Steingraber is all too well aware of how environment affects our bodies. Her latest book, *Having Faith*, is based on her experiences as a mother of two very young children. And *Living Downstream* drew much from her 1979 diagnosis of bladder cancer at age 20—a disease she calls "a quintessential environmental disease."

"My autobiography continues to drive my science," she says. "Most public health scientists do their work because they have a personal connection."

Department of Agriculture (USDA). Another telling example: Just two companies now grow about 75 percent of carrots sold in North America.

As the number of farms has declined over the past 50 years, the value of international trade in food has tripled. Accordingly, the farmer's share of each food dollar has steadily dropped over the last 50 years, from 41 cents in 1950 to 30 cents in 1980 to about 15 cents today. Food distributors and brokers are making the lion's share of the profits rather than farmers.

Organic agriculture can be a lifeline for small farmers because it offers an alternative market in which food crops are more profitable. Buying organic and sustainably produced foods from local farms puts your food dollars directly into the hands of small family farmers rather than into the pockets of international food companies.

Support a True Economy

Organic and sustainably produced foods may seem expensive, but you can't get a better value for your money. Keep in mind that industrially produced food incurs several hidden costs. Your tax dollars pay for federal farm subsidies that keep conventional food prices low. You also pay indirectly for mass-produced food when your tax dollars go toward cleaning up hazardous waste and repairing environmental damage caused by industrial agriculture and animal farming.

Grass-fed beef makes a good example of sustainably produced food that's worth the slightly higher price tag. Grass-fed cattle takes longer to reach slaughter weight and the meat needs to age to make it juicy, so grass-fed beef is more expensive than grain-fed. But grass-fed beef incurs none of the hidden health costs associated with grain-fed beef, such as soil and water pollution, antibiotic-resistant bacteria, and *E. coli* poisoning from crowded, unsanitary growing conditions.

Plus, when you buy organic or sustainably produced food, more of your money is likely to go to the farmer who actually grew or produced the food—especially if you buy locally or direct from farmers' markets. And that represents a more equitable relationship between food producers and food consumers.

Promote Biodiversity

The industrial practice of monocropping single species of commodity crops tripled farm production between 1950 and 1970. But it dramatically reduced the diversity of plant life that could grow in the depleted soil. Organic farming, on the other hand, promotes biodiversity by growing a wide range of plants, including heirloom varieties of vegetables and other produce. These varieties tend to have more complex and interesting colors, shapes, textures, and tastes than the produce you find in most supermarkets.

While eating a variety of plant-based foods promotes biodiversity more directly, even eating pasture-raised beef can help to increase biodiversity. After being weaned as calves, most feedlot cattle never set hoof on pastureland. Pasture-raised cattle, however, typically graze over a range of grasslands. Researchers from Colorado State University found that the rotational grazing of grass-fed cattle encourages diverse plant life. Over a 55-year period, the researchers studied plant life on Colorado rangelands that had been either ungrazed by cattle or grazed lightly, moderately, or heavily. The most diverse plant life was found on the moderately grazed rangeland. Even the heavily grazed pasture had greater biodiversity than the ungrazed areas, which were overrun with a single species of prickly pear cactus.

Eat to Live

Eating great-tasting food is one of life's basic pleasures. Good food satisfies us, nourishes us, and sustains us far into the future. So why ruin a great-tasting meal with the suspicion that it may be tainted or contaminated in some way? Especially when worry-free alternatives are in plain sight?

Buying responsibly produced, high-quality food can give you great peace of mind. That may mean regularly or occasionally choosing fruits and vegetables labeled "organic," eggs labeled "free-range," chicken or beef labeled "pasture-raised," or milk labeled "rBGH-free." Even when you can't find 100 percent organic food, you have plenty of other healthy, environmentally sound choices. This book helps you navigate your way through those choices.

FEDERAL LEGISLATION
The Food Quality Protection Act and Its Shortcomings

Federal law is rarely perfect. And pesticide laws are no exception. To understand why, here's a quick look at how pesticides are currently regulated. The Environmental Protection Agency (EPA) is responsible for registering or licensing pesticide products for sale and use in the United States. However, both the EPA and the Food and Drug Administration (FDA) share the responsibility of establishing legal limits, or "tolerances," for pesticide residues in food. This shared role can make it difficult to implement new pesticide regulations.

For instance, the 1996 Food Quality Protection Act (FQPA) amended federal pesticide policy in three critical ways. First, it made human health risks a top priority. Previously, the EPA balanced the profits of pesticide companies against public health risks in making some decisions. Second, the act provided special protections for infants and children. Before FQPA, tolerances for pesticide residues in food were based on adult consumption only. Under FQPA, tolerances are set according to the diet and behavior of children, who are much more susceptible to the toxic effects of pesticide exposure. Third, the act recognizes multiple sources of pesticide exposure over time, rather than looking only at the isolated effects of each pesticide. As a result, certain classes of pesticides such as organophosphates are considered more dangerous.

The FQPA was a great step forward in ensuring a safe food supply for all Americans, particularly children. It helped to cut home uses of organophosphate pesticides and reduce exposures to these chemicals. However, because its key provisions address pesticide tolerances, which are regulated by both the EPA and FDA, government has been slow to implement the act. Eight years later, studies show that our food supply still contains toxic levels of pesticides. That's why it's important to use caution when choosing foods for your family, especially fresh produce. If you can't buy organic, choose produce with the least pesticide residues, such as bananas, broccoli, cabbage, cauliflower, corn, kiwi, mangoes, onions, peas, pineapple, plums, and watermelon. To stay informed on this and other food policy developments, sign up to receive *Fresh Choices Quarterly* at FreshChoices@generationgreen.org or call 800-652-0827.

Fruit

Apple orchards and berry farms stretch across the rolling hills near my home in eastern Pennsylvania. When summer weather finally makes its way to the area, my son August begs me to take him berry picking at the "U-Pick" farms. These weekend outings are a special time for us. We play hide-and-seek around the blueberry bushes, fill our baskets with the most plump, deep-colored berries, and taste more than a few specimens along the way for "quality control."

Most of these farms don't grow their blueberries organically. But I don't mind so much. Blueberries are one of the fruits lowest in pesticide residues, according to recent analyses of government data by the Environmental Working Group. I know that these blueberries won't pose a significant health threat to my family. Besides, the experience of picking berries with my family—organic berries or not—is more important to me than avoiding pesticides every single time we eat. Organic would be ideal, but it's hard to find organic U-Pick berry farms in my area. Until it becomes easier, I'm going to keep on picking blueberries from conventionally grown crops.

Apples, however, are another story. As much as I love them, apples have some of the highest pesticide residues of any fruit. American children under age 1 consume 15 times more apple products relative to their weight than most adults and older kids, which means that kids are exposed to many more of the harmful pesticides used on apples.

Only one of the orchards in my area grows organic apples, and they don't open the farm for customers to pick the apples themselves. So we buy organic apples, apple juice, and applesauce whenever possible. We're not fanatics though. We sometimes give in to the apple-picking urge and visit the conventional orchards. I don't think it's going to kill us to eat those apples now and then. But on those rare occasions, I always peel the apples to remove surface pesticides and lower the risks of exposure.

Apples and blueberries paint a fair picture of the range of pesticide residues on various fruits and the relative health risks. The bottom line is that some conventionally grown fruits are more likely to contain high residue levels, making it wise to buy organic when you can. Others, however, are relatively low in pesticides, giving you more leeway if you need to buy the conventionally grown version.

Smart Picks among Conventionally Grown Fruit

While Americans ate 28 percent more fresh fruit in 2000 than in the 1970s, current U.S. Department of Agriculture (USDA) figures show that we could be doing better. Less than 40 percent of American adults and only 26 percent of children over the age of 1 eat the recommended two to five servings of fruit a day. And there are plenty of reasons why we should try to do better.

Simply put, fruits are among the most nutritious foods on the planet. They contain virtually no fat, and they're loaded with fiber, vitamins, minerals, and health-protecting antioxidants. They also give you the satisfying sweetness of sugar without the empty calories of most other sweets. And fruit may even help you lose weight. USDA researchers recently found that people who eat more fruit tend to have a lower body mass index (a measure of your weight relative to your height) and lower overall weight.

So what fruits should you choose when organic isn't available? A number of fruits tend to be low in pesticide residues and have little negative impact on the environment. Coincidentally, they also tend to be higher in valuable nutrients than other varieties. Here's the rundown on which conventionally grown fruits you can choose with confidence.

Tropical Fruits

Whenever you need healthy fruit fast, reach for bananas, plantains, pineapples, mangoes, papayas, or kiwifruits. Compared with other types of fruit, tropical fruits are sprayed less and have lower pesticide concentrations. They're also some of the most nutritious fruits available to us.

One banana supplies nearly 400 milligrams of potassium. Research shows that eating bananas a few times a week can help to lower your lifetime risk of high blood pressure, heart attack, and stroke. Bananas are also a good source of other electrolytes, which help to replace and regulate fluids lost during exercise. After your next workout, replenish yourself with a banana and some water instead of a bottle of sports drink. (Ditto when the kids come in from a full day of play.) Or try the Orange Banana Smoothie on page 38. If you find bananas labeled "Rainforest Alliance Certified" in your market, grab 'em. While not strictly organic, these bananas are grown using environmentally responsible practices you can feel good about.

Kiwis make another highly nutritious and low-pesticide choice. In fact, kiwis contain more nutrients per calorie than any other fruit. Two kiwis supply more potassium than a banana, as much fiber as grapefruit, and twice as much vitamin C as an orange. These little powerhouses are also high in glutamate and arginine, two amino acids that have been shown to help your body secrete growth hormones that reduce the effects of aging. Plus, a kiwi packs easily and has a refreshingly tart-sweet citrus-like flavor that kids tend to like.

Can't find kiwis? Try mangoes instead. Mangoes are low in chemical residues yet high in vitamin C, fiber, and beta-carotene. One mango provides 6 grams of fiber. That's more than what you'll get in a cup of cooked oat bran.

If kiwis, mangoes, or papayas are too hard to find in your area, try pineapple—another tropical fruit that's usually lower-pesticide than many other fruits. Fresh pineapple contains bromelain, an enzyme that aids digestion by breaking down proteins. (That's one reason why pineapples go so well with pork—bromelain acts as a natural meat tenderizer.) And pineapples are high in immunity-boosting vitamin C. One cup of pineapple chunks supplies 40 percent of your daily vitamin C needs, while

8 ounces of pineapple juice supplies 100 percent. For an even bigger shot of vitamin C, look for fresh "golden" pineapple imported from Costa Rica. It's sweeter and juicier, and it has more than four times the vitamin C of regular pineapple.

Melons

Most melons are low in pesticide residues and high in important nutrients. Both honeydew melons and cantaloupe provide high amounts of potassium and vitamin C and

Fruit Swap

Research from Consumers Union (publishers of *Consumer Reports*) and the Environmental Working Group shows that much of the health risks associated with pesticides are concentrated in a relatively small number of fruits. Here's how to substitute those fruits with less contaminated fruits that supply a similar amount of key nutrients.

HIGH-PESTICIDE FRUIT	KEY NUTRIENT	HEALTHIER ALTERNATIVE
Apples	Vitamin C	Bananas, grapefruit, kiwi, tangerines, watermelon
Apricots	Vitamins A and C, potassium	Grapefruit, tangerines, U.S. cantaloupe (in season from May to December), watermelon
Cantaloupe (Mexico)	Vitamins A and C, potassium	U.S. cantaloupe, watermelon
Cherries (U.S.)	Vitamin C	Blackberries, blueberries, grapefruit, kiwi, tangerines, U.S. cantaloupe
Grapes (Chile)	Vitamin C	U.S. grapes (in season from May to December)
Peaches	Vitamins A and C	Canned peaches, grapefruit, tangerines, U.S. cantaloupe, watermelon
Pears	Vitamin C	Bananas, grapefruit, kiwi, tangerines, watermelon
Red raspberries	Vitamin C	Blackberries, blueberries, grapefruit, kiwi, tangerines, U.S. cantaloupe
Strawberries	Vitamin C	Blackberries, blueberries, grapefruit, kiwi, tangerines, U.S. cantaloupe

a fair amount of fiber. Cantaloupe also contains beta-carotene, which can help protect against cancer.

Some imported cantaloupe has been linked to outbreaks of salmonella poisoning, but it's such a healthy fruit, there's no reason to avoid it. To help reduce any salmonella risk, scrub the rind of cantaloupe under running water like you would a potato. A quick scrub before cutting into cantaloupe helps to eliminate any bacteria on the rind that could be carried to the fruit via the knife.

For the lowest pesticide residue among melons, sink your teeth into a slab of juicy watermelon. One of summer's supreme eating pleasures, watermelon also makes terrific soup. Try a sweet and spicy change of pace with the Watermelon Gazpacho on page 42.

Grapefruit and Other Citrus Fruits

Grapefruit carries a fairly low pesticide risk and ranks high in nutritional benefits. Grapefruit provides several powerful antioxidants that have been shown to help relieve cold symptoms, prevent cancer, and heal bruises. The fruit's high pectin content also supplies plenty of fiber, which can help lower cholesterol and reduce risk of heart disease.

While these may sound like age-related diseases, new research shows that health-boosting fruits such as grapefruit may help kids, too, to ward off cancer and heart disease in the long run. Give your kids a healthy head start by getting them in the habit of eating low-pesticide citrus like grapefruit, tangerines, and mandarin oranges.

Among citrus fruits, navel oranges are slightly higher in residues, but most of the pesticides are concentrated in the peel. If you're eating the fruit only, conventionally grown versions are reasonably safe. But if you plan to use the peel of oranges (or lemons or limes), the best bet for reducing pesticide exposure is to buy organic. As for orange juice, tests by the Consumers Union show that pesticide risks in conventional orange juice are fairly low.

Blueberries

You won't find a healthier berry than a blueberry. While most commercial berries are extremely high in insecticide residues, blueberries are among the lowest of any fruit. Plus, these little treasures are low in calories and high in vitamin C, potassium, and fiber. They're also the number one source of antioxidants in the produce aisle. The compounds in blueberries can help prevent heart disease, urinary tract infections, and certain forms of cancer, as well as improve vision from a disease called macular degeneration. Recent studies even show that blueberries can play a role in boosting your memory and slowing the aging process.

When they're in season (July to September), keep blueberries in the fridge for tossing into cereal, whipping into fruit shakes, or making pies, crisps, and cobblers. Freeze them to enjoy during the rest of the year. Or try dried blueberries, which taste great in muffins and other quick breads. Blueberries pair well with poultry, too. Check out Citrus-Grilled Chicken with Blueberry Mango Salsa on page 137.

California Grapes

Most U.S.-grown grapes come from California and test low in pesticide residues. Look for them in markets from May to December. The other four months of the year, however, choose organic grapes to help protect your health. Imported grapes (usually shipped in from Chile) are available in U.S. markets year-round, but USDA data shows that 88 percent of imported grapes have high pesticide residues.

Whenever you reach for an organic or low-pesticide grape, you'll also reap some important health benefits. Grapes provide a fair amount of vitamin C and potassium and some boron, a mineral that can help strengthen your bones. Grapes also contain the natural plant chemical ellagic acid, which has been shown to help prevent cancer in laboratory studies by breaking down hydrocarbons, the cancer-causing substances in cigarette smoke and exhaust fumes.

Grapes are a natural for snacking and in fruit salads, but try them other ways, too. If you're concerned your fresh grapes may go bad before you get to eat them, toss them into a freezer bag and freeze them. On a hot day, pop a few frozen grapes into your mouth for a refreshing snack. Or add fresh grapes to sauces. Try the recipe for Mahimahi with Grape Sauce and Mint on page 110.

And there's more good news about grape juice. Most bottled and canned grape juices carry a low pesticide risk, according to tests conducted by Consumers Union. Purple grape juice also provides some of the same heart-protecting flavonoids found in red wine. These compounds help to lower blood cholesterol by preventing it from sticking to artery walls.

Plums

Many stone fruits (like peaches) are heavily sprayed with synthetic chemicals to ward off insects. But plums rank among the lowest of all fruits for insecticide residues.

Known as a good source of vitamin A and potassium, plums—especially dried plums (also known as prunes)—may even have properties that can stop the growth of the bacteria that cause food poisoning, according to new research. Scientists at Kansas

State University mixed a small amount of plum extract with raw meat and found that it suppressed the growth of 90 percent of harmful bacteria such as *Salmonella* and *E. coli* 0157:H7. The research is still preliminary, but until we find out more, it certainly doesn't hurt to pair plums with meat. Serve up Sautéed Chicken with Sage and Gingered Plums (page 135) or Pork Medallions with Plum Port Sauce (page 175).

Best Fruits to Buy Organic

Many common fruit crops, such as apples, pears, and peaches, are treated with organophosphate pesticides. Chlorpyrifos and azinphos methyl, two of the most widely used, work by impairing the nervous system of insects and other small organisms—and they have been shown to cause brain and nervous system damage as well as interfere with hormones in humans.

The risks of continuous exposure to these organophosphates are highest for children, whose nervous systems are just developing and are more sensitive than those of adults. What's more, young children are among the biggest consumers of many organophosphate-treated fruit products, such as applesauce and pureed baby food peaches.

To avoid unnecessary exposure to high levels of pesticide residue, here are the fruits you should consider buying organic whenever you can.

Apples and Pears

In recent USDA tests, 47 harmful chemicals were found on apple crops. Fortunately, Alar (daminozide) was not among them. Most apple growers stopped using Alar in the early 1990s after a media blitz revealed that apples were exposing American children to this potentially cancer-causing pesticide.

Nonetheless, from 1992 to 2000 (the latest figures available), nearly 93 percent of the apples tested in the USDA's Pesticide Data Program came up high in pesticide residues. One of the chemicals that did show up most often on apples, diphenylamine (DPA), has been shown to cause brain and nervous system damage in laboratory studies.

DPA and 38 other pesticides were also found on 95 percent of the pears tested. And these pesticides do indeed make their way into our bodies when we eat apple and pear products, according to a 2001 report from the Centers for Disease Control and Prevention.

While the risks of these pesticides are highest for children, there's good reason for adults to enjoy organic apples and pears as well. A comparative study from Swiss researchers at the Research Institute of Organic Agriculture, for example, found that organically grown apples are higher in overall quality—specifically, they were better-tasting and more nutritious, testing higher in fiber, disease-fighting compounds, firmness, and overall flavor than conventionally grown apples.

When you can, choose organic pears, apples, applesauce, and apple juice. These are increasingly available in supermarkets and widely available in natural food stores.

Most Stone Fruits

With the exception of plums, stone fruits like peaches, nectarines, and cherries tend to be high in pesticide residues. Recent USDA studies detected 51 pesticides on peaches, 27 on nectarines, and 22 on cherries. Among the chemicals found most often were the potentially cancer-causing fungicide iprodione and the insecticide azinphos-methyl, which can cause brain and nervous system damage.

Look for fresh organic peaches, nectarines, and cherries throughout the summer season. In the off-season, try canned peaches, which tested lower in pesticides than fresh peaches in recent Consumers Union studies.

Strawberries and Raspberries

These soft, sweet berries are among summer's greatest pleasures. They're nutritious, too. Like other berries, strawberries and raspberries provide ellagic acid, which may help prevent certain cancers. But it's smart to buy organic strawberries and raspberries whenever possible.

Strawberries are among the most heavily sprayed fruit crops. USDA tests turned up more than 40 pesticides on strawberries, including high concentrations of captan,

Fruit Juice: Is It Healthy?

Technically, ¾ cup of fruit juice counts as a serving of fruit. But most nutritionists agree that fruit juice—even 100 percent fruit juice—makes a poor substitute for whole fruit. According to the American Academy of Pediatrics (AAP), fruit juice contains no nutritional benefits for infants under 6 months old and can be harmful to adolescents and teens who drink too much.

Sure, fruit juice makes a better choice than soda. At least you get a few vitamins in fruit juice. But juicing removes the fiber, and unless the juice is freshly squeezed and consumed immediately, most of the nutrients are lost. Commercial canned or bottled juices—even those labeled "100 percent juice"—are little more than denatured fruit sugar mixed with water, vitamin C, and other flavorings. They provide mostly empty calories, and some studies show that relying on fruit juice as a beverage can lead to obesity among children.

The American Academy of Pediatrics says it's wise to keep tabs on your child's daily intake of 100 percent juice: no more than 4 to 6 ounces for children 1 to 6 years old and 8 to 12 ounces for children 7 to 18 years old. For infants under 1 year old, breast milk, formula, and plain water are the best beverages.

If your family loves juice, try diluting the juice with water to cut the sugar content. Look for cloudy juices such as pineapple juice and pulpy orange juice. These tend to provide more fiber than clear juices like apple juice. Or buy fruit nectars instead of fruit juice. Fruit nectars are slightly thicker, more flavorful, and usually higher in fiber, protein, and other nutrients. Goya brand makes a line of canned fruit nectars available in the international aisle of most grocery stores.

Note: Whichever juice you buy for your kids, be sure it's pasteurized. Unpasteurized juices can run the risk of containing a form of salmonella, which may lead to serious infections in children.

---

a particularly harmful fungicide that has been linked to cancer and birth defects and may damage the reproductive, nervous, and immune systems.

Red raspberries didn't fare much better in government tests. Pesticides were found on 62 percent of the raspberries studied, including 43 harmful chemicals in all. Captan was found on most of the raspberries tested, as was vinclozolin, a fungicide that can cause reproductive damage and interfere with hormones as well as possibly cause cancer.

Look for organic strawberries and raspberries in season from May through July. For a low-pesticide alternative, try blackberries or blueberries. Or look for huckleberries and black raspberries growing wild in your area.

Orange Banana Smoothie

I'm addicted to this drink. It's simple, creamy, and pure refreshment in a glass. You can use any flavored yogurt you like. Strawberry makes it pink. Blueberry makes it purple. Or toss in a handful of fresh berries instead. This smoothie is great for breakfast, in the lunchbox, or after a workout. I use a handheld stick blender to whip this up in seconds, then just rinse off the stick.

1 container (8 ounces) organic vanilla yogurt

1 cup orange juice

1 fresh or frozen ripe banana, broken into pieces

⅛ teaspoon ground cinnamon (optional)

Pinch of salt

Choice Advice: Regular OJ is fine for this recipe because most pesticide residue in oranges is concentrated in the peel.

In a blender, combine the yogurt, orange juice, banana, cinnamon (if using), and salt. Blend until smooth and frothy, about 30 seconds.

Makes 2 servings

Helping Hand: If you make this shake a regular habit, stock a large (32-ounce) container of yogurt in the fridge, then scoop out about ¾ to 1 cup each time you whip up the shake. You can easily double or triple the recipe.

Energy Bites

Why buy energy bars when you can make them at home for a lot less money? Snack on these little bites whenever you need a pick-me-up. They pack well for road trips, too. Look for the dried fruit in the produce aisle of your grocery store.

½ cup raisins

1¾ cups chopped dried figs

1 cup chopped organic dried apricots

1 cup chopped pitted dates

½ cup crunchy peanut butter

½ cup mini chocolate chips

½ teaspoon ground cinnamon

½ cup dried unsweetened coconut or cocoa powder (optional)

Put the raisins in a bowl. Cover with boiling water and soak until plump, about 10 minutes.

Pluck the raisins out of the water and transfer to a food processor. Add the figs, apricots, and dates and process until finely chopped, about 1 minute. (If you don't have a processor, you can finely mince the fruit instead.) Remove to a bowl and stir in the peanut butter, chocolate chips, and cinnamon. If the mixture is too dry, add up to 2 tablespoons of the raisin-soaking liquid to moisten. Roll into 1" balls with wet hands (to prevent sticking). Roll in the coconut or cocoa (if using).

Makes 24 bites

Helping Hand: If you are sensitive to sulfites (such as those found in wine), look for sulfite-free dried fruits.

RODNEY TAYLOR
A New Look for the School Lunch

School cafeterias have never been the destination place for a decent meal. Today, Rodney Taylor is changing that. As director of food and nutrition services in California's Santa Monica–Malibu Unified School District, Taylor introduced an innovative program that revitalized the lackluster school salad bar. The concept couldn't be simpler: Buy fresh produce from local farmers and prepare it especially for students.

Taylor's program goes one step further by offering students nutrition education classes, farm and farmers' market tours, organic gardening projects, and physical education. "When we are engaged in treating the whole child," says Taylor, "they are smarter and healthier for the experience."

Taylor soon realized that the Farmers' Market Salad Bar, begun as a pilot program in 1997, could help change the nature of school food service. "The key was that the produce was made user-friendly for the kids," he recalls. "The apples were quartered. The strawberries were sliced. And the grapes were already plucked. No one was prodding the kids to eat. They made their own choices, and they actually ate more produce because it was so well presented."

By 2000, the farmers' market fresh fruit and salad bar was rolled out to all 15 schools in Taylor's California school district. In the first year, sales jumped from 30 to more than 100 salad bar meals a day. "The kids love it," says Taylor. "And it supports our goal of helping students to become lifelong healthy eaters." The U.S. Department of Agriculture is so impressed with Taylor's work that they've asked him to consult with other schools to help develop similar nutrition-based programs around the country.

Citrus Salsa

This salsa comes straight from Rodney Taylor's department of food and nutrition services in California's Santa Monica–Malibu Unified School District. "With oranges, grapefruit, tangerines, and lime juice," says Taylor, "it may be the most refreshing thing you ever lay your lips on." Serve with baked organic tortilla chips. Or try it over grilled fish.

2 organic navel oranges, peeled and seeded

2 tangerines, peeled and seeded

1 Ruby Red grapefruit, peeled and seeded

1 organic red bell pepper, seeded and chopped

1 organic jalapeño pepper, seeded and chopped

½ small red onion, chopped

½ cup chopped fresh cilantro or basil

Juice of 2 limes

Cut the oranges, tangerines, and grapefruit into small pieces and put in a large bowl. Stir in the bell pepper, jalapeño pepper, onion, cilantro or basil, and lime juice. Serve immediately or refrigerate for up to 1 day.

Makes about 5 cups

Helping Hand: To easily seed and chop a pepper, hold the pepper by its stem and cut the flesh off the core. Discard the core, seeds and all. To chop a jalapeño pepper without touching it, seed as described and then use the flat blade of a paring knife to hold the pepper steady on the cutting board while chopping with your chef's knife.

Watermelon Gazpacho

Andrew Schloss, the king of convenience cooking, first showed me how to make this recipe. It's so simple and refreshing, I had to share it here. Made in a food processor, the gazpacho comes together pretty easily. Just be sure not to puree the ingredients or you'll have to serve this as a smoothie instead! Use short "pulses" to finely chop the ingredients in the processor.

6 cups seedless watermelon cubes (6 pounds whole watermelon)

½ peeled and chopped seedless cucumber

½ organic yellow bell pepper, seeded and chopped

3 scallions, chopped

1 large clove garlic, minced

2 tablespoons lime or lemon juice

1 tablespoon extra-virgin olive oil

½ teaspoon hot pepper sauce

1 cup cold raspberry-cranberry juice

3 tablespoons chopped fresh mint

In a large food processor, combine 3 cups of the watermelon, the cucumber, bell pepper, scallions, garlic, lime juice or lemon juice, oil, and pepper sauce. Process with short pulses until the mixture is just finely chopped.

Add the remaining watermelon, raspberry-cranberry juice, and mint. Process with pulses until just finely chopped.

Makes 8 servings

Helping Hands: If you use a whole watermelon to make this recipe, cut the melon into a basket shape by removing two large quarter-wedges from the top half, leaving a 2"-wide handle over the middle. Scoop out the watermelon with an ice cream scoop, leaving a shell about ½" to 1" thick. Fill the watermelon basket with the gazpacho and serve with a ladle.

If your processor holds less than 3 cups liquid at the fill line, make this entire recipe in two batches to avoid any spills. Follow the directions above, using half of the ingredients to make the first batch. Remove that batch to a large bowl and repeat the process to make the second batch.

Summer Fruit Salad
with Spiced Yogurt Sauce

Here's one of my favorite everyday fruit salads. Feel free to vary the ingredients. Replace the cantaloupe with honeydew melon or use organic raspberries instead of blueberries. The secret's really in the sauce, which heightens the flavor of the fruit.

1 U.S.-grown cantaloupe

2 navel oranges, peeled and sectioned, sections cut in half

8 ounces fresh blueberries

3 cups organic or California seedless green grapes

1 tablespoon sugar

1½ cups organic vanilla yogurt

4 ounces crème fraîche or another ½ cup yogurt

½ teaspoon ground cinnamon

¼ teaspoon grated nutmeg

¼ teaspoon ground ginger

Cut the cantaloupe in half and remove the seeds and strings. Using a melon baller, scoop the fruit into balls (or chop into bite-size pieces with a knife). Put the cantaloupe, oranges, blueberries, grapes, and sugar in a serving bowl. Toss to mix.

In a medium bowl, whisk together the yogurt, crème fraîche (or additional yogurt), cinnamon, nutmeg, and ginger. Spoon over the top of the salad.

Makes 6 servings

Nutrient Boost: To add protein, fiber, and vitamin E, sprinkle each serving with a tablespoon or two of chopped walnuts or pecans. Walnuts also contain ellagic acid, an antioxidant that helps to prevent cancer.

Mango Orange Sorbet

Banana and coconut milk deepen the sweetness of mango in this simple sorbet. I like to serve this with gingersnap cookies to complement the Indian flavors. Look for canned coconut milk in the Asian or international section of your grocery store. You can use either the reduced-fat or regular variety. You can also use frozen mango chunks, which are available in the frozen fruit section of many supermarkets.

4 cups fresh or frozen mango chunks

1 fresh or frozen banana

⅓ cup sugar

½ cup coconut milk

2 tablespoons grated organic orange zest

1 tablespoon amaretto (optional)

Big pinch of ground ginger

Put the mango, banana, sugar, coconut milk, orange zest, amaretto (if using), and ginger in a food processor. Process until smooth, stopping to scrape down the sides occasionally, about 2 minutes.

Pour into a shallow metal pan. Cover and freeze until frozen solid, at least 4 hours or overnight. Break the mixture into chunks with a sturdy knife (or if your pan is somewhat flexible, twist the opposite corners and push up from the bottom to loosen the whole frozen sheet from the pan; then break it into chunks). Process in a food processor until soft and snowy but not melted, about 1 minute. Stop occasionally to make sure there are no big chunks in the mixture.

Mound into bowls and serve.

Makes 6 servings

Helping Hands: To peel and pit a fresh mango, stand the fruit upright on a cutting board. Slice down through the flesh on one of the flatter sides, guiding the knife as close around the oval-shaped pit as possible. Repeat on the other side to make two disks of fruit plus a third centerpiece containing the pit. For the centerpiece, cut off the peel and then cut the fruit off the pit; discard pit and peels.

Hold one of the remaining disks in your hand and very carefully score the flesh almost all the way down to the peel in a checkerboard pattern. Be careful not to let the knife pierce through the mango skin and into your palm. Push up through the center of the peel side of the disk to expose the cubes of flesh. Cut the flesh away from the peel and discard the peel. Repeat with the other disk.

Tropical Ice Pops

My son August loves to help make these frozen treats—and eat them. Once everything's in the blender, he gets to turn the machine on and off—a big thrill the first time he did it at age 3. A pretty easy job, too, with a touch of timing required! Of course, the best part is licking the melting juice off the stick in the hot summer sun.

1 can (11 ounces) Mandarin oranges in juice, drained

¾ cup pineapple juice

½ cup orange sherbet, softened

½ cup organic low-fat piña colada or coconut yogurt

3 ounces organic cream cheese, at room temperature

Choice Advice: Mandarin oranges are among those citrus fruits with the least pesticide residue, according to USDA and Food and Drug Administration data.

Put the oranges, juice, sherbet, yogurt, and cream cheese in a blender or food processor and blend until smooth. Pour into eight 3-ounce freezer-pop cups or paper drinking cups. Insert a wooden craft stick in the center of each cup. Place on a baking sheet (if using flat-bottomed cups) and freeze until firm.

Makes 8 pops

Best Fruit for Baby

For infants 6 to 12 months old, commercial baby food is the number one source of exposure to pesticides in food. The most common culprits are applesauce, apple juice, pears, and peaches. That doesn't mean you should stop buying baby food. Several brands of organic baby food are widely available in grocery stores. These make the best bet for your baby's health. And when organic isn't an option, put the emphasis on baby food made with low-pesticide fruits such as bananas, blueberries, and plums. Or make baby food at home. Puree, mash, or cut up other low-pesticide fruits like kiwi, mangoes, pineapple, tangerines, and watermelon.

Grilled Fruit Wraps with Gingered Yogurt Dip

The raw heat of the grill caramelizes the sugar in these fruits and creates incredible flavor. I take everything out to the grill so the wraps can be assembled without running back to the kitchen. These can be eaten out of hand once they cool off a bit.

2 ripe organic peaches or nectarines, halved and pitted

4 thick slices fresh or canned pineapple

2 almost-ripe bananas, peeled

2 teaspoons sugar

¼ teaspoon pumpkin pie spice

½ cup organic vanilla yogurt

1 teaspoon minced crystallized ginger

6 flour tortillas (8" diameter), preferably whole wheat

Choice Advice: If you can't find organic peaches or nectarines for this recipe, replace them with just-ripe mangoes because they are lower in pesticide residue. Brush with oil before grilling 2 to 3 minutes on the cut side. (See page 44 for tips on cutting mangoes.)

Coat a grill rack with cooking spray and preheat the grill to medium. Place the halved peaches or nectarines, pineapple slices, and peeled bananas directly on the grill rack. Grill until soft and seared on both sides, 3 to 4 minutes per side (slightly less time for the banana if it's ripe), using a spatula to turn the fruit. Chop the fruit and drain any accumulated juices into a small bowl (you'll get more juice with really ripe fruit). Scrape the fruit into another bowl. Stir the sugar and pumpkin pie spice into the fruit. Stir the yogurt and ginger into the accumulated juices.

Divide the fruit filling among the tortillas. Roll up, folding the short sides over the filling first and then rolling over the long sides to completely enclose. Secure at the seam with a toothpick and coat all over with cooking spray. Grill seam-side up until golden, 30 seconds to 1 minute. Carefully turn over and grill the other side until golden. Let cool slightly, cut in half, and serve with the yogurt sauce for dipping.

Makes 4 to 6 servings

Helping Hands: Be sure to scrape your grill rack clean before putting on the fruit. Charred steak flavor doesn't go well here.

Look for minced crystallized ginger in jars in your grocery store's spice aisle. Or buy sliced crystallized ginger in bags at a natural food store and then mince before using. If you can't find it, the recipe works just as well without it.

Brown Butter Poached Pears

When butter melts, cooks gently, and begins to turn golden brown, the milk solids gradually become toasted, giving the butter a deep, almost nutty flavor. This recipe uses brown butter to cook sliced pears, then adds honey, vermouth, and citrus juices to make a simple sauce. If you can get your hands on some organic ice cream (or frozen yogurt), it's highly recommended here. Ben & Jerry's rBGH-free vanilla does the trick.

½ organic orange

½ organic lemon

¼ cup honey

¼ cup vermouth

¼ cup water

4 tablespoons organic butter

4 almost-ripe organic Anjou or Bosc pears, cored and sliced

2 teaspoons cornstarch

2 tablespoons brandy

1 teaspoon vanilla extract

1 cup organic or rBGH-free vanilla ice cream (optional)

Grate the zest from the orange and lemon and put in a medium bowl. Squeeze the juices from both fruits into the bowl and then stir in the honey, vermouth, and water. Set aside.

Melt the butter in a large skillet over medium heat. Cook until the butter turns a medium golden brown, 2 to 3 minutes. Add the pears and cook, stirring frequently, until the pears just begin to soften, 2 to 3 minutes. Pour in the juice mixture and bring to a boil over high heat. Reduce the heat to medium-low and simmer, stirring occasionally, until the pears are tender, about 3 minutes. Using a slotted spoon, remove the pears to four small serving bowls and set aside.

Dissolve the cornstarch in the brandy and vanilla. Stir into the pan and cook until slightly thickened, about 1 minute. If using the ice cream, add a scoop to each serving bowl and then spoon the sauce over the pears and ice cream.

Makes 4 servings

Broiled Figs with Goat Cheese and Basil

Figs taste luxuriously good eaten out of hand. It's also fun to dress them up a little. The mild sharpness of goat cheese and the lingering perfume of basil bring out a fig's sweeter side. If you like, mash up fresh raspberries with a little sugar to make a sauce for serving on the side.

8 ripe fresh figs, halved from top to bottom

4 teaspoons brown sugar

1 tablespoon minced fresh basil

1 log (4 ounces) goat cheese, cut into 16 rounds or pieces about ¼" thick

Preheat the broiler. Put the figs, cut side up, on a baking sheet and sprinkle evenly with the brown sugar. Broil until the sugar melts, 1 to 2 minutes. Sprinkle evenly with the basil and top each fig half with a round of goat cheese. Broil just until the cheese melts and browns slightly, 2 to 3 minutes. Serve warm.

Makes 4 servings

Helping Hand: Fresh figs are in season from early summer through midfall. They're sweet and sticky on the inside, so dip your knife in hot water to help reduce stickiness when cutting. You could also chill the figs for an hour or so in the refrigerator to help "set" the sugars and reduce stickiness. If the round sides of the figs are very plump, cut off a sliver to help each fig half sit flat.

Stemilt Fruit

You may have seen the "Stemilt: Responsible Choice" label on fruits like apples, pears, and cherries. This label provides some assurance that the fruit was grown with fewer harmful pesticides than conventionally grown fruit.

Fruits carrying the Stemilt label make a decent alternative to organic because they are grown using integrated pest management (IPM), an approach to managing agricultural pests that relies on pesticide use as a last resort. Under the Stemilt program, pesticides are categorized into three tiers. The most harmful pesticides in the top tier are prohibited. However, the program administrators provide no other details about the other tiers of pesticides, so the label doesn't exactly guarantee that certain harmful chemicals are avoided.

To completely avoid fruit grown with pesticides, look for the organic label, which Stemilt also began to use on certain fruits in fall 2003.

Lemon Pear Turnovers

This elegant dessert is perfect for company or a special occasion—especially with a scoop of vanilla or chocolate ice cream. Look for puff pastry in the frozen bread aisle of most supermarkets.

½ organic lemon

2 organic almost-ripe Anjou or Bosc pears, peeled, cored, and chopped

2 tablespoons organic butter

2 tablespoons sugar

¼ teaspoon ground cinnamon

2 teaspoons cornstarch

1½ tablespoons water

1 sheet frozen puff pastry, thawed

1 pasture-raised or organic egg

1 tablespoon organic milk

Grate the zest from the lemon and set aside. Squeeze the lemon juice into a medium bowl, add the pears, and toss to coat.

Melt the butter in a medium skillet over medium heat. Add the pear and lemon mixture and bring to a simmer. Stir in the sugar, cinnamon, and reserved lemon zest. Simmer until the pears are just tender, about 3 minutes.

Dissolve the cornstarch in the water and stir into the skillet. Stir until the mixture thickens, about 1 minute. Remove from the heat and cool to room temperature, then refrigerate to cool completely.

Meanwhile, cut the sheet of puff pastry into a grid to make four 6" squares. Beat the egg with the milk and brush the mixture over the squares. Cover the remaining egg mixture and refrigerate.

Divide the filling among the pastry squares, mounding in the center. Lift one corner of the pastry over the filling to meet the opposite corner and make a triangle. Crimp the open edges with the tines of a fork to seal. (If you have a little extra filling, save it to serve over ice cream or frozen yogurt.) Cover and refrigerate the turnovers for 2 hours or up to 8 hours. (You could also freeze them for several months and defrost them before baking.)

Preheat the oven to 400°F. Brush the turnovers all over with the remaining beaten egg (or additional beaten egg if you've frozen the turnovers). Bake on a baking sheet until puffed and brown, about 15 minutes.

Makes 4 turnovers

Greg Higgins
Teaching People about Food and Community

For chef Greg Higgins, food isn't only about fabulous flavor. It's about stimulating a vibrant community. At Higgins Restaurant and Bar in Portland, Oregon, the chef has been cultivating his local food community for the past 20 years. Even the restaurant's beautiful open kitchen encourages customers to stop by, chat about food, and see how their meals are being prepared.

Higgins puts a premium on developing and maintaining relationships among his suppliers, his staff, and his customers. He does this, in part, because the chef considers it his job to teach people about food, not just to serve it to them. "Chefs have been thrown into this role as tastemakers," he says, "and it comes with an ethical responsibility." For Higgins, that means buying and serving food that has been grown and produced under healthy, sustainable conditions.

While organic is important, it's not Higgins' only consideration. His focus is on high-quality food that is grown responsibly. "In the 1970s, I began to see a suspicious change in fruits and vegetables," he recalls. "Food just didn't taste like what I remembered when I was a kid. So I started my obsession with connecting with growers."

The chef doesn't require his suppliers to be certified organic. Instead, he asks them questions. By talking with suppliers, Higgins has encouraged many growers to produce extraordinarily high quality food that surpasses government regulations for organic production. Greener Pastures Poultry in the nearby town of Noti provides chicken and turkey that is pasture-raised on a diet of natural forage. River Run in Clatskanie, Oregon, produces the restaurant's grass-fed certified Angus beef. And all of the seafood at Higgins Restaurant is sustainably harvested from the nearby northern Pacific coast. From the wild mushrooms to the pinot noir wine, the food served at Higgins Restaurant and Bar comes primarily from the local food community of Oregon's Willamette Valley.

Chef Higgins' ultimate goal is to nurture a sense of shared responsibility for the food we all produce and enjoy. "It's up to individuals to create a healthy, sustainable food system," he says. "Government regulations haven't been malicious; they've just been careless." The chef recommends buying food at local farmers' markets and talking to farmers whenever you can. Or if you can't talk to farmers directly, then "get to know your grocer," he says. Once you've had a conversation, you can encourage him or her to carry the types of products that you want to spend your money on.

Higgins' outstanding recipes have been featured in several cookbooks, and the chef has appeared nationwide to promote sustainable cuisine. He is also a board member of Chefs Collaborative, a national organization that mirrors his food philosophy by educating people about food production and encouraging chefs as well as the public to enjoy locally, responsibly produced food. In 2002, Higgins won a prestigious James Beard Award as Best Chef of Northwest America.

Greg Higgins' Baked Braeburn Apples with Walnut Filling

At Higgins Restaurant and Bar in Portland, Oregon, chef Greg Higgins loves to use locally grown apples. In these dressed-up baked apples, he fills hollowed-out Braeburns with sweetened cream and egg to make a deliriously good custard. Drizzle the baked apples with the warm pan juices and serve with a scoop of vanilla ice cream.

6 organic Braeburn apples
1 cup organic apple cider
½ cup organic heavy cream
¼ cup sugar
¼ cup pure maple syrup
1 pasture-raised or organic egg
½ teaspoon vanilla extract
¼ teaspoon ground cinnamon
⅛ teaspoon salt
⅔ cup walnuts, toasted and chopped

Level off the base of the apples with a knife so that the apples stand upright; cut off only as much as necessary. Use a melon baller or small spoon to dig out the apple seeds and core, making a cavity about 1½" in diameter. Leave the base intact.

Pour the cider into a baking pan just large enough to hold the apples. Set the apples in the pan.

Preheat the oven to 375°F.

Put the cream and sugar in a small saucepan. Bring to a boil over medium-high heat.

In a medium heatproof bowl, whisk together the maple syrup, egg, vanilla, cinnamon, and salt. Gradually whisk the hot sweetened cream into the egg mixture. Stir in the walnuts and spoon the mixture evenly into the apples.

Bake until the apples are tender and the custard is set, 30 to 35 minutes. Serve warm with the pan juices.

Makes 6 servings

Helping Hands: To toast the walnuts, bake them in the preheating oven until fragrant and toasty, about 5 minutes.

If you can't find organic Braeburn apples, use your favorite baking apple, such as Gala, Jonathan, Macoun, or Granny Smith.

What to Pick When

You can get most fresh fruits year-round in U.S. supermarkets. But a strawberry shipped to you in January will never be as deeply red and dripping with succulent juice as a ripe strawberry picked in late May or June.

Stick with fresh fruit in season and you'll be sure to get it at its most plump and luscious. It'll probably be less expensive, too—especially since it won't have to be shipped from as far away! Keep in mind that weather, climate, and seasons vary from region to region.

Here's a quick look at which popular fruits to buy when. Dried fruits for the winter months are also listed to encourage eating fruit all year long.

MONTH	FRUIT TO LOOK FOR
January	Grapefruit, oranges, tangerines, lemons, kiwi, dried berries, raisins, other dried fruits such as dates
February	Grapefruit, oranges, tangerines, lemons, kiwi, dried berries, raisins, other dried fruits such as dates
March	Bananas, grapefruit, oranges, lemons, kiwi, pineapples
April	Bananas, grapefruit, pineapples, rhubarb
May	Bananas, pineapples, rhubarb, strawberries
June	Apricots, bananas, blackberries, cherries, limes, pineapples, raspberries, rhubarb, strawberries, watermelon
July	Apricots, blackberries, blueberries, cherries, grapes, limes, peaches, nectarines, raspberries, cantaloupe, honeydew melon, watermelon
August	Blackberries, blueberries, raspberries, grapes, limes, peaches, nectarines, plums, pears, cantaloupe, honeydew melon, watermelon
September	Apples, pears, blueberries, grapes, peaches, plums, cantaloupe, watermelon
October	Apples, pears, dried berries, raisins, other dried fruits such as dates
November	Apples, pears, tangerines, lemons, kiwi, cranberries, dried berries, raisins, other dried fruits such as dates
December	Apples, pears, grapefruit, oranges, lemons, tangerines, cranberries, dried berries, raisins, other dried fruits such as dates

Cherry Almond Cobbler

Most cobblers consist of sweetened fruit topped with some sort of cake, biscuit, or other pastry dough on top. In this one, a loose batter goes on the bottom, and the fruit is scattered over top. This is my favorite type of cobbler. It was inspired by a recipe in the now-classic *New Southern Cooking* by Nathalie Dupree.

⅓ cup organic butter

¼ cup whole grain pastry flour or unbleached all-purpose flour

⅓ cup sugar

1 teaspoon baking powder

¼ teaspoon salt

¼ cup organic buttermilk

½ teaspoon almond extract

1 pint organic sour cherries, pitted and halved

Choice Advice: If you can't find organic buttermilk, add ¾ teaspoon lemon juice to ¼ cup organic milk. Let stand for 5 minutes before using.

Preheat the oven to 350°F. Put the butter in a 9" deep-dish pie plate or shallow 2-quart baking dish. Put the pan in the oven until the butter melts, about 5 minutes.

Meanwhile, whisk together the flour, ¼ cup sugar, the baking powder, and salt in a medium bowl. Whisk together the buttermilk and almond extract, then whisk the mixture into the dry ingredients just until moistened, leaving a few lumps.

Pour the batter over the melted butter in the pan. Scatter the cherries on top of the batter. Sprinkle with the remaining sugar. Bake until browned around the edges and a toothpick inserted in the center comes out clean, about 45 minutes.

Makes 6 servings

Food Lore: Researchers at Michigan State University discovered that sour (tart) cherries are an excellent source of compounds with antioxidant and anti-inflammatory properties. The antioxidants can help protect against cancer and heart disease, while the anti-inflammatories can help relieve arthritis pain. The researchers concluded that 20 sour cherries a day can keep pain related to arthritis and inflammation at bay.

Caramelized Nectarine and Blueberry Galette

A sort of free-form pie, a galette is made on a flat baking sheet instead of in a pie pan. The edges of the pie dough are folded over the filling, leaving the center open. Galettes have a rustic look and feel that make you want to add a scoop of vanilla ice cream and dig in. I developed this one for a benefit dinner that Generation Green held a couple years ago.

6 ripe organic nectarines

½ cup sugar

10 tablespoons cold unsalted organic butter

2 cups unbleached all-purpose flour or whole-grain pastry flour

½ teaspoon salt

2 ounces cold organic cream cheese, cut into pieces

1 tablespoon lemon juice

⅓ cup ice water

¼ cup crushed anise biscotti, almond biscotti, or plain dry bread crumbs

½ teaspoon ground allspice

1 tablespoon organic 2% milk

½ cup fresh blueberries

Cut the nectarines in half lengthwise, twist to separate the halves, and remove the pits. Pour the sugar into a shallow bowl. Dip each nectarine half, cut side down, into the sugar, coating generously. Set aside.

Melt 2 tablespoons butter in a large heavy skillet over medium heat.

Add the fruit, cut side down, to the skillet and cook until the sugar melts and turns deep golden brown, 5 to 8 minutes. Using a wide spatula, invert each half onto wax paper to cool, spooning any excess caramel over the fruit.

In a large bowl, mix the flour, salt, and 2 tablespoons sugar from the bowl. Cut the remaining 8 tablespoons butter into ½" cubes. Using a pastry cutter or your fingers, cut the butter and cream cheese into the flour until they form pea-size pieces among the flour.

In a cup, combine the lemon juice with 2 tablespoons ice water. While stirring gently with a spoon, sprinkle in the lemon juice mixture and just enough additional ice water so that the dough can be gathered into a ball. Gently press the ball into a disk in the bowl, cover loosely with a large piece of parchment paper, and refrigerate for 15 minutes.

Preheat the oven to 425°F.

Remove the parchment paper and put the disk of dough on top of it. Quickly roll the dough out to a 14" circle. Transfer to a large flat baking sheet or the back of a rimmed baking sheet. Sprinkle the dough evenly with the crushed biscotti or bread crumbs. Put one nectarine half, cut side down, in the center of the dough. Arrange the remaining halves, cut side down, in a circular pattern around the center piece, leaving a 2" border of dough at the edges. Sprinkle the fruit with the allspice and 2 tablespoons sugar. Fold the border of dough over the edge of the fruit.

Brush the surface of the dough with the milk and sprinkle with the remaining 1 tablespoon sugar. Bake for 15 minutes. Reduce the heat to 375°F and scatter the blueberries evenly over the nectarines. Bake until the fruit is tender and the crust is light brown, 20 to 25 minutes more. Let cool for 10 minutes, then slice into wedges.

Makes 8 servings

Helping Hands: A sprinkling of crushed biscotti helps to absorb excess moisture from the fruit and keep the crust from getting soggy. You'll need about two large biscotti. Break them up and put them in a food processor. Then process until finely crushed.

To get a nice flaky pastry crust, keep all of the dough ingredients—especially the butter—as cold as possible. It also helps to handle the dough very little.

Look for parchment paper near the aluminum foil in your grocery store.

Chapter 3

Vegetables

If you want the freshest vegetables you can find (and don't have the time or space for your own garden), shopping at local farm markets is one of the best ways to get them. Buying locally grown vegetables helps to bring you closer to the rhythm of the seasons and strengthens your personal connection to the food you eat. Small, local markets may also give you the opportunity to try a wide variety of vegetables, including gorgeous heirloom varieties you may have never tasted before.

One particular type of farm operation that's worth seeking is anything that refers to itself as "community supported agriculture" or a CSA. In most CSAs, "members" of the farm pay some money up front to cover the costs of growing food and may also be asked to pitch in with some of the hands-on activities from time to time. Then they simply show up at the farm and collect a weekly bag of locally grown, lovingly handled, and incredibly delicious food that may include vegetables, fruits, cheeses, eggs, poultry, baked goods, and more. It's a fun way to shop.

Buying locally also helps avoid unnecessary pollution due to long-distance shipping and reduces pesticides sprayed on foods for shipping and storage. And by shopping locally, you'll enrich your local economy and put your money into the hands of small family farmers.

Best of all, buying locally makes shopping for the freshest seasonal veggies a cinch. As the owner of my local CSA, George DeVault, once told me, "If it's not coming up at the farm, it's not in season."

A Harvest of Low-Pesticide Veggies

Another plus of buying locally is that many small farms grow vegetables organically. That means the farmers don't use petroleum-based fertilizers, genetically modified plants, or harmful synthetic pesticides. These farmers work hard to build healthy soil, avoid polluting nearby waterways, and reduce the impact of farming on wildlife.

New research shows that buying organic vegetables will vastly reduce your family's exposure to toxins. But when you can't buy organic, you don't have to throw your principles and your health out the window. Certain conventionally grown vegetables are sprayed with fewer pesticides than others or retain less residue. Here's a field guide to conventionally grown vegetables that are low in pesticides, according to USDA data. If organic isn't an option, focus on these instead. The best news: The conventionally grown vegetables lowest in environmental toxins tend to be the highest in health-boosting nutrients.

Asparagus

When springtime rolls around, reach for one of the season's first fresh vegetables: asparagus. This vegetable is a harbinger of the garden's rebirth in more ways than one. Asparagus is high in folate, a B vitamin that can help prevent birth defects. Researchers found that pregnant women who get 400 micrograms of folate a day can cut their children's risk of developing brain and spinal cord defects (neural tube defects) by 50 percent. Five asparagus spears provide about 110 micrograms of folate, nearly 30 percent of the recommended daily amount of folate for pregnant women. Asparagus spears also test low for residues of most pesticides.

Avocados

The U.S. Department of Agriculture (USDA) has been tracking environmental contaminants in food crops since the late 1980s. According to the USDA's Pesticide Data Program, avocados have the lowest levels of the fewest number of pesticides of all crops examined. That fact alone makes avocados attractive. But their rich, buttery texture and mild, inviting flavor make them truly irresistible. Even better, they're a great source of healthy monounsaturated fats that can help to prevent heart disease. Technically fruits, avocados are treated more like vegetables. Try mashing some up for your infant or child. Or round out your next Mexican meal by serving Guacamole with Fresh Tortilla Chips (page 78).

Crucifers

Broccoli, cauliflower, brussels sprouts, and cabbage all belong to the same food family, known as cruciferous vegetables. Numerous studies show that crucifers offer the best cancer protection due to their complex mix of antioxidants like beta-carotene, sulforaphane, and indole-3-carbinol (I3C). Researchers have found that the compound I3C in broccoli, cabbage, and brussels sprouts is particularly effective in lowering levels of harmful estrogens that can cause breast cancer. Plus, cruciferous vegetables rank consistently low in pesticide residues even when grown by conventional, chemical-dependent methods, according to analyses of government data by the Environmental Working Group. To get more of these healing foods into your diet, try the recipes for Garlicky Lemon Broccoli (page 73) and Nell Newman's Cauliflower and Parmesan Soup (page 85).

Eggplant

Here is yet another fruit (actually a berry) that gets cooked more like a vegetable. But no matter how you cook it, eggplant makes for good eating. And that's especially good because, according to recent analyses of government pesticide data by the Environmental Working Group, conventionally grown eggplant ranks among the vegetables lowest in harmful environmental contaminants.

Grilling brings out the latent sweetness of eggplant and adds a roasty, caramelized flavor. Try grilling a few slabs brushed with a little olive oil, salt, and pepper. Serve them as a side dish or in a grilled vegetable sandwich. Look for smaller eggplants, as

In Season = Incredible Flavor

Like fruits, vegetables taste best at peak ripeness. Vegetables in season also sell for lower prices since they don't need to be shipped in from far away. You can buy many vegetables year-round in U.S. supermarkets, but try to get in the habit of using only those vegetables that are at peak ripeness during any particular month. That means focusing on things like broccoli and kale in wintertime, asparagus and potatoes in the spring, corn and tomatoes in the summer, and pumpkins and mushrooms in the fall. Check the list below to find out what other vegetables are in season throughout the year. There are more than you might think!

MONTH	VEGETABLES TO LOOK FOR
January	Broccoli, carrots, celery, collard greens, endive, kale, parsnips, potatoes, rutabagas
February	Broccoli, carrots, celery, endive, parsnips, rutabagas
March	Artichokes, avocados, beets, broccoli, carrots, celery, dandelion greens, endive, parsnips, rutabagas, spinach
April	Artichokes, asparagus, avocados, beets, carrots, celery, dandelion greens, parsnips, potatoes, radishes, spinach
May	Asparagus, broccoli, carrots, celery, dandelion greens, green beans, parsnips, peas, potatoes, radishes, scallions, summer squash, watercress, wax beans
June	Asparagus, beets, broccoli, cabbage, carrots, chicory, cucumbers, dandelion greens, green beans, lettuces, mustard greens, okra, parsnips, peas, potatoes, radishes, scallions, spinach, summer squash, tomatoes, wax beans
July	Beets, broccoli, cabbage, cauliflower, chard, corn, cucumbers, eggplant, green beans, lettuces, lima beans, mustard greens, okra, onions, parsnips, peas, peppers, radishes, scallions, summer squash, tomatoes, turnips, wax beans
August	Beets, cabbage, cauliflower, chard, corn, cucumbers, eggplant, green beans, lettuces, lima beans, onions, parsnips, peas, peppers, radishes, summer squash, scallions, tomatoes, turnips, wax beans
September	Beets, cabbage, cauliflower, chard, corn, cucumbers, eggplant, lettuces, lima beans, onions, parsnips, peas, peppers, potatoes, pumpkins, radishes, summer squash, tomatoes, turnips
October	Beets, broccoli, brussels sprouts, cabbage, cauliflower, chard, escarole, lettuces, lima beans, mushrooms, parsnips, peas, peppers, potatoes, pumpkins, radishes, rutabagas, turnips, winter squash
November	Broccoli, brussels sprouts, cabbage, carrots, celery, endive, mushrooms, parsnips, potatoes, rutabagas, turnips
December	Broccoli, brussels sprouts, carrots, celery, collard greens, endive, kale, mushrooms, parsnips, potatoes, rutabagas, turnips

they tend to become bitter with age. Or try Japanese or Italian eggplants, which are usually smaller, sweeter, less bitter, and more tender.

Okra

Popular in the South, okra is a key ingredient in gumbo both for its flavor and because it releases a viscous liquid when cooked that helps to thicken the stew. These tapered green pods contain a powerful cancer-fighting antioxidant called glutathione. Researchers at Emory University found that people with the highest intake of glutathione were half as likely to develop oral and throat cancers as those with low levels of the antioxidant. Apparently, glutathione works by ushering cancer-causing chemicals away from your cells and out of your body via the urine. Okra also supplies a fair amount of fiber and vitamin C, without the pesticide load carried by many other vegetables. If you're new to okra, try the recipe for Turkey Gumbo with Sausage and Escarole (page 142). Many people find the sticky texture of okra unusual at first, but if you flash-fry or quickly sauté okra, it doesn't become quite as stringy. Give it a shot and taste for yourself.

Onions

It's a good thing onions are healthy or we'd be in big trouble. Onions are among the top five veggies eaten by Americans, according to USDA consumption figures. These root vegetables show up in countless salads, snacks, sandwiches, and sauces. That's where they supply us with dozens of healing compounds such as flavonoids, which help to keep cholesterol from sticking to artery walls, and sulfur compounds, which lower levels of blood fats called triglycerides and inhibit the allergic response that occurs with asthma. Thankfully, conventionally grown onions offer all these health benefits without the drawbacks of harmful pesticide residues.

Peas

Whether they're in butter sauce, accompanying mashed potatoes, or in soups or casseroles, peas find their way into many American meals. They're also one of the veg-

Smart Alternatives to High-Pesticide Veggies

Most Americans—particularly children—should eat more vegetables. But not all vegetables have a clean bill of health. Some, such as peppers, are treated with loads of pesticides, while others retain more residues from the soil. Here are the four vegetables with the highest pesticide residues, plus a few smart alternatives, according to USDA data. Each alternative is a good source of the main nutrient found in the high-pesticide food.

HIGH-PESTICIDE FOOD	KEY NUTRIENTS	HEALTHY ALTERNATIVES
Spinach	Vitamins A and C, folic acid	Asparagus, broccoli, brussels sprouts, cabbage, chard, romaine lettuce
Peppers (sweet and hot)	Vitamins A and C	Asparagus, broccoli, brussels sprouts, carrots, romaine lettuce, tomatoes
Celery	Carotenoids	Broccoli, carrots, radishes, romaine lettuce
Potatoes	Vitamin C and potassium	Asparagus, broccoli, brussels sprouts, cabbage, cauliflower, eggplant, radishes

etables that infants and young children eat most often. Thankfully, peas provide lots of heart-healthy fiber (4 grams in half a cup!) without significant pesticide residues.

Radishes

Most American markets carry small round red-skinned radishes, but look for mild-flavored white daikon radishes, too. They add a pleasantly juicy crunch when shredded for salads and stir-fries. According to the latest government data, all radishes are low in harmful chemical residues.

Sweet Corn

Botanically speaking, corn is a grain, but we eat it like a vegetable. Whatever you call it, corn provides many of the health benefits that both veggies and grains are known for, particularly cholesterol-lowering fiber and folate, a B vitamin that may help to reduce heart disease risk. Corn also contains a special plant chemical (or "phytochemical") called lutein, which may reduce your risk of colon cancer and age-related vision loss. Sweet corn ranks among those vegetables high in nutrients and low in pesticide residues. To find out more about corn that is genetically modified, see page 219 in the Beans, Nuts, and Grains chapter.

Best Vegetables to Buy Organic

Every year, more than 500 million pounds of pesticides are applied to conventional U.S. agricultural crops, and laboratory tests confirm that their residue regularly shows up in our vegetables. In addition, other harmful chemicals that persist in soil and water from year to year also show up in these tests.

A landmark study from the National Research Council found that the chemical residues on commonly eaten vegetables like potatoes can be particularly dangerous for young children and infants whose bodies are more vulnerable to their effects. Some pesticides are potentially harmful to children's nervous systems, while others have been linked to childhood cancer or to developmental problems, weakened immune function, and disrupted hormone function.

According to tests conducted by Consumers Union (publishers of *Consumer Reports*), organic vegetables are significantly lower in pesticide residues when compared with conventionally grown. And when researchers at the Environmental Working Group recently analyzed pesticide data from the USDA, they found that five vegetables had consistently higher levels of the most harmful agricultural pesticides (spinach, bell peppers, chile peppers, celery, and potatoes). Whenever possible, buy organic versions of these vegetables to reduce your exposure to harmful toxins.

Spinach

While most greens such as chard, collard greens, beet greens, and mustard greens don't pose much of a pesticide risk, spinach tests higher in harmful chemical residues than any other vegetable. Government pesticide data turned up 40 pesticides on spinach, and most of those pesticides were found on nearly 85 percent of the spinach samples tested.

One chemical that regularly shows up on spinach is the insecticide dichloro-diphenyl-trichloroethane, also known as DDT. While this pesticide isn't actually applied to spinach crops, it shows up in our food because it has persisted in soil and water from its heavy use in the early 1940s. It takes about 8 years for the human body to metabolize just half of the DDT it consumes. As a result, DDT builds up in the body over time.

Problems related to extensive DDT use began to appear in the late 1940s. Many insects developed a resistance to the pesticide, and DDT appeared to be highly toxic to fish. DDT has since been classified as a carcinogen, and it has also been linked to birth defects. The Food and Drug Administration banned all uses of DDT in 1973. Nonetheless, it still shows up in vegetables like spinach.

While it's difficult to completely avoid exposure to persistent contaminants like DDT, it's a good idea to buy organic spinach whenever you can. Organic spinach gives you plenty of cancer-fighting carotenoids and blood-building iron without the unwanted burden of so many synthetic chemical residues. Most grocery stores carry organic spinach in the refrigerated produce section or among the bagged salad mixes. Look for baby spinach leaves, which tend to have the sweetest flavor and rarely need to have their small stems removed.

Peppers

Both sweet bell peppers and hot chile peppers test high for pesticide residues. Current USDA tests reveal 45 different pesticides on bell peppers and a variety of environmental contaminants on 54 percent of chile peppers sampled. One of the pesticides found most often on peppers is endosulfan, an insecticide that disrupts hormone function. Other common substances on peppers include methamidophos and acephate, both of which have been shown to cause brain and nervous system damage in laboratory studies. Some studies suggest that acephate may also contribute to the development of certain cancers.

Why not make a healthier choice when organic peppers are widely available? If you can't find them locally, check the list of retailers on page 276. Or grow them organically yourself. Sweet and hot peppers both grow easily in backyard gardens or in pots.

Whatever you do, don't give up eating them. Peppers are high in vitamin C and beta-carotene, both of which help to boost your immune system.

Celery

These crunchy stalks are among America's top 10 favorite vegetables. They're widely used both raw and cooked to make everything from soups and salads to stews and casseroles. That's why it's so important to look for organic celery when you can. Nearly 90 percent of conventionally grown celery tests high in harmful chemical residues, including permethrins, chlorothalonil, and acephate. All three of these pesticides have been linked to certain cancers in laboratory studies. Look for organic celery in your supermarket or farmers' market. Most large grocery stores now carry organic celery. If you can't find it locally, check the retailers on page 276 for other ways to get it.

Potatoes

Americans eat more potatoes than any other vegetable. In fact, spuds account for more than 25 percent of all the vegetables eaten by children (and most of those come in the form of french fries). Take a moment to think about all of the potato foods we commonly eat: hash browns, baked potatoes, mashed potatoes, potato salad, potato chips. The potato shows up in countless popular American foods as the star ingredient or as a supporting player. Spuds seem so unassuming and innocent, yet potatoes are among the foods highest in chemical residues. Recent USDA data found 38 different contaminants on potatoes, including hormone-disrupting pesticides such as endosulfans and the insecticide thiabendazole, which can cause brain and nervous system damage.

Do your family a big, health-inspired favor and buy organic spuds whenever the opportunity presents itself. Or if you see potatoes labeled "Protected Harvest," they make a good alternative to organic. While not grown strictly according to national organic standards, these potatoes are not genetically engineered and are grown with techniques that reduce pests naturally. As a result, they are exposed to fewer pesticides. (For more information about genetically modified crops, see 216.)

Look for organic or Protected Harvest spuds at organic farmers' markets or some larger supermarkets. Another pleasant bonus is that these markets tend to carry more interesting varieties than the typical russets and Yukon Golds found in grocery stores. Pick up some colorful blue-fleshed potatoes, red-fleshed potatoes, and small, tender fingerlings for a delicious change of pace.

Vegetables for Vitality

No matter which vegetables you like best, it's a good idea to eat more of them. In 2002, Oxford researchers looked at more than 30 years of studies and concluded that eating more vegetables can lower your risk of developing cancer. They also confirmed the findings of other long-term studies showing that specific compounds in plants can help prevent other chronic diseases, such as heart disease, asthma, and diabetes.

America's Favorite Vegetables

Most Americans gravitate toward the same few vegetables: potatoes, lettuce, tomatoes, and onions, for example. It's interesting that you can find all of these in just about any meal at McDonald's! Of course, that's not the best way to eat your veggies. Baked or roasted potatoes (with the skins on) offer a lot more fiber and nutrients than french fries. But the news isn't all bad: Broccoli and cabbage made the list, and they are among the most nutritious vegetables available to us.

Here are America's top 10 veggies, in order of popularity.

1. Potatoes	6. Celery
2. Iceberg lettuce	7. Corn
3. Tomatoes	8. Broccoli
4. Onions	9. Green cabbage
5. Carrots	10. Cucumbers

Many nutritionists recommend eating more vegetables to maintain a healthy weight. The idea is that if you're eating more vegetables, which tend to be low in calories and fat, you're eating less of the highly processed, high-calorie foods that can cause you to gain extra weight. This advice applies to both adults and children. Unfortunately, the latest figures indicate that more than 80 percent of kids don't get the recommended three to five servings of vegetables a day. Given that the number of overweight American children has increased by more than 50 percent over the last 20 years, nutritionists are urging parents to include more vegetables in the family meal plan.

To eat more vegetables, try fitting them into your day whenever you can. They are so versatile you can put them almost anywhere. Mix sautéed veggies into rice or pasta dishes. Or replace some of the meat in your favorite main dishes with vegetables. Add mushrooms and peppers to meat loaf. Serve fresh salsa over fish. Snack on carrots instead of crackers. If you're planning meals with finicky kids in mind, try putting veggies in unexpected places, like shredded zucchini into quick bread. And if all else fails, try drinking vegetable juice cocktail instead of fruit juice or soda. Of course, you can also try some of the healthy recipes in this chapter.

Tapenade Phyllo Tartlets

Olives aren't really vegetables; they're fruits. But we treat them more like vegetables, and they star in the Mediterranean spread known as tapenade. Here, the classic mixture of olives, capers, and other seasonings fills phyllo shells to make a simple appetizer that's impressive enough to serve to company.

1 cup pitted Kalamata olives

2 tablespoons drained capers

1 clove garlic, minced

1 cup pine nuts

1 tablespoon extra-virgin olive oil

1 tablespoon lemon juice

1 teaspoon chopped fresh thyme or
    ½ teaspoon dried

¼ teaspoon ground black pepper

2 cups fresh parsley leaves

3 boxes (2.1 ounces each) mini
    phyllo shells, thawed

Put the olives, capers, garlic, pine nuts, oil, lemon juice, thyme, pepper, and parsley in a food processor. Blend until the ingredients are finely minced but not completely pureed into a paste, 15 to 30 seconds.

Refrigerate in a resealable bag for at least 4 hours or up to 24 hours. Bring to room temperature.

Preheat the oven to 350°F. Cut off a corner of the bag and pipe about 2 teaspoons of the filling into each of the 45 phyllo shells. Bake until heated through, 5 minutes.

Makes 45 mini tartlets (about 2 cups filling)

Helping Hand: Frozen mini phyllo shells are perfect for making appetizers without the fat of traditional pastry. Look for them in the frozen bread section of your grocery store.

Beet and Blue Cheese Puffs with Arugula

This appetizer is a total indulgence. Creamy pesto sauce and rich blue cheese spill out of light and crisp puff pastry shells. The beets and arugula add a few redeeming nutrients, but I was really after their contrasting sweet and peppery flavors in this combination. If you can find Chioggia beets, use those. Kids love to see their beautiful pink and white striped rings when cut crosswise. I wonder . . . if you count the rings, will they tell you how many weeks old the beet is?

6 young beets with tops, gently scrubbed

1 tablespoon lemon juice or white vinegar

4 frozen puff pastry shells

2 tablespoons organic butter

¼ cup unbleached all-purpose flour

2 cups organic 2% milk, warmed

3 tablespoons prepared pesto

3 tablespoons crumbled imported blue cheese

1 gently packed cup young arugula leaves

Salt and ground black pepper

2 tablespoons walnuts or pine nuts, toasted and chopped

1 tablespoon chopped fresh basil (optional)

Cut off the beet tops, leaving 1" of stems attached to the bulb. Reserve the beet greens for another use. Put the beets in a medium saucepan and add water to cover. Add the lemon juice or vinegar and bring to a boil over high heat. Reduce the heat to medium-high and boil until the beets are just fork-tender, 20 to 30 minutes. Drain the beets and set aside to cool. When cool, trim off the beet stems and roots. Rub off the beet skins if they are thick; if they are thin, don't bother. Finely chop the beets and set aside.

Meanwhile, preheat the oven to 400°F. Put the pastry shells on a baking sheet with the tops up. Bake until puffed and golden, 20 to 25 minutes.

Rinse out the pan used for the beets and return it to medium heat. Melt the butter in the pan. Whisk in the flour and cook for 1 to 2 minutes. Gradually whisk in the milk, whisking constantly to break up any lumps. Cook and whisk until thickened and simmering, 3 to 5 minutes. Stir in the pesto and blue cheese. Add the beets and arugula and cook until the arugula is just wilted, about 1 minute. Taste and add salt and pepper as necessary.

Put the hot pastry shells on small plates. Remove the tops with a fork. Spoon the filling evenly into each shell, allowing some to spill over the side and onto the plate. Garnish with the walnuts or pine nuts and basil (if using).

Makes 4 servings

Helping Hands: This is a fork-and-knife kind of appetizer. For a finger food, spoon the filling into about 40 frozen phyllo shells (available in the frozen section of most supermarkets) and bake until the shells are crisp, about 5 minutes.

Try to use young beets between the size of a golf ball and a racquetball for this dish. They're the most tender and sweet. If your beets are bigger, use one or two less than called for here.

If you love this flavor combination, it makes a special weeknight meal, too. Just skip the puff pastry shells, thin the sauce with a little more milk, and serve it over cooked linguine instead.

National Farm-to-School Movement Is on a Roll

Back in the mid 1990s, a number of people in different pockets of the country had a similar idea. Why not support our small farms and improve the food served to our schoolchildren at the same time? Schools could get fresher, more nutritious food and strengthen the local economy by purchasing from local farmers. Genius!

But it's been a long, arduous process to coordinate school food services, administrators, farmers, legislators, and the public—and to convince them that it will work. Fortunately, in 2000, the USDA gave the movement a substantial grant and has since facilitated connections between school food service, state departments of agriculture, and other important groups. Also, the 2002 Farm Bill encourages school food service officials to buy locally whenever possible.

These are great strides for a movement that offers tremendous health and social benefits for our children. Farm-to-school programs provide better-tasting food, but they also help children eat more fruits and vegetables. By focusing on healthy alternatives to the fast food and soft drinks sold in many schools, these programs help to combat the recent increases in childhood diseases such as obesity and type 2 diabetes.

Farm-to-school programs are currently operating in California, Florida, Georgia, Iowa, Kentucky, Massachusetts, New Mexico, New York, North Carolina, Pennsylvania, and Vermont. Programs are underway elsewhere, so to find out more about efforts in your area, look up the Community Food Security Coalition on the Web at www.foodsecurity.org.

Hot Greens with Ginger, Soy, and Sesame

This is one of my favorite ways to prepare greens. Use beet greens, mustard greens, spinach, or your favorite cooking greens. I like to use beet greens freshly cut from the tops of beets. These make a fantastic side dish for any Asian-flavored entrée.

1 bunch (about 1 pound) beet greens or other cooking greens

1 tablespoon extra-virgin olive oil

2 cloves garlic, minced

2 teaspoons minced fresh ginger

¼ teaspoon crushed red pepper flakes

1 tablespoon organic tamari or soy sauce

½ teaspoon toasted sesame oil

1 tablespoon sesame seeds, toasted

Cut the whole bunch of greens crosswise into 3" lengths. If using beet greens or another green with sturdy stems, set the stems aside.

Heat the olive oil in a deep, wide sauté pan over medium heat. When hot, add the stems and cook, stirring now and then, until they are just beginning to get tender yet still have good crunch, 2 to 3 minutes. Add the greens, garlic, ginger, and pepper flakes. Cook and stir until the greens just begin to wilt, about 1 minute. Remove from the heat and stir in the tamari or soy sauce and sesame oil. When thoroughly incorporated, divide the greens among plates and top with the sesame seeds.

Makes 4 small servings

Helping Hand: To easily toast the sesame seeds, put them in the sauté pan you'll be using and toast over medium heat until they smell fragrant, 2 to 3 minutes. Pour the seeds into a bowl, heat the olive oil in the pan, and continue with the recipe.

Garlicky Lemon Broccoli

Here's my family's standard side dish for broccoli. It's so simple, I hardly consider it a recipe. But my kids love eating broccoli this way, so there must be something to it. Hopefully, your whole family will like it, too.

2 heads broccoli, cut into florets (about 5 cups)

Juice of ½ lemon

3 tablespoons extra-virgin olive oil

2 cloves garlic, finely minced

½ teaspoon salt

⅛ teaspoon ground black pepper

Pinch of crushed red pepper flakes (optional)

Choice Advice: Cruciferous vegetables like broccoli, cauliflower, and brussels sprouts rank consistently low in pesticide residues when grown by conventional methods.

Put the broccoli in a steamer basket set over a pan of simmering water. Cover and steam until the broccoli is crisp-tender, 3 to 4 minutes.

Meanwhile, squeeze the juice from the lemon into a large bowl. Whisk in the oil in a slow, steady stream until thoroughly blended. Whisk in the garlic, salt, pepper, and pepper flakes (if using). Add the hot broccoli and toss to coat with the dressing.

Makes 4 servings

Helping Hands: To quickly cut a head of broccoli into florets, cut off the stalk crosswise just below the base of the florets' small stems. The bottom layer of florets will fall away from the stalk. Continue cutting across the stems of the florets until all are removed. You can use the pieces of stem in this recipe, too. Just cut them into ½" pieces so they're cooked through when the florets are ready.

When buying fresh broccoli, look for heads with a dark purple color. These contain the most beta-carotene, which can help prevent heart disease, cancer, and cataracts.

LaDonna Redmond
Making Healthy, Organic Food Available to All

Soon after LaDonna Redmond's son, Wade, was born, he developed severe allergies to dairy products, eggs, and shellfish. After he endured numerous hospitalizations and emergency room visits, LaDonna read everything she could about managing her son's allergies. She began to look for healthy food in her Chicago neighborhood of Austin. But it was nowhere to be found. "Here, I could get McDonald's or Kentucky Fried Chicken," she says, "but I couldn't get whole-grain bread or an organic tomato."

Around the same time, LaDonna learned that two children in Austin had heart attacks and four died of stroke. She firmly believed that the food in her community was contributing to health problems among residents. To solve the problem, LaDonna, a longtime community activist, set her sights on a new mission: to make sure that healthy, organic food is available and affordable for everyone in urban neighborhoods such as Austin.

In 1999, LaDonna and other community residents founded the Austin Black Farmers' Market to provide the community with organic meat and high-quality produce from local farmers. She also established the Institute for Community Resource Development (ICRD) to promote local organic farmers and develop urban agriculture. "People of color come largely from agricultural backgrounds, and folks have always grown food in their backyards," explains LaDonna. "We have expanded on that and converted large, vacant spaces into urban farms. We are using the plots to create access to healthier food."

ICRD has been funded by the Chicago Community Trust and the W. K. Kellogg Foundation. Through a partnership with Loyola University, ICRD was able to expand its outreach. Loyola University and ICRD are collaborators on the Chicago Food System Project, which was awarded a $698,000 grant by the W. K. Kellogg Foundation in 2002. The project has established nutrition education programs in two Austin schools and helped to influence food policy in forums such as the Annual Illinois Food Summit and the Illinois Sustainable Food Policy Council. "If we don't get the attention of policy makers," says LaDonna, "we'll continue to do these kinds of programs over and over again, not making any real impact or lasting change."

LaDonna's latest addition to her Chicago community is a community-owned grocery store that features local organic produce, informs Austin people about food and health, provides jobs for residents, and distributes healthy food to grocery stores and restaurants throughout West Side Chicago. "I'm really focused on getting people in touch with their communities and the land their food comes from," she explains. To continue educating Illinois residents and policy makers about issues of race, class, and access to healthy food, LaDonna is now working with Loyola University to establish the Center for Urban and Regional Ecology.

Warm Potatoes with Mustard Herb Dressing

When the hot potatoes hit this mustard dressing, they immediately start soaking up flavor. Spicy mustard, aromatic dill and tarragon, and rich olive oil become infused into the surface of the spuds. Let the spuds sit covered for a few minutes to soak up more flavor. The dish tastes best warm, but you could serve it cold or at room temperature.

12–14 medium organic red potatoes, scrubbed and cut into bite-size pieces

3 tablespoons extra-virgin olive oil

1 tablespoon country-style Dijon mustard

1 tablespoon brown mustard

1 tablespoon chopped fresh tarragon

1 tablespoon chopped fresh dill

½ teaspoon cracked black pepper or ¼ teaspoon ground

½ teaspoon salt

Put the potatoes in a steamer basket and set over a pan of simmering water. Cover and steam over medium heat until the potatoes are fork-tender, 10 to 12 minutes.

Meanwhile, mix together the oil, Dijon mustard, brown mustard, tarragon, dill, pepper, and salt in a medium bowl. Add the hot potatoes and mix. Serve warm.

Makes 4 servings

For Baby: Set aside a few of the cooked potatoes before mixing with the dressing. Let cool slightly, then peel off the skins. Mash the spuds with a splash of olive oil. To thin further, mix in some breast milk or formula.

If your baby is a little older and has teeth, set aside some of the fully dressed potatoes. Let the spuds cool slightly and then mash them or cut them into very small pieces before serving to your little one.

Pesto Cream Green Beans with Almonds

Tom Aczel, a good friend of mine, always grows the tastiest green beans in his backyard organic garden. He prefers to grow the thin French "haricots verts" and always ends up with more of these beans than he can eat. One of his green bean gift bags ended up on my table as described below. Since then, this has become my preferred way to serve up Tom's haricots.

8 ounces green beans, preferably thin haricots verts

2 tablespoons Basic Basil Pesto (on opposite page) or prepared pesto

1½ tablespoons organic light cream, heavy cream, or half-and-half

⅛ teaspoon salt

⅛ teaspoon ground black pepper

2 tablespoons chopped almonds

Put the green beans in a steamer basket and set over a pan of simmering water. Cover and steam over medium heat until the green beans are crisp-tender, 2 to 4 minutes.

Meanwhile, mix together the pesto, cream or half-and-half, salt, and pepper in a medium bowl. Add the hot green beans and toss to mix. Put in a serving bowl or on plates and sprinkle with the almonds.

Makes 4 servings

Basic Basil Pesto

We always grow basil in our backyard garden. To remember the magic of this fresh herb all year long, I make pesto and freeze it. Purists will scoff because pesto is at its best when freshly made. There's no disputing that. But during the winter months when fresh basil is harder to come by, I prefer my own frozen pesto to the jarred stuff you find in grocery stores.

1 large clove garlic

5 loosely packed cups fresh basil leaves

1 cup grated Parmigiano-Reggiano cheese

6 tablespoons pine nuts

1/3 cup extra-virgin olive oil

1/2 teaspoon salt

1/8 teaspoon ground black pepper

Choice Advice: If you don't have Parmigiano-Reggiano cheese on hand, you'll still sidestep the issues surrounding rBGH if you substitute another imported grating cheese such as Grana Padano or Asiago or a domestic sheep's milk cheese such as Pecorino Romano.

Put the garlic in a food processor. Process until finely chopped, about 10 seconds. Add the basil, cheese, and pine nuts. Process until finely chopped, about 20 seconds. With the processor on, pour the oil through the feed tube in a slow, steady stream, processing until the mixture forms a loose paste, about 20 seconds. Add the salt and pepper through the feed tube and process until blended.

Use immediately or freeze in an airtight container for up to 1 year. Use a melon baller to scoop out frozen pesto as necessary.

Makes 1 cup

Helping Hand: When adding frozen pesto to hot dishes, such as pasta, the heat of the dish will thaw the pesto. If using frozen pesto for a sandwich or other cold dish, remove the amount of pesto you need and thaw that amount at room temperature. Or for a quick thaw, microwave the pesto in 5-second increments.

Guacamole with Fresh Tortilla Chips

Rich, buttery-tasting avocados are one of summer's most delicious fruits. They're also high in calories and fat. Fortunately, most of the fat is the heart-healthy monounsaturated kind. To lower the calories, this version of guacamole replaces some of the avocados with tomatillos (Mexican green tomatoes). The chips are also lower in fat and salt than store-bought varieties.

GUACAMOLE

2 Hass avocados, pitted and peeled

1 tablespoon lime juice

3 tomatillos, husked, rinsed, and finely chopped

1 small tomato, finely chopped

1 organic jalapeño pepper or 2 serrano peppers, seeded and chopped

¼ cup chopped onion

1 clove garlic, minced

3 tablespoons chopped fresh cilantro

¾ teaspoon salt

TORTILLA CHIPS

8 yellow and/or blue corn tortillas

½ teaspoon salt

½ teaspoon chipotle chile powder (optional)

Choice Advice: In the late 1980s, the USDA and FDA examined 42 common food crops for pesticide residues. Avocados had the lowest levels of the fewest number of pesticides of all crops examined.

To make the guacamole: Mash the avocados in a serving bowl with a fork. Stir in the lime juice, tomatillos, tomato, pepper, onion, garlic, cilantro, and salt. Serve immediately or cover with plastic wrap pressed onto the surface and refrigerate for up to 4 hours.

To make the chips: Preheat the oven to 375°F. Stack the tortillas into two stacks of 4 tortillas each. With a large knife, cut each stack like a pizza into 8 wedges (for a total of 64 chips). Lay the chips in a single layer on large baking sheets. Coat both sides of the chips with cooking spray and sprinkle with the salt and chipotle powder (if using). Bake until crisp and lightly browned, 12 to 15 minutes. Serve in a paper-lined basket with the guacamole.

Makes 8 servings

Helping Hands: Tomatillos have a tart, citrusy flavor, sort of like a lime crossed with a tomato. They are available in most supermarket produce sections near the chile peppers or in Mexican groceries. Look for them in midsummer. Peel off the papery husk and rinse under cool water before chopping.

To quickly pit and peel an avocado, cut it in half from top to bottom through the peel and around the pit. Twist apart the halves and place the half containing the pit in your palm or nest in a towel. Whack the pit with the knife blade and then twist the knife to lift out the pit. Knock the pit off the knife with a spoon. Use the spoon to scoop the avocado from its peel.

Chunky Tomato Salsa

This lively salsa also goes by the name of *pico de gallo* or "rooster beak." It's certain to give you a fresh peck on the cheek! Leave in the chile seeds for even more bite.

2 tomatoes, seeded and finely chopped

3 organic jalapeño peppers, seeded and finely chopped

1 small clove garlic, minced

⅓ cup finely chopped onion

¼ cup chopped fresh cilantro

2 tablespoons lime juice

½ teaspoon salt

Mix together the tomatoes, peppers, garlic, onion, cilantro, lime juice, and salt in a serving bowl. Let sit for 1 hour to blend the flavors.

Makes 8 servings

Helping Hand: To make Roasted Tomato Salsa, roast the whole tomatoes in a heavy skillet over medium heat until blackened all over. Remove and let cool. Add the chiles and unpeeled garlic to the skillet and pan-roast until the chiles are blackened all over and the garlic is soft and blackened in spots (the garlic will take a little longer than the chiles). Peel the tomatoes and garlic; chop the chiles. Mix in a bowl with the remaining ingredients.

The Green and the Red

Lettuce and tomatoes are among America's most frequently eaten vegetables (even though, botanically speaking, tomatoes are considered a fruit). Fortunately, both foods make relatively healthy choices and aren't very high in pesticide residues.

For more nutritious lettuce, pick darker green varieties, such as romaine. Or go even further and try greens like spinach and arugula in salads and on sandwiches. In general, the darker the green leaf, the more vitamin C, vitamin A, folate, and iron you'll get.

Tomatoes are also high in vitamin C, and they're loaded with a red pigment called lycopene. This powerful antioxidant can help prevent several forms of cancer, including prostate, colon, stomach, breast, and lung cancers.

What about genetic engineering? Most lettuces and tomatoes currently sold are not genetically altered, but one tomato variety bears the distinction of the being the world's first genetically engineered food approved for human consumption. In 1994, the Flavr Savr tomato hit U.S. markets, promising better taste and appearance. Unlike most conventionally grown tomatoes, the Flavr Savr was engineered so that it could be allowed to ripen on the vine yet stay firm during shipping without bruising or rotting.

Unfortunately, the Flavr Savr didn't live up to its name. It neither tasted better nor lasted longer than conventional tomatoes. Within 2 years, it was taken off the market. For the best-tasting tomatoes, try vine-ripened organic tomatoes from a local grower.

Jicama Fennel Salad with Lime Orange Dressing

The anise-flavored fennel and the citrus in this salad really wake up the taste buds. So does the peppery bite of watercress! If you can't find fresh watercress in the herb section of your grocery store, use a torn-up head of buttercrunch lettuce. In that case, you might want to double or triple the hot pepper sauce for extra kick.

1 small jicama, peeled and cut into 2" long matchsticks (about 3 cups)

1 medium fennel bulb, trimmed and cut into 2" long matchsticks (about 3 cups)

3 large organic navel oranges

⅓ cup extra-virgin olive oil

Juice of 1 lime

½ teaspoon salt

¼ teaspoon grated nutmeg

¼ teaspoon ground fennel seeds (optional)

¼ teaspoon hot pepper sauce (or more to taste)

⅛ teaspoon ground black pepper

2 bunches watercress, stems trimmed

¼ cup chopped fresh basil

1 tablespoon sliced almonds

In a large bowl, combine the jicama and fennel.

Peel and section 2 oranges. Cut each section into quarters and add to the bowl.

Squeeze the juice from the remaining orange and the lime into a small bowl. Whisk in the oil in a slow, steady stream until incorporated. Whisk in the salt, nutmeg, fennel seeds (if using), pepper sauce, and black pepper. Pour over the jicama and toss.

Divide the watercress among salad plates. Top with the jicama mixture. Pour any remaining dressing evenly over the salads and sprinkle each with the basil and sliced almonds.

Makes 6 servings

Helping Hands: To trim fennel, cut off the stems and fronds where they turn pale green and the white bulb begins. Save the stems and fronds for another use (toss them into a stock or sauce for a delicate anise flavor; the fronds also make a beautiful garnish). Trim off the base of the bulb and cut it in half through the base. To make curved matchsticks, cut or pull off the naturally crescent-shaped slices from the core of each half.

To avoid the somewhat bitter membranes in the oranges, make *suprêmes* out of the sections. Start with the whole orange and cut off ½" from the top and bottom just to expose the flesh. Stand the orange on one of the cut sides and cut off the peel all the way around the orange. Stand the rindless orange on end and run the knife on either side of each segment in a V-shape to remove each segment from its surrounding membrane. Put the resulting orange flesh, or suprêmes, in the bowl and squeeze any juice from the cut scraps.

Mesclun Salad with Pears and Apricot Balsamic Vinaigrette

Use fresh or bagged organic salad greens for this easy side salad. Mesclun sometimes goes by the name of "spring mix" and is usually a blend of tender young greens such as mizuna, tatsoi, and arugula. Any combination of mild and bitter greens will do.

6 tablespoons apricot nectar

1 tablespoon balsamic vinegar

1½ tablespoons extra-virgin olive oil

⅛ teaspoon Dijon mustard

⅛ teaspoon salt

5–6 cups mixed organic baby salad greens

1 tablespoon lemon juice

½ teaspoon sugar

1 small ripe organic pear (Anjou or Bosc), cored and chopped

2 tablespoons pecans, toasted and broken into pieces

4 ounces goat cheese, crumbled

Choice Advice: If your salad greens contain spinach in the mix, it's best to buy organic.

Put the nectar and vinegar in a large bowl. Whisk in the oil in a slow, steady stream. When the oil is fully incorporated, whisk in the mustard and salt. Add the greens and toss to coat. Divide the dressed greens among salad plates.

Whisk together the lemon juice and sugar in a medium bowl. Add the pear and toss to coat. Scatter the pear and pecans over the greens. Top with the cheese.

Makes 4 servings

Helping Hands: Look for canned apricot nectar in the juice aisle of your grocery store. Or look in the international aisle; Goya makes a popular line of fruit nectars. In this recipe, the nectar makes a lower-fat vinaigrette by thickening the dressing so you can use a bit less oil. If you can't find apricot nectar, try peach nectar or mango nectar.

To easily crumble a log of goat cheese, scrape it with a fork over the salad.

To toast pecans, lay them in a single layer on a baking sheet and bake at 300°F just until toasty and fragrant, 3 to 5 minutes. Watch carefully to avoid burning.

Potato Corn Chowder

This thick soup tastes rich and luscious even though it uses reduced-fat milk and just a smidgen of butter. The secret is the cornmeal used for thickening, which boosts the corn flavor and creates a creamy texture similar to that of polenta.

2 teaspoons organic butter

½ onion, chopped

1 clove garlic, minced

½ organic red bell pepper, seeded and chopped

2 large GMO-free or organic Yukon Gold potatoes, cut into ½" cubes

½ teaspoon dried rosemary, crumbled

1 bay leaf

3 cups vegetable broth or pasture-raised or organic chicken broth

¼ cup stone-ground organic yellow cornmeal

1 cup organic 2% milk

1 cup fresh or frozen corn kernels

¼ teaspoon ground black pepper

Salt

Melt the butter in a medium soup pot over medium heat. Add the onion, garlic, and bell pepper to the pan. Cook until soft, about 5 minutes. Add the potatoes, rosemary, bay leaf, and broth. Bring to a boil over high heat. Reduce the heat to medium and simmer until the potatoes are tender, about 12 minutes.

Whisk the cornmeal into the milk and then stir into the soup. Cook until thickened, about 5 minutes. Stir in the corn and black pepper and cook for 2 minutes. Taste and add salt to taste. Remove and discard the bay leaf.

Makes 4 to 6 servings

Helping Hands: To add a flavorful (and healthy) garnish to this soup, crumble some cooked vegetarian bacon over top. Vegetarian bacon has half the fat and none of the cholesterol of cured pork bacon. More important, it's got none of the hormones, antibiotics, or nitrates. It's not real bacon, of course, but it tastes good in this chowder. Look for vegetarian bacon in the frozen meat or breakfast section of your supermarket.

Fresh corn kernels are best here. Cut fresh kernels from 2 or 3 cobs, then scrape the "milk" from the cobs using the back of the knife blade. Add the kernels and milk to the soup.

Creamy Tomato Rice Soup

After playing outside during chilly autumn afternoons as a kid, I found nothing warmed me up more than a bowl of creamy tomato soup and a grilled cheese sandwich. In this version, pureed cooked rice thickens the soup instead of cream. This steaming bowl is the perfect place to crumble a few of your favorite crackers.

2 tablespoons organic butter

1 onion, chopped

1 cup chopped carrots

1 organic celery rib, chopped

1 can (28 ounces) diced tomatoes in juice

1½ cups vegetable broth or pasture-raised or organic chicken broth

1 teaspoon dried basil or marjoram

¼ teaspoon ground black pepper

1¼ cups cooked white rice

1 cup organic 2% milk

Melt the butter in a medium soup pot over medium heat. Add the onion, carrots, and celery. Cook until the vegetables begin to soften, about 5 minutes. Add the tomatoes, broth, and basil or marjoram. Bring to a boil over high heat. Lower the heat to medium-low and simmer until the flavors are blended, 15 to 20 minutes.

Remove from the heat and stir in ½ cup rice. Puree the soup in a blender or food processor (in batches if necessary).

Return the soup to medium-low heat and stir in the milk and the remaining ¾ cup rice. Heat through and serve.

Makes 6 servings

Helping Hand: I use canned tomatoes here because I usually fix this dish in the fall, after tomatoes are long gone from the vine. Of course, if fresh tomatoes are in season when you make it, use those instead. You'll need about 3 cups of peeled, cored, and chopped tomatoes (about 1½ pounds). For the rice, I like medium-grain white rice, but long-grain, short-grain, or quick-cooking rice will also work.

NELL NEWMAN
A Lifelong Environmentalist

Bubbling with enthusiasm, Nell Newman told me a few years ago about the new snack she'd been taste testing: creamy, chocolate-filled Newman-O's, her organic version of Oreos. "You've got to try them," she gushed.

These cookies are one of the latest additions to Nell's organic line of snack foods, Newman's Own Organics. Launched in 1993, Nell's company started as a division of her famous "Pa" Paul Newman's food business, Newman's Own.

Newman's Own Organics is the perfect marriage of Nell's passion for food and her commitment to sustainable agriculture. A lifelong environmentalist, Nell holds a B.S. in human ecology, has worked for the Environmental Defense Fund, and is former executive director of the Ventana Wilderness Sanctuary in California.

After years of reestablishing threatened peregrine falcons and bald eagles in California, Nell saw just how devastating pesticides could be. "The eggs of these birds had such high levels of contaminants that they were too thin to hatch," she says. Nell even had her own blood tested. "The test came back showing low levels of DDT, PCBs [polychlorinated biphenyls], and chlordane. Although I know that everybody has background levels of contaminants in their blood, it still concerned me," she confided. "It hits home with people when I tell them that I've got these contaminants in my body...and that everybody does."

That's when Nell found her calling: to support sustainable agriculture by giving profits away to environmental groups. Since the company has become independent, Newman's Own Organics has followed in the parent company's footsteps and donated after-tax profits to charity through a grant process. "I'm thrilled to be able to support sustainable agriculture on both ends," she says. "We buy organic ingredients to support organic farmers, and then we donate profits to sustainable ag groups like the Organic Farming Research Foundation."

So far, Newman's Own Organics has given away more than $2 million.

Nell Newman's Cauliflower and Parmesan Soup

Nell Newman, owner of Newman's Own Organic foods, loves to dream up new recipes. This soup originated during one of Nell's refrigerator-cleaning sprees, in which she throws all her leftovers into a pot, heats them, and waits to see what happens. The result here is a fantastically fresh-tasting, slightly lemony, creamy soup. Use fresh green peas if you can. They make a world of difference in the flavor.

2 cups water

1 cup millet or white rice, rinsed

6 cups vegetable broth or pasture-raised or organic chicken broth

1 onion, chopped

1 large head cauliflower, cut into bite-size pieces

¾ cup grated Parmesan cheese

Juice of ½ lemon

1 cup fresh or frozen peas

¼ cup chopped fresh dill or ¾ teaspoon dried

Salt and ground black pepper

Bring the water to a boil in a medium saucepan over high heat. Add the millet or rice. Reduce the heat to low, cover, and cook until the grain is soft, about 15 minutes. Set aside, covered, for 5 minutes and then fluff with a fork.

Meanwhile, in a large soup pot, combine the broth, onion, and cauliflower. Bring to a simmer over medium heat and cook until the cauliflower is tender, 8 to 10 minutes. Transfer the mixture to a blender or food processor in batches and puree until smooth. Return to the pot and heat gently over low heat. Stir in the cheese, lemon juice, peas, cooked millet or rice, and dill. Cook for 5 minutes. Taste and add salt and pepper as necessary (which will depend on how highly seasoned your broth is).

Makes 8 servings

Helping Hands: A high-protein staple grain in Asia and Africa, millet looks like a tiny oval, ivory-colored seed. Look for it in the rice aisle of your supermarket or natural food store. If you can't find it, rice makes a fine substitute.

If you have a handheld stick blender, by all means use that instead of transferring the soup to an upright blender to puree.

Pantry Minestrone

My wife, Christine, has a gift for improvising this soup with whatever we have on hand, and you can, too. If you don't have white beans, use chickpeas. If you don't have ditalini, use small shells. If you have extra zucchini, throw that in, too. You get the idea. Big hunks of bread and a salad complete the meal.

1 cup ditalini pasta

1 tablespoon extra-virgin olive oil

1 small onion, chopped

2 cloves garlic, minced

1 carrot, chopped

2 organic celery ribs, chopped

1 organic red bell pepper, seeded and chopped

½ teaspoon dried Italian seasoning

½ teaspoon dried rosemary, crumbled

1½ cups vegetable broth or pasture-raised or organic chicken broth

1 can (14 ounces) diced tomatoes in juice

1 cup cooked or rinsed canned small white beans

Choice Advice: Be sure to use organic celery. If you can't find it, replace with another root vegetable or 2 or 3 tablespoons of chopped fresh parsley.

Cook the pasta in salted boiling water until slightly undercooked, about 6 minutes. The pasta should still be a little chewy and white in the center, because it will cook further in the soup. Drain and set aside.

Meanwhile, heat the oil in a medium soup pot over medium heat. Add the onion and garlic and cook, stirring occasionally, until softened, about 4 minutes. Add the carrot, celery, and pepper. Cook until slightly softened, about 4 minutes. Stir in the Italian seasoning, rosemary, broth, and tomatoes. Simmer until the flavors blend, about 15 to 20 minutes. Add the beans and pasta and simmer until heated through, 3 to 5 minutes.

Makes 4 servings

Cheesy Potato Onion Pie

Years ago on a rainy day in England, my aunt Catherine served this dish, and I fell in love. How can you go wrong with potatoes and cheese? Make this pie in the fall when you want to warm up the kitchen and fill up with a satisfying meal. If you have the time, make the crust for this pie with any standard deep-dish piecrust recipe. I call for a store-bought crust to cut down on prep time. Store-bought crusts are also lower in fat than most homemade ones because commercial machines can roll the dough very thinly, using less pie dough overall.

2 tablespoons organic butter

1 large leek, cleaned and chopped

½ small onion, chopped

1 small clove garlic, minced

10 small organic Yukon Gold potatoes, peeled and chopped

2 cups organic 2% milk

½ cup shredded Gruyère cheese

1 tablespoon chopped fresh thyme

1 teaspoon Dijon mustard

½ teaspoon salt

½ teaspoon ground black pepper

½ cup shredded organic sharp Cheddar cheese

1 prepared deep-dish piecrust, prebaked

2 pasture-raised or organic eggs, separated

⅛ teaspoon paprika

Preheat the oven to 350°F.

Melt the butter in a deep, wide sauté pan over medium-low heat. Add the leek, onion, and garlic and cook, stirring occasionally, until the vegetables are tender, about 8 minutes. Stir in the potatoes and enough milk to almost cover the potatoes. Bring to a boil over high heat. Reduce the heat to medium and simmer, stirring occasionally, until the potatoes are tender, about 10 minutes.

Partially mash the potatoes with a potato masher in the pan. Stir in the Gruyère, thyme, mustard, salt, and pepper. Remove from the heat to cool slightly.

Meanwhile, lay the Cheddar over the bottom of the prepared crust.

Stir the egg yolks into the potato mixture. Beat the egg whites with clean dry beaters in a medium bowl until almost-stiff peaks form when the beaters are lifted. Gently fold the whites into the potato mixture, then scrape the filling over the Cheddar in the crust. Dust the top with paprika and bake until puffed and golden, about 20 minutes.

Makes 8 servings

Chiles Rellenos Gratin

Stuffed chiles are among the gringo favorites of Mexican food. The American version—jalapeño "poppers" stuffed with cheese, breaded, and fried—is now standard bar food across the United States. But there are so many other ways to enjoy stuffed chiles. Here, roasted poblano chiles are stuffed with an herbed filling of sautéed scallions, corn, red bell peppers, and pine nuts. The chiles are then covered with a spicy cream sauce, topped with a mixture of cornmeal and bread crumbs, and baked. I like to serve this in a large gratin dish, but if you're having a more formal affair, serve it in individual baking dishes, allowing two rellenos per dish.

8 organic poblano chile peppers

4 tablespoons organic butter

1 organic red bell pepper, seeded and chopped

1½ cups fresh or frozen corn kernels

5 scallions, chopped

2 tablespoons pine nuts

2 cloves garlic, minced

1 cup crumbled queso fresco or shredded reduced-fat organic sharp Cheddar cheese

2 tablespoons chopped fresh cilantro or parsley

1 teaspoon salt

¼ teaspoon ground red pepper

½ teaspoon ground cumin

⅛ teaspoon grated nutmeg

3 tablespoons unbleached all-purpose flour

2 cups organic 2% milk

1 tablespoon lime juice

½ cup plain dry bread crumbs

¼ cup stone-ground organic yellow cornmeal

Preheat a grill, broiler, or gas burner to high.

Roast the chile peppers on the grill, under the broiler, or over the flame until just blistered and blackened all over, about 3 minutes per side. Set in a bowl covered with a kitchen towel until just cool enough to handle (the chiles should still hold their shape). Remove and discard the skins.

Make a 2"-long slit in each chile. Use a melon baller or spoon to scrape out and discard the core and seeds. Set the chiles in a 2-quart gratin or baking dish coated with cooking spray.

Heat 1 tablespoon butter in a large nonstick skillet over medium heat. Add the bell pepper and cook until tender, about 4 minutes. Add the corn, scallions, pine nuts, and garlic and cook until heated through, 2 minutes. Remove from the heat and stir in ¾ cup cheese, the cilantro or parsley, ½ teaspoon salt, and ⅛ teaspoon ground red pepper. Spoon about ⅓ cup filling into each chile.

Preheat the oven to 350°F.

In the same pan used to cook the filling, melt the remaining 3 tablespoons butter over medium-low heat. Whisk in the cumin, nutmeg, and the remaining ⅛ teaspoon ground red pepper. Cook for 30 seconds. Whisk in the flour and whisk frequently until the

RAFFI
A Lover of True Voices

An internationally renowned children's troubadour, Raffi has become a friend to millions of children and their families. His song "Baby Beluga" is among the most popular children's songs ever recorded. For Raffi, children are an immeasurable source of inspiration because of their "true voices."

Raffi is deeply committed to the principle of doing more to nurture and care for our young. "As a children's entertainer and advocate," says Raffi, "I have been guided by the belief that honoring children is fundamental. It should be the framework for evaluating all actions, both private and public." Raffi believes that environmental protection for young children is a human-rights issue, and this belief has led him to action.

Raffi is president of a triple bottom-line company called Troubadour Music. He is also the founder of Child Honoring, an original philosophy connecting the personal, cultural, and planetary aspects of life, a unifying principle for restoring human and natural communities. His *Covenant for Honoring Children* is widely circulated in child health and development circles. Raffi has given talks on child honoring in settings as diverse as the New York Academy of Medicine, Parliament Hill in Ottawa, Ontario, the World Bank, and Harvard University.

mixture browns well, about 5 minutes. Gradually whisk in the milk until smooth. Cook until thick, about 4 minutes. Whisk in the remaining ½ teaspoon salt and the lime juice.

Pour the sauce evenly over the chiles. Mix together the bread crumbs, cornmeal, and the remaining ¼ cup cheese. Sprinkle evenly over top. Bake until bubbly, about 20 minutes. Turn on the broiler and broil until the top is lightly browned, about 1 minute.

Makes 8 servings

Helping Hand: I find it easiest to peel roasted chiles from the tip (tapered end) to the stem end.

Chapter 4

Fish and Shellfish

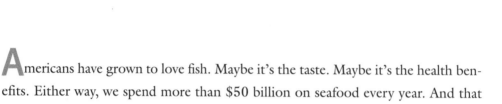

Americans have grown to love fish. Maybe it's the taste. Maybe it's the health benefits. Either way, we spend more than $50 billion on seafood every year. And that figure is rising. Fish is popular worldwide, too. Men, women, and children around the world eat more fish than any other type of animal protein, according to the United Nations Food and Agriculture Organization (FAO).

To most seafood lovers, there seems to be an ever-growing abundance and variety of fish and shellfish. However, the FAO estimates that two-thirds of the world's major marine fisheries are currently overfished or depleted. In 2001, a long-term study published in *Science* magazine concluded that extinction of ocean life due to overfishing had a greater impact on our coastal ecosystems than all other forms of human interference, including pollution, declining water quality, and even changes in climate (global warming) caused by human activities. In North America, the evidence is clear right off our shores. Atlantic cod supplies off the coasts of New England and Canada are perilously low. Wild Atlantic salmon is now on the endangered species list. And in Maryland, blue crabs are becoming increasingly scarce.

We simply haven't managed our oceans well enough. "None of the conservation groups were focusing on fish," says Dr. Carl Safina, vice president for marine conservation and founder of the Living Oceans Program at the National Audubon Society. "There were the save-the-dolphins people and the save-the-seals people, but no one was saving the fish." Dr. Safina admits that progress has been made in the past 20 years, but a lot of work lies ahead for ensuring the long-term abundance of seafood and the health of our oceans.

In response to declining fish supplies, fish farming or "aquaculture" efforts boomed around the globe throughout the 1980s and 1990s. Aquaculture continues to outpace the growth of all other animal food production, according to current FAO figures. Overall, fish farms have been relatively successful with some varieties of seafood, such as catfish and tilapia, but disastrous with others, such as salmon and shrimp. Drawbacks of aquaculture include excessive pollution from overcrowded open net pens in coastal waters, disease outbreaks, and destruction of nearby marine ecosystems, all of which have added to the problem of declining wild fish stocks rather than improving it.

In addition, the health of our oceans is not the only issue—recent studies suggest that even the healthfulness of fish appears to have declined in recent years. In 2002, for example, the U.S. Food and Drug Administration (FDA) issued an advisory recommending that all pregnant women completely avoid four types of fish: shark, swordfish, king mackerel, and tilefish. Tests show that these fish can harbor enough mercury to cause developmental abnormalities in infants. Other fish have tested high in harmful environmental contaminants such as dioxins and polychlorinated biphenyls (PCBs).

Eat the Purest Seafood

Eating seafood has certainly become more problematic in recent years. But there's no reason to completely avoid the fish counter. If you choose fish and shellfish carefully, the nutritional benefits far outweigh the risks. Here's a buying guide so you can enjoy your favorites without any snags.

Sustainably Harvested Wild Fish

For your health and the long-term survival of commercial fish supplies, sustainably harvested wild fish makes the best overall choice among seafood. Plus, wild fish usually taste better than farmed.

Certified Sustainable Seafood

In 1997, the London-based Marine Stewardship Council (MSC) began a labeling program to promote sustainable fisheries around the world. According to the MSC's basic definition, sustainable fisheries "ensure that the catch of marine resources is at the level compatible with long-term sustainable yield, while maintaining the marine environment's biodiversity, productivity, and ecological processes." Fisheries that meet the Council's detailed criteria can put the MSC logo on their products.

The MSC is similar to the independent agencies that certify organic agricultural products, such as Oregon Tilth. Since the program is relatively young, only a few fisheries have been certified. But if you see the MSC label on a type of seafood, you can be sure it makes an ecofriendly choice. To date, the label can be found on Alaskan salmon, Burry Inlet cockles, Lock Torridon nephrops, New Zealand hoki, South West mackerel (a handline fishery), Thames herring, and Western Australian rock lobster.

Most varieties of wild fish are relatively low in total fat and high in protein. Wild fish also provide fair amounts of iron and vitamin B_{12} and are high in heart-healthy omega-3 fatty acids. Two credible, long-term studies show strong evidence that the omega-3s in fish can help reduce your risk of developing heart disease, the number one cause of death in America. Researchers involved in the long-running Nurses Health Study, which has been analyzing the diets, lifestyles, and health of nearly 85,000 nurses since 1976, recently concluded that women who ate fish two to four times a week cut their risk of heart disease by 30 percent, compared with women who rarely ate fish. A similar study, the Physicians' Health Study, has been tracking the experience of about 22,000 male doctors since 1982. Scientists leading the men's study found that those with higher blood concentrations of omega-3 fatty acids were more than 80 percent less likely to die from a heart attack.

As important health benefits like these have become better known, many Americans have begun to eat more fish. Current estimates indicate we eat about 15 pounds of fish per person per year, a gradual increase since the early 1980s that is expected to grow. However, as the demand for fish grows, both the worldwide and the domestic wild fish supply become increasingly threatened by overfishing.

Simply put, overfishing results from catching more wild fish than can be replaced by the natural reproductive cycle of the species. Demand for some particular types of fish is partly to blame, as are destructive fishing practices that include certain kinds of fishing gear. For example, bottom trawls—huge, heavy nets dragged across the ocean floor—have destroyed thousands of miles of marine habitats, making it more difficult for fish to reproduce or hide from larger predators. Larger, long-lived fish, such as Patagonian toothfish (marketed as Chilean sea bass), have also had severe trouble recovering from rampant overfishing. The same holds true for most other big, wild fish that reproduce late in life, such as sharks and tuna.

Better fisheries management and increasing awareness in the food industry is slowly beginning to help the situation. In the meantime, you can make a big difference by choosing wild fish species that are relatively abundant and well managed. Believe it or not, your fish choices have a substantial impact on current demand and influence the types of fish that get ordered from fish suppliers for restaurants and grocery stores.

In 1997, for instance, environmental and consumer groups helped spread the message of depleted North Atlantic swordfish supplies with a campaign called "Give Swordfish a Break." Since then, fewer consumers and chefs have been buying and serving swordfish, and North Atlantic swordfish are slowly beginning to recover. Recently, a similar campaign called "Take a Pass on Chilean Sea Bass" has let consumers know that Chilean sea bass are overfished and has begun the long process of recovery for this wild fish species.

Ideal choices for well-managed, sustainably harvested species include wild Alaskan salmon, Pacific halibut, Atlantic striped bass, and mahimahi. Canned albacore tuna is also an option since most of it is caught by trolling, one of the less destructive fishing practices. These fish come from sustainable fisheries, defined loosely as those that responsibly manage wild fish populations to restore abundance and ensure the survival of plentiful fish stocks for future generations to enjoy. See "Safe and Sustainable Seafood" on page 99 for other types of sustainable fish.

Whenever you shop or eat out, get in the habit of asking a few questions before buying wild fish: Where is the fish from and how was it caught? Does it come from a sustainable fishery? (In general, hook-and-line caught, pole-caught, and trolled fish are more sustainably harvested than trawled fish.)

Responsibly Farmed Fish

As wild fish stocks continue to deplete, fish farms have grown tremendously to meet demand. According to current figures from the United Nations, more than one-quarter of the seafood eaten worldwide is raised on farms rather than caught from the seas. Fishing industry analysts predict that, by the year 2020, fish farms or aquaculture operations will surpass capture fisheries in supplying the majority of seafood to the world.

In 2001, U.S. aquaculture accounted for 800 million pounds of the nation's food supply. Several varieties of farmed fish make safe and sustainable choices. But some are riddled with health and environmental problems, so it's wise to choose carefully.

Overall, intensive fish farms are vulnerable to many of the same problems seen in intensive hog- and cattle-feeding operations, or feedlots. Overcrowding and growth-promoting feed unnaturally stress the animals to the point of poor health. Unsanitary conditions can arise, which may allow parasites and diseases to spread rapidly and may also allow huge amounts of contaminated waste to be released into nearby waters, leading to excessive and damaging pollution. In addition, the food used in many aquaculture operations is commonly derived from wild fish, indirectly contributing to the depletion of wild fish stocks.

To illustrate many of these related problems, let's consider the specifics of a typical salmon farm. An average operation confines about 250,000 salmon in metal or open mesh net pens out in coastal waters and produces about 2 metric tons of waste per day, about the same amount humans would produce in a small city. Because the open net pens float in the ocean, any mismanaged waste, pollution, disease, or escaped fish from these farms directly affects surrounding marine ecosystems. Escaping fish can create problems, too. Diseased fish or new varieties of genetically engineered fish (which grow twice as fast) could weaken wild fish species through increased competition for food and interbreeding with wild fish populations.

Salmon feed also poses a few health risks. Most farmed salmon are fed a high-fat, high-protein diet of processed fishmeal and fish oil supplements. This body-building diet accelerates their growth but comes at a significant price. Salmon feed tends to be high in harmful environmental contaminants like dioxins and PCBs. These man-made toxins are the product of industrial waste and eventually end up in ocean waters, where they concentrate in the fatty or oily parts of fish. The toxins are further concentrated in the fish oil that is then compressed into salmon feed pellets. As a result, farmed salmon tend to be higher than wild salmon in cancer-causing dioxins and PCBs. In 2003, a study from the Environmental Working Group found that U.S. farmed salmon have about 16 times the PCBs found in wild salmon, 4 times the levels in beef, and 3.4 times the PCBs found in other seafood. This study confirmed the findings of previous research in Canada and the United Kingdom, concluding that farmed salmon is likely the most PCB-contaminated protein source in the U.S. food supply.

USDA figures also show that farmed varieties of salmon have nearly twice the fat, twice the saturated fat, and fewer beneficial omega-3 fatty acids than wild salmon. With a lowered health profile and concerns over disease, pollution, and waste management—plus a noticeable drop in flavor—farmed salmon may seem like something to avoid. However, that's easier said than done. More than 70 percent of fresh salmon eaten in the United States is, in fact, farmed. And all salmon labeled as "Atlantic" comes from farms. So if you're a salmon fan, your best bet is to look for fresh—or even canned—salmon from Alaska, for both its flavor and its health benefits. If Atlantic salmon is your only option, look for salmon that comes from salmon farmers who rotate their fish pens to reduce disease, pollution, and predator problems.

Fortunately, other varieties of farmed fish are less problematic. Aquaculture has had good results with catfish, tilapia, rainbow trout, and striped bass. Most catfish are farmed on land in ponds that don't produce excessive pollution. Likewise, striped bass have been responsibly farmed in ponds and tanks since the early 1960s. About half of the striped bass sold in markets comes from closed, nonpolluting aquaculture systems. (Flavor aficionados take note: Farmed striped bass is actually a hybrid of wild striped bass and white bass, which weakens the flavor in the farmed variety a bit.) The best choices among farmed fish are those that come from closed, nonpolluting farms such as ponds and tanks.

Sustainably Harvested Wild Shellfish

If well-managed and responsibly harvested in the wild, shellfish make a good choice for health and ocean conservation. Not to mention flavor!

In the mid to late 1980s, many people avoided shellfish because they were considered to be high in cholesterol, which is linked to an increased heart disease risk. Researchers now agree that having two to three servings of shellfish per week is unlikely to significantly raise blood cholesterol. Here are two reasons why. First, because of better testing methods, we now know that shellfish actually contain less cholesterol than previously thought. Shrimp, for instance, is the shellfish highest in cholesterol, yet a typical 3-ounce serving contains nearly 25 percent less cholesterol than what you'll get if you eat a single egg. Second, shellfish contain virtually no saturated fat, which we know is the real culprit in raising heart disease risk—much more so than dietary cholesterol.

Because shellfish serve as one of nature's water filters, they do accumulate pollutants and toxins in their flesh that can potentially make you sick—especially if you eat raw shellfish—but the health risk for most adults is relatively low. Coastal shell-fishing

Safe and Sustainable Seafood

Fish and shellfish generally make healthy food choices, but some species are contaminated with excessive pollutants or overfished to the brink of extinction. Deciding which seafood makes the best overall choice for your health and the environment can be incredibly complicated. Here's a look at the top catches on both counts. Put the emphasis on these fish and shellfish to improve your health without leaving our oceans irreparably depleted. If you don't see "farmed" or "wild" after a particular fish, either type makes a viable option. These lists are based on consumption recommendations from the Natural Resources Defense Council, Environmental Defense, the National Audubon Society, the Monterey Bay Aquarium, and the U.S. Food and Drug Administration. Since our oceans are in constant flux, check with these organizations for regularly updated information on healthy, sustainable seafood choices. Or visit www.generationgreen.org.

FISH

Anchovies

Bluefish

Catfish (U.S. farmed)

Char (arctic farmed)

Cod (Pacific or hook-caught Atlantic)

Halibut (Alaskan or Pacific)

Herring (Atlantic)

Mackerel (Atlantic or Spanish)

Mahimahi

Rainbow trout (farmed)

Sablefish (black cod)

Salmon (wild Alaskan—chinook, chum, coho, pink, or sockeye)

Sardines

Striped bass (farmed or wild Atlantic)

Tilapia

SHELLFISH

Clams (farmed)

Crab (Dungeness, stone, or blue—from anywhere but the Chesapeake Bay)

Crawfish

Mussels (Mediterranean or farmed blue)

Oysters (Japanese Pacific, European, or farmed Eastern)

Prawns (trap-caught spot prawns)

Scallops (Atlantic farmed)

waters are carefully monitored and closed to shell fishing when found to be high in toxins. Legally harvested shellfish come to market with tags certifying that they were harvested from unpolluted waters. To be sure, especially if you'll be eating raw shellfish, ask the seller if the shellfish comes from certified unpolluted waters. Keep in mind the risk of food-borne illness from eating raw shellfish is greater for children, the elderly, and those with compromised immune systems.

Even though shellfish are a healthy food and reasonably safe to eat, all wild shellfish are not necessarily good choices for the environment. One particular favorite on the American seafood menu—shrimp—has led to more environmental destruction from overfishing than any other fish or shellfish. In part, that's because wild shrimp are usually harvested with harmful bottom trawls that disrupt ecosystems as they scour the ocean floor, leaving a wake of destroyed coral reefs, sponges, and anemones in their path. While all fishing gear typically ends up catching some extra species of fish in every haul, bottom trawls are the worst. For every pound of shrimp harvested, 5 pounds of unwanted fish are discarded. A recent study by the National Academy of Sciences found that bottom trawling is a major cause of declining fish stocks and threatened marine life in U.S. waters.

In the Gulf of Mexico, shrimp trawling has depleted the red snapper stocks and rendered them an unsustainable seafood choice. Because sea turtles have been similarly threatened by shrimp trawling, some new trawls have an escape hatch for the turtles. Shrimp harvested this way are sometimes labeled "turtle-safe shrimp."

Fortunately, other shellfish varieties are harvested using more ecologically sound methods. Spot prawns, a type of shrimp, are increasingly caught with traps instead of bottom trawls off the coast of California, which makes them a viable alternative to most other shrimp. Atlantic northern pink shrimp are another good choice, if you can find them (most are exported to other countries). Other well-managed wild shellfish include Dungeness crab, stone crab, blue crab (from anywhere but the Chesapeake Bay, where they are overfished), and crawfish. See the list on page 99 for more types.

Responsibly Farmed Shellfish

Most shellfish eaten in the United States comes from farms. The good news is that farmed mollusks such as blue mussels, Atlantic scallops, and clams make reasonably healthy and ecofriendly choices. On the whole, these farmed shellfish are raised without significantly damaging wild fish populations or creating excessive pollution.

Shrimp are another story, however. During the aquaculture boom of the 1980s and 1990s, shrimp farms quickly expanded, primarily in regions near Southeast Asia. Now, the majority of shrimp eaten in the United States is imported farmed shrimp. The problem is that the shrimp farm industry's rapid growth and poor regulation in

Switch Fish

Eating healthy, responsibly harvested seafood doesn't have to be a shell game. Just switch fish, replacing excessively polluted or overfished varieties with those that are responsibly managed and less contaminated.

INSTEAD OF	CHOOSE
FISH	
Atlantic cod	Alaskan pollock, hook-and-line-caught cod, or sablefish
Atlantic halibut	Pacific halibut
Atlantic salmon	Wild Alaskan salmon
Grouper	Mahimahi or striped bass
Haddock	Striped bass or tilapia
Orange roughy	Catfish
Pacific rockfish	Striped bass
Patagonian toothfish (Chilean sea bass)	Striped bass
Red snapper	Striped bass
Swordfish	Pacific halibut or striped bass
Tuna, canned	Canned mackerel
Tuna, fresh	Bluefish or striped bass
SHELLFISH	
Chesapeake Bay blue crab	Any other blue crab
Dredged clams	Farmed clams
Dredged scallops	Farmed scallops
Lobster	Crawfish
Shrimp	Atlantic northern pink shrimp or trap-caught spot prawns

developing countries led to considerable habitat destruction, water pollution, and even soil degradation.

According to a 2001 report by the Washington, D.C., advocacy group Environmental Defense, shrimp farms have also contributed to the depletion of worldwide fish stocks. Shrimp farms are often located along miles of coastal mangrove forests, which are important nurseries for wild fish that reproduce among the mangrove root systems. When these farms are intensively managed, their resulting pollution and disease problems affect the surrounding nurseries. In addition, wild fish near shrimp farms are also caught and turned into feed for growing the shrimp. While the shrimp farming industry begins to reform itself, it's wise to choose your shrimp carefully. Trap-caught spot prawns from California make the best overall choice. As for other farmed shellfish, put the emphasis on blue mussels, Atlantic scallops, and clams.

Local Catch

Fish caught in local waters may seem like a good alternative to problematic farmed or wild seafood. But be alert. Local waters are not always safe and may have elevated levels of mercury or other environmental contaminants. Find out which areas of your state are safe by checking local advisories through the Environmental Working Group (www.ewg.org). You can also take a peek at "Low-Mercury Seafood" on page 104 to find out which fish are generally lowest in mercury around the nation.

Smaller Varieties

As a general rule, large, longer-lived fish like shark and tuna accumulate more environmental contaminants, such as dioxins or PCBs, in their muscle tissue. Stick with smaller, younger fish like pollock and cod, and you'll reduce your exposure to these toxins.

Dioxins and PCBs enter our water supply as a result of industrial waste burning and pollution, and they eventually make their way up the food chain as small fish eat

HOLD THE MERCURY, PLEASE

In the realm of unsafe seafood, mercury-tainted fish has captured the attention of American consumers. Though mercury is a naturally occurring element, it is also a by-product of burning oil, fuel, or coal—particularly from coal-fired power plants, our most widely used source of electricity.

Once mercury is released into the air from industrial emissions, it eventually returns to waterways, where it accumulates. It's currently estimated that between 60 and 75 percent of the mercury in U.S. waterways results from man-made pollution, according to Environmental Protection Agency (EPA) data. What's more, bacteria in our water supply can cause chemical changes that transform mercury into a highly toxic form called methylmercury. From there, methylmercury makes its way up the food chain from fish to humans, where it builds up in the body's muscle tissue.

A 2003 report from the EPA found that nearly 5 million American women of childbearing age had at least 5.8 parts per billion (ppb) of mercury in their blood as of 2000. That's about 8 percent of U.S. women aged 16 to 49. A level of 5.8 ppb may not sound like much, but the EPA says children born to women with blood concentrations of mercury above 5.8 parts per billion are at risk of adverse health problems, including reduced developmental IQs, problems with motor skills, and damage to the cardiovascular, immune, and reproductive systems. In 2000, the National Academy of Sciences issued a report estimating that current Food and Drug Administration (FDA) mercury standards put 60,000 unborn children at risk of toxic exposure annually.

Many scientists and public policy organizations are urging the FDA to tighten its mercury regulations. Until that happens, women and children should be cautious. Most adult men—and women who are not pregnant—can safely follow the American Dietetic Association and American Heart Association recommendations of eating fish twice a week for heart health. But pregnant women and young children should put the emphasis on fish with lower levels of mercury.

toxic algae and big fish eat the smaller fish. Both contaminants have been linked to health problems in fish and humans. Dioxins are potent carcinogens, and PCBs are the suspected cause of developmental delays and lower IQs in the children of women who frequently ate contaminated fish from the Great Lakes region during pregnancy. Researchers from the University of Illinois recently found that PCBs can also impair the learning and memory capacity of adults.

Freshwater fish tend to carry high levels of dioxins and PCBs because they are closer to the source of these chemical pollutants. Check local fish advisories before eating wild-caught freshwater varieties. Among wild marine fish, lower your exposure by choosing smaller types such as Alaskan pollock and hook-and-line–caught cod.

Fish High in Omega-3 Fatty Acids

Here's some great news for fish lovers: You *can* get all the heart-healthy benefits of the omega-3 fatty acids in fish without worrying about other health risks or contributing to overfishing. Some of the least problematic fish that are high in omega-3s include wild Alaskan salmon, canned pink salmon, albacore tuna, Atlantic mackerel, sardines, anchovies, and herring. See the recipes in this chapter for some delicious ways to enjoy healthy, ecofriendly fish and shellfish.

Cajun Catfish in Cornmeal

If your kids like fish sticks, they'll love these crunchy fillets. And you'll love them, too, since farmed catfish makes a responsible seafood choice. You could also use hook-caught Atlantic cod. To make these fillets more spicy, bump the ground red pepper up to ½ or ¾ teaspoon.

½ cup unbleached all-purpose flour

2 pasture-raised or organic eggs

½ cup stone-ground organic yellow cornmeal

½ cup plain dry bread crumbs

1½ teaspoons Cajun or Creole seasoning

¼ teaspoon ground red pepper

4 farm-raised catfish fillets (about 6 ounces each)

3 tablespoons peanut oil or GMO-free vegetable oil

4 lemon wedges

Hot pepper sauce

Put the flour in a large shallow bowl or plate. Beat the eggs in a similar-size bowl or plate. In a third bowl or plate, mix together the cornmeal, bread crumbs, seasoning, and pepper.

Wash the fillets in cold water and pat dry. For each fillet, dredge the fish in the flour, patting off any excess. Then dip the fish into the eggs to coat both sides. Put the fish into the cornmeal mixture, then use your dry hand to press the breading all over the fish. Lay the breaded fillets on a baking sheet.

Heat the oil in a large heavy skillet (such as cast iron) over medium heat for at least 3 minutes. When the oil is very hot, carefully add the fillets without crowding (cook in batches if necessary). Cook the fillets, turning once, until golden brown on both sides and just slightly translucent in the center, about 5 minutes per side.

Serve with the lemon wedges for squeezing and pepper sauce for extra kick.

Makes 4 servings

Helping Hand: If you can't find Cajun or Creole seasoning at your market, make it yourself. To get about 4 teaspoons, mix together 1 teaspoon paprika, 1 teaspoon ground black pepper, ¾ teaspoon garlic powder, ½ teaspoon dried thyme, ½ teaspoon dried oregano, ½ teaspoon onion powder, ⅛ teaspoon mustard powder, and ⅛ teaspoon ground red pepper (or more to taste).

Grilled Salmon
with Pineapple Ginger Salsa

Here's a reason to get outside and fire up the grill. The salsa takes just a few minutes of chopping, and the fresh flavor is totally worth it. Look for wild Alaskan salmon in season in the spring and summer.

1½ cups fresh or canned pineapple, finely chopped

1 small cucumber, peeled, seeded, and chopped

½ small organic red bell pepper, seeded and chopped

1 organic jalapeño pepper, seeded and minced

¼ red onion, chopped

¼ cup chopped fresh basil

1 tablespoon minced fresh ginger

Juice of 2 small limes

1 heaping tablespoon brown sugar

4 wild Alaskan salmon steaks (4 to 6 ounces each)

1 tablespoon peanut oil or olive oil

Salt and ground black pepper

In a medium bowl, combine the pineapple, cucumber, bell pepper, jalapeño pepper, onion, basil, ginger, lime juice, and brown sugar. Set aside.

Preheat the grill to medium-hot.

Pat the salmon dry and rub the oil into both sides of the fish. Sprinkle lightly with salt and pepper. Grill until the fish is just slightly translucent in the center, 3 to 4 minutes per side. Serve the salsa over the fish.

Makes 4 servings

Helping Hand: To quickly seed a cucumber, cut it in half lengthwise and scoop out the seeds with a melon baller or spoon. If you like hot, hot salsa, chop the whole jalapeño pepper—seeds and all. To broil the salmon instead of grilling it, preheat the broiler and broil 4" from the heat until the fish is just opaque, 3 to 4 minutes per side.

Nutrient Boost: For more vitamin C (and color), replace ¾ cup of the pineapple with 1 mango, peeled, seeded, and chopped.

Food Lore: Salmon and shrimp are the most popular seafood in American restaurants. In 2001, shrimp replaced canned tuna as America's favorite seafood overall.

Salmon and Fennel Salad Sandwich

Black bread adds a faintly sweet note to this easy seafood salad sandwich. If you can't find it, use any other sturdy dark bread such as pumpernickel. The loaf should be large and round or oval-shaped so that each slice can be cut in half to make the top and bottom pieces of the sandwich.

3 tablespoons reduced-fat mayonnaise

2 tablespoons lemon juice

1 tablespoon organic sour cream

1 tablespoon chopped fresh dill

8 slices black bread

8 romaine lettuce leaves, each torn in half

2 cans (6 ounces each) Alaskan pink or sockeye salmon, drained and flaked

½ fennel bulb, trimmed and finely chopped

Choice Advice: All salmon labeled "Atlantic" is farm-raised, so be sure to look for Alaskan salmon to get the most health benefits.

In a medium bowl, whisk together the mayonnaise, lemon juice, sour cream, and dill. Spread about a teaspoon of this mixture over each slice of bread and then cut the bread slices in half. Line each half with the lettuce leaves.

Stir the salmon and fennel into the remaining mixture in the bowl. Mound onto half of the bread and top with the remaining bread to make sandwiches.

Makes 4 servings

Helping Hands: To trim fennel, chop off the stems just where they begin to turn white at the bulb. Cut the bulb in half lengthwise (through the bottom and stem ends). Use only half of the bulb for this recipe. Trim off and discard the bottom end of the bulb. Then place the bulb cut side down and chop like an onion.

Canned salmon (especially less expensive brands) often contains small bones. Most of these bones are soft enough to eat—and they're a good source of calcium! If the bones bother you or if you see some bigger bones, simply pick them out. You can also use cooked wild Alaskan salmon for this sandwich. You'll need about 1½ cups of chunks. This could come from leftover grilled, broiled, or sautéed salmon steaks or fillets.

Mustard-Glazed Striped Bass

Also known as rockfish, striped bass tastes moist, sweet, and firm. Look for wild striped bass, which has a richer flavor than the farmed variety. The wild version was once depleted but has made a comeback as a result of responsible management by fisheries. In this recipe, a preheated roasting pan gives the fillet a delectably crisp skin.

4 striped bass fillets (each about 5 ounces and ¾" thick)

1 lemon

3 tablespoons reduced-fat mayonnaise

1½ tablespoons grated Parmigiano-Reggiano cheese

1 tablespoon chopped fresh dill

1 tablespoon country-style Dijon mustard

¼ teaspoon ground black pepper

2 teaspoons extra-virgin olive oil

Wash the fish and pat dry. Put on a large piece of wax paper or foil, skin side down.

Cut the lemon in half crosswise and squeeze the juice from one half into a small bowl. Cut the remaining lemon half into four wedges and set aside. Add the mayonnaise, cheese, dill, mustard, and pepper to the bowl and stir until combined.

Spread the mustard mixture evenly over the top of the fillets.

Adjust your top oven rack so that it's 4" to 6" from the heat. Preheat the broiler. Use a paper towel to rub the oil into the bottom of a shallow roasting pan or rimmed baking sheet (it should be big enough to hold all the fillets in a single layer). Preheat the pan under the broiler until very hot, 1 to 2 minutes.

Quickly transfer each fillet from the wax paper or foil to the hot pan, skin side down. Broil until just slightly translucent in the center, 6 to 8 minutes. Lift the fillets from the roasting pan with a spatula and transfer to a platter or plates. Serve with the lemon wedges for squeezing.

Makes 4 servings

Helping Hand: My favorite reduced-fat mayonnaise is Hellmann's Just 2 Good! It doesn't taste like anything has been reduced, even though it has no cholesterol and only 2 grams of fat per tablespoon.

Striped Bass Kabobs with Soy and Lemon

This recipe comes from Dr. Carl Safina, vice president for marine conservation and founder of the Living Oceans Program at the National Audubon Society. When he grills, Dr. Safina often turns to firm-fleshed striped bass instead of swordfish or tuna, which are overfished. Serve these easy kabobs with cooked rice.

2 tablespoons extra-virgin olive oil

2 tablespoons organic tamari or soy sauce

1 tablespoon lemon juice

1 pound striped bass fillets (about 1" thick), cut into bite-size pieces

1 pint cherry tomatoes

8 ounces mushrooms

1 organic green bell pepper, seeded and cut into bite-size pieces

1 teaspoon lemon-pepper seasoning

1 tablespoon chopped fresh oregano or 1½ teaspoons dried

Soak 8 to 12 bamboo skewers in water for at least 30 minutes.

Mix the oil, tamari or soy sauce, and lemon juice in a 2-quart shallow dish or resealable plastic bag. Add the fish, cover or seal, and refrigerate for 30 minutes to 1 hour.

Preheat the grill to medium.

Thread the marinated fish, tomatoes, mushrooms, and peppers on separate skewers. Brush the kabobs all over with the marinade and then sprinkle evenly with the lemon-pepper seasoning and oregano.

Grill the kabobs, turning occasionally. The vegetables should be heated through and have faint grill marks, 5 to 6 minutes. The fish should be just slightly translucent in the center, 6 to 8 minutes.

Makes 4 servings

Mahimahi with Grape Sauce and Mint

This firm, darker-fleshed fish also goes by the name of dolphinfish. But mahimahi, its Hawaiian name, helps to avoid confusion with the dolphin that is a mammal. Here, the mild, sweet flavor of this fish gets a boost from a simple pan sauce made from wine and grapes, garnished with a touch of mint.

4 mahimahi fillets (each about 7 ounces and 1" thick)

Salt

¼ teaspoon ground black pepper

¾ cup unbleached all-purpose flour

3 tablespoons organic butter

2 teaspoons chopped shallot

1 cup dry white wine

1 cup fish stock or organic chicken stock

24 California or organic seedless green or red grapes, halved lengthwise

1½ teaspoons chopped fresh mint

Preheat the oven to 350°F.

Sprinkle the fillets all over with ¼ teaspoon salt and the pepper.

Put the flour in a shallow bowl or plate and dredge the fillets in the flour, patting off any excess.

Melt 2 tablespoons butter in a large ovenproof skillet over medium heat. When the butter is hot and bubbly, add the fillets, round side down, and cook until just cooked ¼" up from the bottom, 2 to 3 minutes. Carefully flip the fillets with a spatula and transfer the skillet to the oven. Bake until the fish is just slightly translucent in the center, 7 to 9 minutes. Remove the fillets to a platter or plates and cover with foil to keep warm.

Put the pan over medium-high heat and add the shallot, cooking until just soft, 10 to 15 seconds. Pour in the wine and boil over high heat for 2 minutes, scraping the bottom of the pan. Add the stock and boil until the liquid reduces to about ¾ cup, 4 to 6 minutes. Reduce the heat to medium-low and stir in the grapes, the remaining 1 tablespoon butter, and a big pinch of salt. Let cook gently for 1 minute. Spoon the sauce over the fish and sprinkle with the mint.

Makes 4 servings

Baked Cod with Tomatoes, Tarragon, and Chard

Huge gillnets and trawls have severely depleted cod stocks in the Atlantic. But hook-and-line–caught Atlantic cod are harvested in a way that doesn't needlessly endanger the fish supplies. The taste of this fish is so straightforward that it needs only a bit of butter, tarragon, and tomato to bring the flavor alive in the oven. And it takes only minutes to prepare.

½ pound green chard, stems removed, leaves coarsely chopped

4 tablespoons organic butter or extra-virgin olive oil

1 small shallot, minced

½ teaspoon salt

¼ teaspoon paprika

2 tablespoons chopped fresh tarragon

4 hook-caught Atlantic cod or Pacific cod fillets (6 to 7 ounces each)

1 large tomato, sliced

4 lemon wedges

Choice Advice: If hook-caught cod isn't fresh at your market, use another mild white fish such as tilapia.

Preheat the oven to 400°F. Put the chard into a shallow 2-quart baking dish to make a bed of greens.

Put the butter or olive in a small saucepan and heat over medium heat until the butter melts or the oil is hot. Stir in the shallot, salt, paprika, and tarragon.

Wash the fillets in cold water and pat dry. Arrange the fish over the chard in the dish and brush all over with the tarragon mixture, reserving about 2 teaspoons. Lay the tomato slices over the fish and brush with the reserved tarragon mixture.

Bake until the chard is wilted and the fish is just barely translucent in the center, 12 to 15 minutes. Use a spatula to transfer portions of fish and chard to plates. Serve with the lemon wedges for squeezing.

Makes 4 servings

Helping Hand: Reserve the chard stems for another use or serve along with this dish. They're terrific sautéed or braised with a little chicken or vegetable broth, salt, and pepper.

Greg Higgins' Grilled Alaskan Halibut with Garden Salsa

Most of the fish chef Greg Higgins serves in his restaurant comes from the Oregon coast. "But we use halibut from Alaska," says Higgins, "because migrating halibut isn't as flavorful." The ingredients for the salsa come from Greg's homegrown organic garden. To complete the meal with wine, serve a chilled Oregon pinot gris.

MARINADE

¼ cup organic tamari or soy sauce

1 organic jalapeño pepper, sliced

½ teaspoon sugar

4 Alaskan halibut fillets (6 to 7 ounces each)

POLENTA

4 cups water

1 cup stone-ground organic yellow cornmeal

2 teaspoons minced garlic

1 organic jalapeño pepper, seeded and minced

½ cup grated Parmigiano-Reggiano cheese

Salt and black pepper

GREG'S GARDEN SALSA

2 cups diced vine-ripened heirloom tomatoes

½ cup diced sweet onion

2 organic sweet chile peppers (such as red Anaheim), seeded and diced

1 organic hot chile pepper (such as jalapeño), seeded and minced

Juice and minced zest of 1 organic lemon

1 teaspoon minced garlic

½ cup chopped fresh cilantro

Salt and black pepper

1 tablespoon extra-virgin olive oil

To make the marinade: In a shallow dish or resealable plastic bag, combine the tamari or soy sauce, sliced pepper, and sugar. Add the halibut, cover or seal, and refrigerate for 2 to 3 hours, turning the halibut in the marinade once each hour.

To make the polenta: In a heavy nonreactive saucepan, combine the water, cornmeal, garlic, and jalapeño pepper. Bring to a gentle simmer over medium heat, stirring frequently to avoid lumps. When the polenta is thick and smooth (after 20 to 25 minutes), reduce the heat to low, add the cheese, and season to taste with salt and pepper. Remove from the heat and cover to keep warm, stirring occasionally.

To make the salsa and finish the dish: In a medium bowl, combine the tomatoes, onion, sweet chile peppers, hot chile pepper, lemon juice and zest, garlic, and cilantro. Season to taste with salt and pepper.

Preheat a grill (preferably charcoal) to medium-hot.

Remove the halibut from the marinade and blot dry on paper towels. Brush the fish with the oil and grill, turning once, until just slightly translucent in the center, about 5 to 7 minutes total. Serve the halibut on the polenta topped with the salsa.

Makes 4 servings

Helping Hand: Alaskan halibut has a firmer flesh than Atlantic halibut and grills up beautifully without falling apart. But if you have a grill basket, put the fillet in the basket anyway to make the fish easier to turn on the grill.

Detox Your Catch

If you eat your own catch—or someone else's—there are easy ways to protect your health when enjoying a fish dinner. Follow these simple rules.

- Avoid eating the fattier parts of fish, such as the skin, dark meat, and belly flap. Dioxin, PCBs, and other toxic chemicals concentrate in these fatty parts.
- Broil, roast, or grill fish on a rack so that fat can drip away.
- Focus on eating smaller fish like salmon and striped bass. Larger, longer-lived fish (such as tuna, shark, and swordfish) contain higher concentrations of pollutants such as mercury.
- When you eat whole crabs, minimize exposure to contaminants by discarding the green gland (the mustard). Similarly, avoid eating the green liver (tomalley) of whole lobster.

RICK BAYLESS
A Love for Local Flavors

If you ever have the opportunity to take a cooking class with Rick Bayless, grab it. You'll learn a truckload about Mexican cooking techniques from a master chef. Better yet, you'll learn about ingredients—from how they're grown to how they're prepared—which can actually help you enjoy the taste of food more.

Rick's enthusiasm for ingredients is infectious. He first visited Mexico at age 14 and discovered dishes like squash blossom soup and chicken in almond sauce. A college major in Latin American literature and culture anchored the chef's attraction to Mexico's people, places, and food. In 1980, Rick finally gave up the long-distance relationship and moved to Mexico with his wife, Deann. As they traveled to every state in the Mexican republic, Rick and Deann developed a deep respect for each region's ingredients, flavors, and communities. "Through those years, we absorbed that same generosity of spirit that had seduced me when I was 14," he says, "that love for life and color and flavor."

You can see, feel, and taste that "generosity of spirit" in both of Rick and Deann's wildly successful Chicago restaurants, Frontera Grill and Topolobampo. The fabulous food, drinks, and service flow as freely as the admiration for the people who grow the restaurants' ingredients—the farmers themselves. Rick has spent more than 20 years developing close relationships with local farmers. He buys directly from small producers who approach agriculture like artisans and responsible land stewards.

Rick also grows organic produce at home—2,000 square feet of chemical-free vegetables and flowers. This produce often makes its way onto dinner plates at the restaurants. Growing organically has challenged and deepened the chef's commitment to sustainable agriculture. "I've gained a massive appreciation for organic farmers—the kind all farmers were before the advent of chemical solutions," he says. "They are some of the smartest people on the planet."

Rick also promotes "sustainable cuisine" as a board member of the Chefs Collaborative, a national network of chefs and food professionals who educate and inspire the public to improve the quality of our food supply by buying food from local, ecologically minded growers. His restaurants and cookbooks have won several major awards, and in 1995, Rick was named Chef of the Year by the James Beard Foundation and the International Association of Culinary Professionals. He is an active participant in Share Our Strength, the nation's largest hunger advocacy organization, and has recently established the Frontera Farmer Foundation to further celebrate and support the work of Chicago's sustainable farmers. Rick has been inducted into the Who's Who of American Food and Drink, and in 1998, he was chosen as the Beard Foundation's Humanitarian of the Year. In 2003, Rick continued to share his passion for high-quality, responsibly produced food in the third season of his critically acclaimed PBS television cooking show, *Mexico—One Plate at a Time.*

Rick Bayless's Grilled Shrimp Ceviche

Ceviche: tender morsels of the freshest fish or seafood gently pickled in lime juice to preserve the freshness of the catch a little longer, tossed with a variety of succulent summer vegetables. Ceviche is as much a place as a dish, and the place is far from home. In the shade or full sun, it's casual, spirited beach food. Food that makes folks feel the thick, salty-smelling coastal air with just one bite of its bracing freshness.

1 generous pound peeled trap-caught spot prawns or medium-size turtle-safe shrimp (about 24 pieces)

½ cup lime juice plus several lime slices

½ medium white onion, finely chopped

⅓ cup chopped fresh cilantro plus several sprigs

½ cup ketchup

1–2 tablespoons bottled hot sauce (like Frontera Tangy Toasted Arbol Hot Sauce)

1 cup diced peeled cucumber or jicama (or ½ cup of each)

1 small ripe avocado, pitted, peeled, and cubed

2 tablespoons extra-virgin olive oil (optional)

½ teaspoon salt

Tostadas, tortilla chips, or saltine crackers

Preheat a gas grill or prepare a charcoal grill. Soak 8 bamboo skewers in water for at least 30 minutes.

Skewer the shrimp, about 6 per skewer; thread a second skewer through the shrimp so they won't turn on the grill. Coat generously with cooking spray. Grill, turning once, until opaque, about 4 minutes total. Let the shrimp cool completely. Cut the cooked shrimp into ½" pieces and place in a large glass bowl. Toss with the lime juice, cover, and refrigerate to chill.

Rinse the onion by placing the chopped pieces in a small strainer, running them under cold water, and then shaking the strainer gently to remove excess liquid. Add to the shrimp bowl, along with the cilantro, ketchup, hot sauce, cucumber or jicama, avocado, and 2 tablespoons olive oil (optional). Taste and season with salt if you think it needs any. Cover and refrigerate if not serving immediately.

Spoon the ceviche into martini glasses, juice glasses, or small bowls; garnish with sprigs of cilantro and slices of lime. Serve with tostadas, tortilla chips, or saltines to enjoy alongside.

Makes 6 appetizer servings

Steamed Mussels with Pernod Cream Sauce

Mussels don't need much flavoring, but why not indulge now and then? This light cream sauce takes them over the top. Pernod, a licorice-flavored liqueur available in most wine and spirits shops, perfectly complements the fresh tarragon.

1 tablespoon extra-virgin olive oil

1 small onion, chopped

4 medium shallots, chopped (about ¼ cup)

⅓ cup Pernod

1½ cups dry white wine

4 dozen farm-raised blue mussels or Mediterranean mussels, scrubbed and debearded

¾ cup organic light cream or half-and-half

1 tablespoon organic butter

2 teaspoons chopped fresh tarragon

¼ teaspoon salt

⅛ teaspoon ground black pepper

Heat the oil in a large, deep sauté pan over medium heat. When hot, add the onion and shallots and cook until just beginning to soften, 2 to 3 minutes. Off heat (to avoid a flare-up), pour in the Pernod and wine. Simmer over medium heat for 1 minute. Add the mussels and cover. Increase the heat to high and steam, shaking the pan once or twice, until the mussels open, 5 to 7 minutes. Discard any unopened mussels. Using a slotted spoon, remove the mussels to a serving bowl and cover with foil to keep warm.

Using a fine-mesh strainer (or a colander lined with a large coffee filter), strain the cooking liquid into a medium bowl. Rinse out the sauté pan and pour the strained liquid back into the pan. Boil over high heat until the liquid is reduced to about 1 cup, 5 to 7 minutes. Reduce the heat to medium-low and stir in the cream or half-and-half, butter, tarragon, salt, and pepper.

Drizzle the sauce over the mussels and serve.

Makes 4 to 6 servings

Helping Hand: To remove grit or sand that may be under the shells, you'll need a pot big enough to hold the mussels. Dissolve about ¼ cup salt in 2 cups warm water and then add 2 tablespoons cornmeal or flour. Add the mussels and enough cold water to cover them. Soak for 2 hours or overnight in the refrigerator. The mussels will actually take in the grain and expel the grit or sand. Before using, rinse the mussels and scrub if scruffy-looking and snip off the "beards" (dark threads) with scissors. If mussels have opened slightly before cooking, tap the shell. They should snap shut. Discard any mussels that don't pass the tap test, as well as any that fail to open during cooking.

Pan-Seared Scallops with Lemon and Sun-Dried Tomato Sauce

Somehow, this appetizer manages to be light and rich-tasting at the same time. The caramelized, almost creamy taste of pan-seared scallops plays well off the sunny yet bold-flavored sauce. For a main dish, serve the scallops and sauce over cooked linguine.

1 tablespoon extra-virgin olive oil

1 pound farm-raised sea scallops

3 cloves garlic, sliced

¼ cup drained oil-packed or soft sun-dried tomatoes, sliced

1 cup dry white wine or sherry

1 cup vegetable broth

3 tablespoons organic butter, cut into pieces

2–3 tablespoons lemon juice

1½ tablespoons chopped fresh basil

Heat the oil in a large, deep skillet over medium-high heat. When hot, add the scallops and cook just until lightly browned and barely translucent in the center, 2 minutes per side. Remove to a plate and cover with foil to keep warm.

Add the garlic, tomatoes, and wine or sherry to the skillet. Boil, scraping the bottom of the pan occasionally, until the liquid is reduced by about half, 5 minutes. Add the broth and boil until the liquid is again reduced by about half, 8 minutes. Reduce the heat to low and stir in the butter. Stir in 2 tablespoons lemon juice and 1 tablespoon basil. Taste and add more lemon juice if you prefer.

Pour the sauce over the bottom of small salad plates. Arrange the scallops over the sauce and sprinkle with the remaining basil.

Makes 6 servings

Helping Hand: Sea scallops are the largest, most common type. They're often soaked in phosphates to help preserve them. If they look bright, shiny, and clustered together, you'll know they've been soaked. For the best flavor, ask for unsoaked or "dry" scallops. They should look pale ivory in color and not clumped together. To prepare scallops for pan-searing, pull off the gristly tendon attached to one side (or leave it on if it doesn't bother you), then rinse the scallops and pat dry. A dry surface on the scallop will help it to brown better.

PEGGY SHEPARD
Working for Environmental Justice

Peggy Shepard lives in northern Manhattan, an area of New York City that includes East, West, and Central Harlem as well as Washington Heights/Inwood. These 7.4 square miles are home to more than 600,000 residents, most of whom are African-American and Latino. Like other African-American and Latino communities around the country, northern Manhattan has a broad range of environmental troubles. Diesel truck and bus traffic pollute the air with fine soot particulates. East and Central Harlem lead the nation in asthma hospitalizations. And to make matters worse, only one grocer in northern Manhattan—home to half a million people—carries organic produce.

To help solve the problem, Shepard cofounded West Harlem Environmental Action, Inc. (WE ACT) in 1988. WE ACT is New York's first environmental justice organization that works to improve the quality of life in communities of color by improving food, water, and air quality.

As WE ACT's executive director, Shepard has a driving interest in protecting communities of color from policies that create dumping grounds in areas where people are less powerful and have the fewest resources to fight back. "WE ACT soon realized that this sort of 'environmental racism' was happening in communities of color around the country," she says.

WE ACT now works for environmental and social justice on a range of issues both locally and nationally. In partnership with Columbia University's Center for Children's Environmental Health, the group helps to identify and control environmental hazards in and around homes and schools, particularly hazards related to food, air, and water quality that can impair child development and impact reproductive health for pregnant women.

Shepard has since been elected to the boards of numerous environmental organizations, such as the Children's Environmental Health Network, the Healthy Schools Network, and Environmental Defense. In 1997, she received the Susan B. Anthony Award from the National Organization for Women (NOW) New York City Chapter. And in January 2002, Shepard was elected the first female chair of the National Environmental Justice Advisory Council (NEJAC) to the U.S. Environmental Protection Agency. She is also a lay member of the National Institute of Environmental Health Sciences Advisory Council.

Baked Oysters
with Almond Watercress Sauce

This recipe comes from Jim Fobel, a great food writer and a careful cook with an ingenious way of combining flavors. If you're a fan of raw oysters with lemon, you'll love the extra shot of flavor in the almond watercress sauce.

2–3 cups kosher salt or rock salt for lining the pan

12 Japanese Pacific oysters, on the half shell

½ bunch watercress, rinsed and patted dry

1 small shallot

1 small clove garlic

2 anchovy fillets

2 tablespoons sliced almonds

2 tablespoons lemon juice

2 teaspoons extra-virgin olive oil

Choice Advice: Look for Japanese Pacific oysters, one of the only varieties that aren't riddled with problems of overfishing, pollution, and ocean habitat destruction from reckless dredging. European oysters and Olympia oysters also make good alternatives to the problematic American oyster.

Preheat the oven to 350°F.

Pour the salt into a large shallow roasting pan or rimmed baking sheet to make an even layer ½" thick. Nestle the oyster shells gently in the salt.

In a food processor, combine the watercress, shallot, garlic, anchovies, almonds, lemon juice, and oil. Process until blended, about 1 minute. Spoon the sauce evenly over the oysters. Bake until the edges of the oysters begin to curl, 4 to 6 minutes.

Makes 4 appetizer servings

Chapter 5

Chicken and Turkey

Chicken is beginning to edge out beef as America's meat of choice. Since 1950, annual chicken consumption in the United States has quadrupled from about 14 pounds per person to about 55 pounds per person, according to current U.S. Department of Agriculture (USDA) figures. The National Chicken Council puts annual consumption even higher, at about 75 pounds per person. Beef consumption, on the other hand, has fallen from its all-time high of 90 pounds per person in the late 1970s to a fairly steady 65 pounds per person today.

Two big things driving poultry sales are low price and low fat. Chicken and turkey are fairly inexpensive sources of protein. After adjusting for inflation, the cost of poultry in 2000 was one-third what it cost in 1935, due to consolidation and streamlining of the production process. Chicken and turkey are also considered healthier choices than red meats. A 3-ounce serving of skinless chicken breast has 142 calories and 3 grams of fat. The same amount of ground chuck has 236 calories and 16 grams of fat. Nutritionists and health experts regularly recommend chicken over beef, especially to help combat the growing problem of obesity among Americans.

We're obviously getting the message. Chicken consumption continues to soar. You'd expect sales of turkey to be up, too. After all, turkey breast is even a little leaner than chicken breast. But annual turkey consumption has remained steady at about 17 pounds per person since the early 1990s. We currently eat four times more chicken than turkey.

Chicken Worth Lickin'

With an increased demand for chicken comes increased chicken production. Today, U.S. poultry production is a $32 billion industry with some 7.5 billion chickens produced annually, according to USDA figures. Such intensive farming of chickens does have its consequences. Huge poultry barns and their enormous amounts of waste have created some problems for public health, local environments, local economies, and the animals themselves. Yet despite these problems, poultry still makes a better choice for the environment than beef, which requires more resources for every pound of meat produced and makes an even bigger impact on our planet. The good news is that you can sidestep many of the issues surrounding poultry production by making wise choices. Here are a few smart picks to seek out at the poultry case.

Chicken and Turkey Raised without Antibiotics

To protect your health and your children's health, buying chicken raised without antibiotics is probably the best choice you can make. Antibiotic resistance has become a major public health concern, due to the overuse of antibiotics in livestock farming as well as in treating human illnesses.

For years, regular antibiotic use in poultry farming has enabled farmers to see their chickens and turkeys grow faster to a marketable size without the risk of infection from unsanitary production facilities. Research by the Union of Concerned Scientists (UCS) found that about 10.5 million pounds of antibiotics are automatically put into poultry feed or water for nontherapeutic uses every year. But over time, harmful bacteria have naturally become resistant to the effects of these antibiotics.

Fluoroquinolones, a specific class of antibiotics, make a good example of how fast antibiotic-resistant bacteria can flourish. In 1995, the FDA approved fluoroquinolones for use in poultry. In intensive poultry operations, this antibiotic helps protect crowded flocks from *E. coli* infection. Since 1995, increased fluoroquinolone use in congested factory farms quickly allowed another bacteria, campylobacter, to become resistant to fluoroquinolone antibiotics. By 2000, the Centers for Disease Control and Prevention (CDC) reported a rapid rise in antibiotic-resistant campylobacter. As a result, campylobacter now contaminates most of the chickens raised in the United States. And it's become a big public health issue because campylobacter is the number one cause of food poisoning in the country. According to the Food and Drug Administration (FDA), at least 50 percent of campylobacter food-poisoning infections are likely caused by eating contaminated chicken. The resistant bacteria can also infect farm workers who handle contaminated meat. Or it can escape into lakes, rivers, and drinking water from animal manure that has been spread over crops as fertilizer or kept in piles of manure. The CDC now estimates that campylobacter causes 2 million illnesses and 100 deaths a year.

In 2000, the FDA proposed a ban on fluoroquinolone use for livestock. Several health organizations supported the move, including the World Health Organization, the American Medical Association, the American Public Health Association, and the American College of Preventive Medicine. Since then, many of the nation's largest poultry producers claim they've stopped using these antibiotics in their poultry, but there is no enforcement infrastructure in place to make sure. And recent studies indicate that antibiotic-resistant campylobacter is still present on poultry sold in stores around the country. The Institute for Agriculture Trade Policy tested supermarket samples of popular poultry brands and found that 100 percent of the whole chickens they tested were contaminated with campylobacter, with about 62 percent of those bacteria resistant to one or more antibiotics. A national study by the Consumers Union, publishers of *Consumer Reports*, also found that 38 percent of all store-bought chicken products were contaminated with campylobacter resistant to one or more antibiotics.

All this scuttlebutt doesn't mean that you should stop eating chicken and turkey. But it does make a good case for reducing antibiotic use and improving hygiene, growing, and slaughter conditions on farms. Until that happens, your best bet for health is to choose pasture-raised or organic poultry. If you can't find organic, look for chicken and turkey labeled "raised without antibiotics" or "no antibiotics administered." Regardless of which type you buy, you can minimize the chance of you or your family becoming ill by following "Safe Poultry and Meat Handling" advice on page 130.

Pasture-Raised Chicken and Turkey

According to the American Pastured Poultry Producers' Association, pasture-raised chickens and turkeys forage for up to 20 percent of their feed. These birds are raised outdoors and are contained using movable fences or portable housing, which is moved regularly to fresh pasture. This old-fashioned type of pasturing raises the birds under clean, healthy conditions that are more natural for the birds and for their local environment than modern concentrated chicken houses and chicken feed.

Pasture production systems also manage waste better, prevent pollution problems, reduce disease, and give the chickens and turkeys a better diet than those confined indoors because much of the feed comes from easy-to-grow grass rather than from pesticide-treated grain.

IT'S ONLY NATURAL?

Chicken or turkey labeled "natural" seems to imply that these lucky birds are raised as nature intended: outside on green pasture that provides the bulk of their diet. In truth, natural is an unregulated labeling term that refers to how a product is processed, not how it is produced. The U.S. Department of Agriculture (USDA) defines natural as simply "a product containing no artificial ingredient or added color and is only minimally processed (a process which does not fundamentally alter the raw product)." So a chicken labeled "natural" won't contain preservatives to keep it looking nice and pink. But it may very well contain antibiotics, because it is probably raised indoors in a crowded chicken house.

Given that the USDA doesn't have an enforcement infrastructure in place, the "natural" label on poultry is even less meaningful, because no one inspects the meat companies that claim to be natural. If you're looking for chicken or turkey that was raised the way nature intended, go for pasture-raised or organic poultry instead.

Pound for pound, this choice may be more expensive compared with your typical chicken, but the benefit to our soil and water is well worth the extra scratch. There are health benefits to you, too. Poultry raised on grass is usually higher in vision-enhancing vitamin A, antioxidant vitamin E, heart-healthy omega-3 fatty acids, and a few other important nutrients. If you can't find organic chicken or turkey, pasture-raised poultry makes a reliable, ecofriendly alternative—and some would argue a better alternative—since USDA regulations do not require that "organic" chickens and turkeys forage on pasture.

Free-Range Chicken and Turkey

In theory, free-range chicken makes a good choice. The term "free-range" conjures images of happy chickens and turkeys foraging freely in wide-open green pastures. But in fact, poultry labeled "free-range" may never come anywhere near a wide-open range. According to the USDA Food Safety and Inspection Service, the definition of free-range or free-roaming is this: "Poultry must be allowed access to the outside." This definition implies that the birds are raised indoors (which they usually are), and it leaves the amount of outside access unregulated. The USDA does have some fine print saying producers can meet the free-range standard by giving their birds 5 minutes of open-air access a day. That's hardly "free-range," and it enables producers to capitalize on the label's popularity without living up to its intended standards.

The fact is, the vast majority of the chicken we eat today, about 98 percent, comes from large indoor poultry operations that bear more of a resemblance to factories than to our idyllic notion of farms. Within the agricultural industry, such facilities are better known by their technical name: confined (or concentrated) animal feeding operations, or CAFOs. According to the Environmental Protection Agency, poultry CAFOs house at least 100,000 broiler chickens or 55,000 turkeys on the floor of a large indoor facility. These chicken houses are usually windowless and lit by continuous low levels of artificial light. For those in the poultry business, the term "free-range" or "free-roaming" typically refers to a bird that comes from a similar indoor chicken house—just with fewer birds.

Therefore, the free-range chicken you buy at the store or at a restaurant could theoretically be a bird that lives in a barn with 20,000 other chickens, all of which have 5 minutes a day to squeeze through a small hole to gain access to a soil-covered slab of concrete outside. That unpleasant scenario illustrates how the intended meaning of "free-range" can be stretched given our present labeling regulations. Revisions to the term are currently under debate at the USDA, but until those regulations are revised, it's a good idea to look for poultry labeled "pasture-raised" rather than "free-range."

Locally Produced Organic Chicken and Turkey

As with other foods, chicken and turkey are healthier for you and for the planet when you buy local and buy organic, and they taste better, too. In several blind taste tests, including tests conducted by the *New York Times* and *Washingtonian* magazine, food

Getting Fresh

Chicken is sometimes labeled "fresh," which implies that it's never been frozen, processed, or preserved. But the reality is that it could have been frozen or "hard chilled." With regard to poultry, the U.S. Department of Agriculture defines fresh as "any raw poultry product that has not been cooled below 26°F." That's several degrees below the freezing point of 32°F, which renders the term "fresh" virtually meaningless to consumers.

The Food and Drug Administration's definition of fresh is much closer to what most consumers expect the term to mean: "food that is raw, has never been frozen or heated, and contains no preservatives." However, that definition applies only to fruits and vegetables, not poultry. If you're looking for a bird that's never been frozen, look for "never frozen" on the label or call the producer directly and ask at what temperature their poultry is kept prior to sale.

critics found organic chickens and turkeys to be superior to conventionally farmed poultry in taste, texture, and color.

Another big benefit is that organically raised chickens and turkeys are not routinely fed antibiotics. A sick bird is treated with antibiotics, is removed from the flock, and cannot be sold as organic. This rule helps to ensure that birds are not given antibiotics to compensate for unhealthy living conditions. Organically raised chickens and turkeys are also given some sort of access to the outdoors and fed organically grown feed, which cannot include meat or seafood by-products (common ingredients in conventional poultry feed). If the birds have access to pasture, it must be free of chemical applications for 3 years before the birds can be certified organic. The following practices are also prohibited from organic poultry production: irradiation, genetic engineering, and the use of chemical fertilizers, sewage sludge as fertilizer, and synthetic pesticides, including herbicides and fungicides.

As for growth hormones, you needn't worry about them showing up in your chicken dinner. Federal regulations prohibit the use of hormones in all poultry production—conventional, organic, or otherwise.

The organic standards take poultry production a huge step forward from conventional methods. Organic production helps to provide Americans with safe and healthy meat from animals raised in an ecologically sound and sustainable way. Reliance on organic feed alone marks a big reduction in potentially harmful substances being added to our environment and, by extension, our bodies.

For instance, one common additive in conventional chicken feed is roxarsone. This form of arsenic is fed to birds to boost weight gain and increase profitability. It also helps fight infections often caused by crowded and unsanitary growing conditions. While only trace amounts of arsenic end up in the meat we eat, significant amounts end up in the millions of tons of chicken manure produced annually. Poultry waste from the mid-Atlantic states of Delaware, Maryland, and Virginia alone introduces between 20 and 50 metric tons of arsenic into the environment every year. And this region is only the fourth-largest poultry producer in the country. Poultry waste is typically kept in fields called windrows or applied directly to corn and soybean crops as fertilizer. Environmental chemists say that, from there, the arsenic in the manure can mobilize during heavy rainstorms to contaminate groundwater and surface water supplies. Studies haven't found high enough levels of arsenic in water to make this a public health problem right now, but it is a growing concern, especially as chicken consumption and production continue to increase.

Conventional chicken feed also contains phosphorus, most of which ends up in the manure and is then applied to fields as fertilizer. As a result, excess phosphorus ends up in the soil and water, where it creates a chemical imbalance that can inhibit proper plant growth and cause water quality problems. In northwest Arkansas, one of the largest poultry-producing regions in the country, chicken manure is a primary source of phosphorous contamination in nearby creeks and rivers. Choosing organic chicken will help to avoid these problems.

Kosher Chicken and Turkey

Jewish dietary laws strictly regulate how animals are processed. Cleanliness and purity are the goals. Kosher poultry is processed in a humane way, mostly by hand, and with meticulous inspections throughout. Bacterial growth is minimized by using cold

Safe Poultry and Meat Handling

Most of the poultry you find in supermarkets is contaminated with some kind of harmful bacteria. Not to worry. Just handle and cook poultry safely to avoid risk of infection. Here are the basics, most of which also apply to beef and pork. For beef and pork cooking times, see page 163.

- When shopping, buy raw poultry and meat last. Refrigerate it as soon as you get home. Set your refrigerator to 40°F or less.
- Refrigerate raw poultry and meat on the bottom shelf in a pan or airtight plastic bag so that juices don't drip onto other foods.
- Avoid storing raw poultry and meat near any food you plan on eating raw, such as fresh fruits or vegetables.
- Use refrigerated poultry and meat within 3 to 5 days or freeze it.
- Defrost frozen poultry and meats in the refrigerator rather than at room temperature. For faster thawing, defrost in a basin of very cold water or in a microwave oven. If you use the microwave, cook the food immediately upon thawing it.
- Immediately after handling raw poultry and meat, use hot, soapy water to wash everything that has come in contact with the meat, including your hands, countertops, cutting boards, knives, and other utensils.
- Always marinate poultry and meat in the refrigerator, even if only for an hour or two.
- Cook stuffing in a separate baking dish rather than inside the bird. When stuffing is inside the bird, it often doesn't reach a safe temperature until the meat is already overcooked and dried out. If you're a die-hard fan of stuffing the bird, wait until immediately prior to cooking to add the stuffing. And then pack it loosely—with about ¾ cup of stuffing per pound of chicken or turkey. Cook the stuffing to at least 165°F in the center. If the bird's done before the stuffing, finish cooking the stuffing in a separate baking dish. This way, you'll still get the rich, moist taste of stuffing drenched in drippings but without risk of food poisoning.
- Eat only thoroughly cooked poultry and meat. To test for doneness, insert an instant-read thermometer into the thickest part of the meat without touching bone to get an accurate reading. Ground chicken and turkey as well as chicken cutlets and livers should be cooked until no longer pink. Other cuts of chicken and turkey should be cooked until the juices run clear when the meat is pierced and the meat has reached the following temperature.

Boneless chicken breasts	160°F
Whole or butterflied chicken or turkey	165°F (tested in a thigh)
Bone-in chicken and turkey parts	170°F

water throughout the process. Koshering also involves brining the poultry meat (soaking it in salt water), resulting in chicken and turkey that may taste a bit more savory and more tender than other varieties. Kosher makes a good choice for safe chicken and turkey that's less likely to be contaminated with harmful bacteria. But koshering refers only to the way the animals are processed—not produced. No restrictions are placed on the kind of feed given to the birds or the use of antibiotics in production.

Lean Cuts of Chicken and Turkey

Despite the health issues surrounding poultry production, chicken and turkey still make a relatively healthy choice. Compared with other meats, chicken and turkey are lower in calories and fat, yet high in protein and B vitamins. The three leanest chicken parts are breasts, drumsticks, and thighs. For lean turkey, choose turkey tenderloins, turkey breast tenders, and turkey London broil (a whole boneless, skinless butterflied turkey breast, available in most grocery stores). When using ground chicken or turkey, be sure to cook the meat thoroughly, as harmful bacteria spread more quickly in ground meats than in whole parts.

Skip the skin on poultry parts to cut calories even further—up to 50 percent. But when using dry heat, as with whole roast chicken or turkey, leave the skin on during cooking to keep the meat moist. Remove the skin just before serving. If you're cooking a whole bird with a spice rub, lemon slices, or other seasonings, put these under the skin to flavor the meat rather than the skin. Rub some of these seasonings inside the bird cavity for extra flavor.

Skipping the skin also means you'll be eating less saturated fat, which can help reduce risk of heart disease and cancer. Plus, you'll reduce your exposure to dioxins, which are known carcinogens that make their way up the food chain, where they tend to concentrate in animal fat.

Buffalo Chicken Nuggets with Blue Cheese Dip

Here's a healthy take on Buffalo wings, complete with blue cheese dip to cool the flames. Older kids and adults love it. For younger children, omit the hot pepper sauce and serve with barbecue sauce or ketchup instead of blue cheese dip.

BLUE CHEESE DIP

½ cup organic fat-free plain yogurt

¼ cup reduced-fat mayonnaise

2 ounces imported blue cheese, crumbled

1 scallion, finely chopped

BUFFALO CHICKEN NUGGETS

½ cup unbleached all-purpose flour

1 teaspoon paprika

1 teaspoon salt

3 pasture-raised or organic egg whites

1 tablespoon organic butter, melted

1 tablespoon mild pepper sauce (such as Frank's)

1½ cups finely crushed cornflakes

½ pound pasture-raised or organic boneless, skinless chicken breasts, cut into 1" pieces

To make the dip: In a small bowl, stir together the yogurt, mayonnaise, blue cheese, and scallion. Cover and refrigerate for 30 minutes or up to 2 days.

To make the nuggets: Preheat the oven to 400°F. Coat a baking sheet with cooking spray.

In a shallow bowl, mix the flour, paprika, and salt. In another shallow bowl, lightly beat the egg whites, butter, and pepper sauce. In a third bowl, spread the cornflakes in a thin layer.

Toss the chicken in the flour, dip in the egg whites, and coat with the cornflakes. Place on the prepared baking sheet and coat with cooking spray. Bake until golden and the chicken is no longer pink, about 30 minutes. Serve with the blue cheese dip.

Makes 6 servings

Nutrient Boost: Serve with organic celery sticks, a good source of fiber, vitamin C, and calcium.

Make It Kosher: Replace the blue cheese sauce with your favorite barbecue sauce and use margarine instead of butter to coat the chicken.

Chicken and Feta Phyllo Tarts

Perfect for parties, these appetizers will have everyone noshing in no time. Don't be put off by the number of ingredients. They're all part of an easy sauté that fills ready-made phyllo shells. The filling takes less than 20 minutes to make, and these bake up in under 10 minutes.

1 tablespoon extra-virgin olive oil

1 onion, finely chopped

2 cloves garlic, minced

1 pound pasture-raised or organic ground chicken

1 teaspoon salt

¼ teaspoon ground black pepper

2 tablespoons unbleached all-purpose flour

⅓ cup white wine

1 tablespoon lemon juice

4 scallions, chopped

3 ounces sheep's milk feta cheese

3 ounces organic reduced-fat cream cheese

2 teaspoons chopped fresh tarragon or 1 teaspoon dried

4 boxes (2.1 ounces each) mini phyllo shells, thawed

2 tablespoons sesame seeds

Heat the oil in a large skillet over medium heat. When hot, add the onion and garlic. Cook until just soft, about 4 minutes. Add the chicken, salt, and pepper. Cook, breaking up the meat with a spoon, until the meat is no longer pink, about 4 minutes. Stir in the flour until evenly distributed. Stir in the wine and cook until thickened, about 2 minutes. Remove from the heat.

Stir in the lemon juice, scallions, feta, and cream cheese. Let cool, then stir in the tarragon. Put the mixture in a pastry bag or resealable plastic bag. If using a bag, cut off a small piece of a corner. Pipe the mixture into the phyllo shells. Sprinkle evenly with the sesame seeds.

Preheat the oven to 350°F. Bake until heated through, 8 minutes.

Makes 60 mini tarts

Helping Hand: Make the filling up to 3 days ahead and store it in the refrigerator. Fill the shells up to 1 hour ahead before heating them.

Chicken and Cheese Enchiladas

These Tex-Mex favorites are perfect for an after-work meal. Look for red enchilada sauce in the Mexican section of your grocery store. Serve with sides of refried beans and rice.

8 corn tortillas

1 tablespoon canola oil

1 pound pasture-raised or organic boneless, skinless chicken breast halves, cubed

½ small onion, chopped

2 cloves garlic, minced

½ teaspoon chili powder

½ teaspoon ground cumin

½ teaspoon dried oregano

4 ounces organic cream cheese or goat cheese

½ cup chunky salsa

¼ cup sliced black olives (optional)

1 cup shredded organic pepper Jack or Cheddar cheese

1 can (10 ounces) red enchilada sauce

Preheat the oven to 350°F. Wrap the stack of tortillas in foil and bake 10 minutes.

Meanwhile, heat the oil in a large, deep skillet over medium-high heat. Add the chicken and onion and cook, turning often, until the chicken is no longer pink in the center.

Stir in the garlic, chili powder, cumin, and oregano. Cook 2 minutes. Stir in the cream cheese or goat cheese and cook over low heat, stirring often, until the cheese melts. Stir in the salsa and olives (if using). Cook until heated through, 2 minutes. Stir in ½ cup of the pepper Jack or Cheddar. Remove from the heat.

Spread a thin layer of enchilada sauce over the bottom of an 11" × 7" baking dish. Spoon about ⅓ cup filling in a column down the center of each tortilla. Roll up and arrange, seam side down, in the baking dish.

Top evenly with the remaining enchilada sauce and pepper Jack or Cheddar. Bake until hot and bubbly, 15 to 20 minutes.

Makes 4 servings

Helping Hand: For Vegetarian Enchiladas, replace the chicken with 12 ounces frozen meatless crumbles. For Beef Enchiladas, use 1 pound pasture-raised or organic extra-lean ground beef and drain off any fat before stirring into the cream cheese mixture.

Sautéed Chicken with Sage and Gingered Plums

Sliced plums sautéed with fresh ginger really make this dish sing. And the whole thing comes together in less than 30 minutes. Perfect for weeknight cooking. If you don't have fresh sage, use ½ teaspoon dried and mix it with the lemon zest.

½ organic lemon

1½ tablespoons finely chopped fresh sage

½ teaspoon salt

¼ teaspoon ground black pepper

Pinch of ground cloves

1¼ pounds pasture-raised or organic boneless, skinless chicken thighs, trimmed of fat

2 tablespoons organic butter

3–4 ripe plums, cut into ½" wedges

2 teaspoons minced fresh ginger

¼ cup organic apple juice

½ cup pasture-raised or organic chicken broth

3 tablespoons plum or cherry jam

2 teaspoons cornstarch

Choice Advice: Unlike most stone fruits, plums rank among the lowest of all fruits for insecticide residues.

Grate the zest from the lemon into a small bowl; reserve the lemon. Mix 1 tablespoon sage, the salt, pepper, and cloves with the lemon zest. Rub the mixture over the chicken, pressing in lightly.

Melt the butter in a large, deep skillet over medium-high heat. When hot, add the chicken, smooth side down, and reduce the heat to medium. Cook until no longer pink in the center, about 4 to 6 minutes per side. Transfer to a platter and cover with foil to keep warm.

Add the plums and ginger to the skillet and cook for 1 minute. Add the apple juice, broth, and jam. Squeeze in about 1 teaspoon juice from the lemon. Cover and cook until the plums are just softened, 1 to 2 minutes. Pour any juices from the chicken platter into the pan. Dissolve the cornstarch in 1 tablespoon cold water and stir into the center of the skillet. Cook, stirring gently, until the entire mixture is bubbly and thickened, about 2 minutes.

Spoon the sauce over the chicken. Garnish with the remaining ½ tablespoon sage.

Makes 4 servings

Make It Kosher: Use olive oil instead of butter.

Chicken and Asparagus Gratin

This is what I call comfort food. Warm, filling, and supremely satisfying straight from the oven. Plus, the asparagus is high in folate and a cancer-fighting antioxidant called glutathione. Who knew? I use half-and-half in the white sauce for extra richness, but if you want this a little lighter, use 2 percent milk instead.

2 pasture-raised or organic boneless, skinless chicken breast halves, cut into bite-size pieces

1 pound asparagus, trimmed and cut into 1" pieces

8 button mushrooms, quartered

1 tablespoon extra-virgin olive oil

¾ teaspoon salt

½ teaspoon ground black pepper

3 scallions, chopped

4 tablespoons organic butter

6 tablespoons unbleached all-purpose flour

2 cups organic 2% milk

1 cup organic half-and-half or 2% milk

2 tablespoons chopped fresh thyme or 1½ teaspoons dried

3 tablespoons grated Parmigiano-Reggiano cheese

2 tablespoons seasoned dry bread crumbs

Move the oven rack to the top third of the oven. Preheat the oven to 400°F.

Mix the chicken, asparagus, and mushrooms in a large roasting pan or on a rimmed baking sheet. Drizzle with the olive oil, ¼ teaspoon salt, and ¼ teaspoon pepper. Toss to coat and spread in an even layer. Roast in the top third of the oven, turning once or twice, just until the chicken is no longer pink and the asparagus is almost tender, about 5 minutes. Scrape into a 1½-quart shallow baking dish. Sprinkle with the scallions.

Reduce the oven temperature to 350°F.

Melt the butter in a medium saucepan over medium heat. Stir in the flour and cook until golden, 2 to 3 minutes. Gradually whisk in the milk until smooth. Add the remaining ½ teaspoon salt and ¼ teaspoon pepper. Gradually whisk in the half-and-half or milk until smooth and bubbly. Cook until thick like gravy, about 2 minutes. Stir in the thyme and pour over the chicken mixture.

In a small bowl, combine the cheese and bread crumbs. Sprinkle evenly over top and bake until bubbly and golden, about 35 minutes.

Makes 6 servings

Helping Hand: To trim asparagus, hold one end of an asparagus spear in each hand and bend the stalk. The spear will naturally break toward the bottom of the stalk where it becomes tough. You can hold a few spears in your hand at a time and bend them together. Cut the asparagus on the diagonal for a more decorative look.

Citrus-Grilled Chicken with Blueberry Mango Salsa

This recipe is all about fresh summer flavors. Orange, lime, cilantro, mango, and blueberries create a rainbow of taste. If you're out at the grill, give these a try. Or if you're going to the beach or on a picnic, take the grilled chicken along with you and serve with the salsa.

2 tablespoons extra-virgin olive oil

4 tablespoons orange juice

3 tablespoons lime juice

5 tablespoons finely chopped red onion

¾ teaspoon salt

¼ teaspoon ground black pepper

4 pasture-raised or organic boneless, skinless chicken breast halves

1 small mango, finely chopped

½ cup fresh blueberries

⅛ teaspoon hot pepper sauce

1 tablespoon chopped fresh cilantro or basil

In a medium bowl or resealable bag, stir together the oil, 2 tablespoons orange juice, 2 tablespoons lime juice, 2 tablespoons onion, ½ teaspoon salt, and the pepper. Add the chicken, turning to coat. Cover or seal and refrigerate for 1 hour or up to 4 hours.

In another medium bowl or bag, combine the mango, blueberries, pepper sauce, and the remaining 2 tablespoons orange juice, 1 tablespoon lime juice, 3 tablespoons onion, and ¼ teaspoon salt. Stir in the cilantro or basil.

Coat a grill rack with cooking spray. Preheat the grill to medium. Grill the chicken 4" from the heat, basting occasionally with the marinade and turning once, until an instant-read thermometer registers 170°F and the juices run clear, 3 to 4 minutes per side. Serve with the salsa.

Makes 4 servings

Helping Hand: To peel and pit a fresh mango, stand the fruit upright on a cutting board. Slice down through the flesh on one of the flatter sides, guiding the knife as close around the oval-shaped pit as possible. Repeat on the other side to make two disks of fruit plus a third centerpiece containing the pit. For the centerpiece, cut off the peel and then cut the fruit off the pit; discard pit and peels.

Hold one of the remaining disks in your hand and very carefully score the flesh all the way down to the peel in a checkerboard pattern. Be careful not to let the knife pierce through the mango skin and into your palm. Push up through the center of the peel side of the disk to expose the cubes of flesh. Cut the flesh away from the peel and discard the peel. Repeat with the other disk.

JESSE COOL
Farmers Are Her Heroes

Jesse Cool has always marched to the beat of her own drummer. Long before "organic" became a buzzword, Jesse was serving up high-quality food prepared with love and grown locally without harmful chemicals at Flea Street Café, her restaurant in Menlo Park, California. Almost 30 years later, Jesse is still cooking to the sustainable beat at Flea Street Café and her new organic restaurants, JZ Cool Eatery and the Cool Café at Stanford University's Cantor Center for Visual Arts.

Jesse's restaurants are each built on a philosophy of nurturing body, soul, community, and planet. "Food has to taste good as well as nourish," she says. "I use organic foods in my restaurants, but having traveled to places where it's not accessible, I know there are broader issues, especially with feeding children. It's important to get kids more connected to the food they eat." To help forge this connection, Jesse recently turned her attention to improving school lunches. She admits that going totally organic is a worthwhile goal but not the central issue in schools. "Changing the way parents and schools feed their kids and helping kids eat better is the real issue," she says.

So how does she recommend doing that? "Plant a garden or grow radishes and carrots in a pot," she says. "Let kids plant the seeds and tend the plants. Let them see how food grows and let them taste the carrots. This alone will get kids back in touch with how real food gets to the table, from growing and handling to cutting and cooking." Of course, she recommends cooking with your kids at home, too. "Put the apron on them. The most important role of the parent is to involve children in the food they eat. That food has a direct relationship to the way kids feel."

In her restaurants, Jesse forges her connection to food by choosing seasonal, organic ingredients from local growers who farm sustainably. When buying fish, she asks questions about how it was caught and avoids species that have been overfished. Her chicken is pasture-raised. And her meats are provided by Niman Ranch, producers of high-quality beef, pork, and lamb that come from animals treated humanely and fed natural feed that doesn't contain growth hormones or antibiotics. "I have a loyal and dedicated connection to the people who produce my food," she explains. "I buy local first, and I've seen where the food comes from. Not buying cheap food grown by low-paid people in other parts of the world where we pollute their environment is a big issue for me."

Jesse also supports local California farms by saving the compostable waste from her restaurants and giving it back to the farmers to enrich their soil. "The farmers are my heroes, my mentors, my teachers," she says. "It's all about teaching people that we are part of the food chain." In 2003, JZ Cool Eatery and Catering Company won a Sustainable San Mateo County Award for its sustainable food philosophy and restaurant practices, including using green cleaning products and posting signs that encourage customers to reduce energy use. To read more about Jesse's food philosophy, look for *Your Organic Kitchen*, her terrific cookbook packed with useful information and recipes that help you eat responsibly.

Jesse Cool's Chicken with Dried Cherries, Olives, and Chiles

Jesse Cool is a master of unique flavor combinations. Once you taste the spicy-sweet salty blend in this dish, you'll be hooked. Bone-in chicken breasts stay juicier when cooked, but you may also use boneless ones.

1 teaspoon paprika

¼ teaspoon salt

¼ teaspoon ground black pepper

4 pasture-raised or organic bone-in chicken breast halves, skin removed

2 tablespoons extra-virgin olive oil

1 small red onion, chopped

1½ cups pasture-raised or organic chicken broth

½ cup organic dried cherries

½ cup pitted Kalamata olives

2 tablespoons honey

1 cinnamon stick, broken in half

1 teaspoon ground cumin

1–2 organic hot chile peppers (such as cayenne, red jalapeño, or habanero), seeded and minced

Preheat the oven to 400°F.

In a small bowl, combine the paprika, salt, and black pepper. Put the chicken in a large, shallow roasting pan. Brush with 1 tablespoon oil and sprinkle with the paprika mixture. Roast until the chicken registers 170°F on an instant-read thermometer and the juices run clear, about 45 minutes.

Meanwhile, heat the remaining 1 tablespoon oil in a medium saucepan over medium heat. Add the onion and cook until soft, about 5 minutes. Add the broth, cherries, olives, honey, cinnamon stick, and cumin. Bring to a boil. Reduce the heat to medium-low and simmer until the cherries are plump and the sauce has thickened, about 20 minutes. Stir in the chile pepper.

When the chicken is cooked, drain any pan juices into the cherry sauce for extra flavor (or skip this step). Remove and discard the cinnamon stick from the sauce.

Arrange the chicken on a serving platter and spoon the sauce over top.

Makes 4 servings

Baked Chicken with Honey and Apples

Rochelle Davis contributed this family favorite recipe. She adapted it from an old recipe by Ron and Nancy Goor. It's tailor-made for Rosh Hashanah, since honey and apples are symbolic foods of the Jewish high holy day. Apples and honey symbolize the hope that the New Year will be sweet, healthy, and happy.

6 pastured-raised or organic bone-in chicken breast halves, skin removed

½ teaspoon ground cinnamon

¼ teaspoon ground black pepper

1 tablespoon extra-virgin olive oil

½ sweet onion, sliced

2 organic Granny Smith apples, peeled, cored, and chopped

1 tablespoon margarine or extra-virgin olive oil

1½ cups organic apple juice

2 tablespoons honey

1 teaspoon salt

Choice Advice: If organic apples aren't available, look for the "Stemilt: Responsible Choice" label, which ensures the most harmful pesticides were not used.

Preheat the oven to 350°F. Put the chicken in a shallow baking dish and sprinkle with the cinnamon and pepper.

Heat the oil in a large, deep skillet over medium heat. Add the onion and cook, stirring occasionally, until tender, about 4 minutes. Add the apples and cook for about a minute. Pour over the chicken.

Melt the margarine or additional oil in the same skillet over medium heat. Stir in the apple juice, honey, and salt. Cook, scraping the bottom of the skillet, for 2 minutes. Pour over the apples.

Bake, spooning the liquid over the chicken occasionally, until the chicken registers 170°F on an instant-read thermometer and the juices run clear, about 45 minutes. Serve with the sauce spooned over the chicken.

Makes 6 servings

Helping Hands: Serve the chicken over cooked rice or noodles.

For a thicker sauce, remove the chicken from the baking dish and pour the juices into a medium saucepan. Bring to a simmer over medium heat. Dissolve 2 teaspoons cornstarch in about 1 tablespoon cold water. Whisk the cornstarch mixture into the pan and cook, stirring frequently, until thickened, 1 to 2 minutes.

Turkey Salad with Orange Mint Vinaigrette

Redolent with the soothing aromas of autumn apples and toasted walnuts, this salad gets a shot of bright flavor from orange zest and fresh mint. The combination is utterly refreshing. Dried cranberries and blueberries bring an extra depth of sweetness.

4 cups pasture-raised or organic chicken broth

1 pound pasture-raised or organic boneless, skinless turkey breast cutlets

½ organic navel orange

1 organic Granny Smith apple, peeled, cored, and chopped

⅓ cup extra-virgin olive oil

¼ teaspoon salt

A few grindings of black pepper

2 tablespoons chopped fresh mint

2 teaspoons chopped fresh chives

1 small head Boston lettuce, leaves separated, rinsed, and dried

¼ cup dried cranberries

¼ cup dried blueberries

½ cup walnuts, toasted and chopped

1½ teaspoons sugar

Bring the broth to a boil in a medium saucepan over high heat. Reduce the heat to medium-low so the broth gently simmers. Add the turkey and cook just until no longer pink in the center, 8 to 10 minutes. Remove to a cutting board. Cool and cut into bite-size pieces. Strain the broth and reserve for another use.

Using a citrus zester, remove the zest from the orange and place in a small bowl. Set aside. Squeeze the juice from the orange into a large bowl. Add the apples and toss to coat. Using a slotted spoon, remove the apples to a plate and set aside, leaving the orange juice in the bowl. Whisk the oil into the juice in a slow steady trickle until fully blended. Whisk in the salt, pepper, mint, and chives. Stir in the turkey and apples.

Line a platter or 4 salad plates with the lettuce. Arrange the turkey salad over the lettuce. Drizzle with any dressing left in the bowl. Top with the cranberries, blueberries, and walnuts. Just before serving, sprinkle the sugar over the reserved orange zest and toss to coat. Garnish the salad with the sweetened zest.

Makes 4 servings

Helping Hands: If you buy commercially prepared chicken broth instead of using homemade, look for the kind in an aseptic box. This type tends to taste better than canned versions. Plus, it comes in a 1-quart box (4 cups), which is perfect for this recipe.

You can use leftover cooked turkey breast for this dish. You'll need 6 to 7 cups bite-size pieces.

Turkey Gumbo with Sausage and Escarole

This thick Southern stew includes okra, a pod vegetable that also goes by the African-derived name "gumbo." Look for it in farmers' markets from late spring through early fall. Or if you live in the South, you can probably get it fresh year-round. If you can't find fresh okra, frozen sliced okra is available in most supermarkets. I briefly sauté the sliced okra to reduce its stringiness yet retain its thickening power.

12 ounces frozen vegetarian Italian sausage links (such as Boca)

3 tablespoons plus ⅓ cup vegetable oil

12 ounces pasture-raised or organic boneless, skinless turkey breast tenderloins

12 ounces fresh or frozen okra, trimmed and sliced ¼" thick (about 2 cups)

1 large onion, chopped

1 large organic green bell pepper, seeded and chopped

2 large organic celery ribs, chopped

2 large cloves garlic, minced

⅓ cup unbleached all-purpose flour

2½ cups pasture-raised or organic chicken broth

1 can (28 ounces) crushed tomatoes

1½ teaspoons dried thyme

¼–½ teaspoon crushed red pepper flakes

2 bay leaves

½ teaspoon salt

½ teaspoon ground black pepper

1 pound California trap-caught spot prawns or medium turtle-safe shrimp, peeled and deveined (optional)

1 pound escarole, coarsely chopped

2 teaspoons filé powder (optional)

Put enough water in a medium nonstick skillet to barely cover the bottom. Add the sausage, cover, and put over medium heat. Cook, shaking the skillet occasionally, until the sausages are thawed, 5 to 6 minutes. Uncover and let any water boil off. Add 1 tablespoon oil and cook, turning the sausages frequently, until they are browned, about 5 minutes. Remove to a cutting board. When cool, slice crosswise.

Meanwhile, heat another 1 tablespoon oil in a large soup pot over medium heat. When hot, add the turkey and cook, turning once or twice, just until no longer pink in the center, about 5 minutes. Remove to a cutting board. When cool, cut into bite-size pieces.

Heat another 1 tablespoon oil in the pot over medium heat. When hot, add the okra and cook, stirring occasionally, until tender, 2 to 3 minutes. Add the onion, pepper, celery, and garlic. Cook, stirring a little, until the vegetables are tender, about 10 minutes. Transfer to a bowl.

Heat the remaining ⅓ cup oil in the pot over medium heat. Gradually whisk in the flour. Reduce the heat a little and cook, whisking frequently, until the liquid mixture (known as a roux) gets a little thick and turns medium brown, about 8 minutes. Watch carefully so you don't burn the roux. It should be a nutty brown. If it burns, clean the pot and start over again with fresh oil and flour. Gradually whisk in the broth, which will thicken and then thin the mixture. Stir in the reserved sausage, turkey, and vegetables. Add the tomatoes (with juice), thyme, pepper flakes, bay leaves, salt, and pepper. Bring to a boil over high heat. Reduce the heat to medium-low and cook at a low simmer, uncovered, for 45 minutes. Remove the bay leaves.

Stir in the shrimp (if using) and escarole. Cook over medium heat until the shrimp are bright pink and the greens are just wilted, 3 to 4 minutes. Remove from the heat and stir in the filé powder. Let stand for 5 minutes. Taste and add more salt and pepper as necessary.

Makes 8 servings

Helping Hands: For an authentic presentation, mound about ½ cup of cooked rice in the center of soup plates. Generously spoon the gumbo around the edges of the rice.

Vegetarian Italian sausage links are available in most supermarkets in the freezer case near the veggie burgers. I use these to avoid the nitrites in sausage. For dinner-type sausages, the best-tasting ones I've found are Boca Italian sausage links.

Turkey tenderloins come from the most tender part of the turkey breast. If you can't find them, use turkey breast cutlets instead.

Filé powder is the pure powdered or ground leaves of the sassafras tree. It's available in the spice aisle of many grocery stores. It's traditional in gumbo to help thicken and flavor the brew. If you can't find it, omit it. Your gumbo will still be thick and flavorful.

Trap-caught California spot prawns are a type of shrimp harvested without undue destruction to our oceans. If you can't find them, you can omit the shrimp altogether from this recipe.

Make It Kosher: Omit the shrimp. The vegetarian sausage already contains no pork, so that makes the recipe kosher as well.

Turkey Piccata with Kale and Sun-Dried Tomatoes

This late-autumn dish gets to the table in a little over 30 minutes and uses only one pan.

1½ pounds pasture-raised or organic boneless, skinless turkey breast

¼ cup unbleached all-purpose flour

¾ teaspoon rubbed dried sage

¾ teaspoon salt

Ground black pepper

4 teaspoons olive oil

2 cloves garlic, minced

¼ cup drained oil-packed or soft sun-dried tomatoes, sliced

¾ pound kale, stemmed and coarsely chopped

2 small organic lemons

1 tablespoon drained capers

¼ cup dry white wine or vermouth

⅔ cup pasture-raised or organic chicken broth

2 teaspoons cornstarch

2 tablespoons organic butter

1 tablespoon chopped fresh parsley

Cut the turkey crosswise into ¼" thick slices.

In a shallow dish, mix together the flour, sage, ½ teaspoon salt, and ¼ teaspoon pepper. Dredge the turkey in the flour mixture to coat both sides, shaking off any excess.

Heat 2 teaspoons oil in a large nonstick skillet over medium-high heat. When hot, add the turkey (in batches if necessary) and cook until browned and no longer pink in the center, about 2 minutes per side. Remove to a plate and cover to keep warm.

Heat the remaining 2 teaspoons oil in the skillet over medium heat. When hot, add the garlic, tomatoes, and half of the kale. Toss quickly in the oil until the kale begins to wilt. Add the remaining kale, tossing all together until the kale is wilted, another minute or so. Reduce the heat to low and season with the remaining ¼ teaspoon salt and a few grindings of pepper. Cook until the kale is tender, 1 to 2 minutes. Remove to a platter or divide among dinner plates. Arrange the turkey over the kale and cover to keep warm.

Grate about ¾ teaspoon lemon zest from 1 lemon and set aside. Squeeze the juice from both lemons and add to the skillet. Add the zest, capers, wine or vermouth, and ½ cup broth to the skillet. Bring to a boil over medium-high heat. Stir the cornstarch into the remaining broth until dissolved. Whisk into the skillet and continue whisking until the mixture thickens, about 1 minute. Whisk in the butter. Pour the sauce over the turkey and sprinkle with the parsley.

Makes 4 servings

Turkey, Gruyère, and Watercress Wraps

These roll up quickly for picnics or road trips. Or serve them for a garden party. To simplify flavors for the kids, use Swiss cheese and iceberg lettuce in place of the Gruyère and watercress. You can also use regular cucumbers instead of English cucumbers, which come wrapped in plastic in most grocery stores. I like English cucumbers because they have fewer seeds and taste a little sweeter.

6 ounces organic cream cheese

2 tablespoons chopped fresh basil or parsley

1 scallion, chopped

4 large flour tortillas (10" diameter), preferably whole wheat

12 ounces thinly sliced cooked pasture-raised or organic turkey breast

6 ounces thinly sliced imported Gruyère or organic Swiss cheese

1 cup shredded carrots

⅓ English cucumber, thinly sliced

2 tomatoes, sliced

1 bunch watercress, stem ends trimmed

In a small bowl, mix together the cream cheese, basil or parsley, and scallion.

Spread the cream cheese mixture evenly over the tortillas. Evenly layer the turkey, cheese, carrots, cucumber, tomatoes, and watercress on the ends of the tortillas closest to you. Roll each sandwich away from you into a tight cylinder. Cut each in half on an angle and secure with toothpicks. (Or roll the wraps into wax paper and cut each whole wrap in half.)

Makes 4 wraps

JANE SEYMOUR
Teaching the Next Generation about Healthy Eating

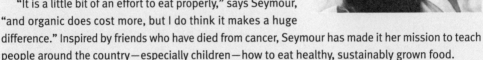

Well-known for her television character Dr. Quinn: Medicine Woman, Jane Seymour actually lives the part. She is the daughter of a real-life doctor, and her sister practices homeopathic medicine. Over the years, healthy food and complementary medicine have become central to Seymour's lifestyle.

"It is a little bit of an effort to eat properly," says Seymour, "and organic does cost more, but I do think it makes a huge difference." Inspired by friends who have died from cancer, Seymour has made it her mission to teach people around the country—especially children—how to eat healthy, sustainably grown food.

The mission starts at home with Seymour's own six children. For the past 10 years, Seymour and her husband, actor and director James Keach, have grown an organic garden on their property in Malibu, California. Their children help to plant the seeds, harvest the food, and cook it, so they can see where their meals come from and how food is grown. "We're teaching the next generation—at least our next generation—what fun it is to grow and eat your own food," says Seymour. "And how easy it is to grow food without harmful pesticides." Seymour also keeps pesticide exposure to a minimum by purchasing organic poultry and meats and using organic pesticides around the house for controlling ants, bees, and the like.

Reducing the environment's toxic load is high on Seymour's list of priorities. But an even bigger issue for the star is America's growing number of obese children and adults. "I travel all over the country," she says. "Most of the kids I see are eating nothing but junk food." She emphasizes how important it is for parents to lead by example. "If your children see you reach for the broccoli, they'll want to do it, too." That philosophy has been working at home. When the actress's twin sons, Kris and Johnny, were just 5 years old, they spontaneously limited their trips to fast-food restaurants and cut their soda drinking to one day a week. "They want to be responsible about it," says Seymour. "And that's the best thing that children could learn."

Seymour gets her message of healthy, organically grown food out to parents and children whenever she can. She works with Mothers for Natural Law, the Make-a-Wish Foundation, and Childhelp USA. And she is honorary chairperson for City Hearts, an organization that enriches the lives of abused and incarcerated youth by teaching the performing arts.

146

Lemon Rosemary Grilled Turkey

This makes a great alternative to the traditional holiday turkey, especially if you like mostly white meat anyway. Serve it with your favorite gravy and stuffing. Or try it any other time of year. It's surprisingly meaty-tasting from the marinade and charcoal grill. You can also use a gas grill or broil the turkey on a rack about 6 inches from the heat, turning and basting as directed.

1 large organic lemon

¼ cup extra-virgin olive oil

1 large clove garlic, minced

2 tablespoons chopped fresh rosemary

½ teaspoon salt

¼ teaspoon black pepper

1 pasture-raised or organic turkey London broil (2 pounds)

Grate the zest from the lemon into a large resealable plastic bag. Cut the lemon in half and squeeze the juice from both halves into the bag. Stir in the oil, garlic, rosemary, salt, and pepper. Add the turkey, seal the bag, and turn to coat completely. Refrigerate for at least 1 hour or up to 8 hours.

Coat a grill rack with cooking spray and preheat the grill to medium. Remove the turkey from the bag and grill, occasionally turning the meat and basting with the marinade, until slightly pink in the center (about 170°F on an instant-read thermometer) and the juices run clear, 15 to 20 minutes total. Discard the remaining marinade. Let the turkey stand 10 minutes so the juices can seep back into the meat. Thinly slice on the diagonal.

Makes 8 servings

Helping Hand: A turkey London broil is a whole boneless, skinless turkey breast that's been butterflied so it lies flat. Most grocery stores carry them, but if yours doesn't, ask your butcher to prepare it for you.

Chapter 6

Beef and Pork

Currently, there are about 1.3 million farms with livestock in the United States. When envisioning that statistic, it would be a mistake to picture them all as quaint operations, set amid rolling hillsides. In fact, many of these operations are more accurately described by the agriculture industry's technical term "concentrated animal feeding operations," or CAFOs. That is because they are designed to maximize profits by getting as many animals to market as quickly and efficiently as possible. Huge beef feedlots, for example, sometimes pack in as many as 100,000 head of cattle. Such intensive production at CAFOs has made a big impact on our water and land, due in part to the enormous amounts of waste produced in such a concentrated area.

In addition, only four huge companies control about 60 percent of pork packing operations and more than 80 percent of beef slaughterhouses in the country. Just one company, IBP, slaughters approximately 40 percent of conventionally raised cattle.

This concentrated production of hogs and cattle consumes enormous amounts of resources for growing vast quantities of grain feed, confining the animals, treating their sicknesses, and processing them. Globally, the modern production of beef and pork has had more impact on the world's land, water, and air than any other type of food production. On the whole, animal agriculture causes 80 percent of the world's annual deforestation, and livestock worldwide consume half of the earth's total grain harvest. According to research from the Center for Science in the Public Interest, the water-pollution impacts of eating hamburger are about 17 times worse than those of eating rice.

Modern Meat

For these reasons, smart choices at the meat case and when eating out will impact the health of your family and the environment more than most other food choices you make. Of course, eating less meat will make the biggest impact. But there are plenty of other ways to keep meat on the menu. Choose beef and pork from farms that raise livestock using responsible, sustainable methods. These growers can provide you and your family with the healthiest, safest meat available—minus the drawbacks of intensive modern livestock farming.

Beef and Pork Raised without Antibiotics

For your health, meat produced without the use of antibiotics makes a good alternative if you can't find organic. Intensive producers of livestock (accounting for most of the meat we buy) routinely rely on antibiotics to promote growth and compensate for the diseases that tend to flourish in livestock feedlots. The problem is that these drugs are administered to ward off potential problems before they occur.

The Union of Concerned Scientists estimates that 70 percent of all the antibiotics used in the United States are fed to otherwise healthy livestock to promote growth and compensate for the stress and health risks of confinement. We use more antibiotics on our food animals than we use on ourselves. The basic concern is that the more that bacteria are exposed to antibiotics, the more resistant they become to these medicines. The massive routine use of antibiotics in food animals results in more antibiotic-resistant infections transmitted to humans, mostly through meat contaminated with drug-resistant microbes. Three different studies in the *New England Journal of Medicine* verified that antibiotic-resistant bacteria are widespread in commercial U.S. meats and can also be found in consumers' bodies. As a result, once-reliable antibiotics are becoming less effective in treating human illness.

The World Health Organization considers antibiotic resistance one of the top three threats to public health and recommends banning all antibiotics in animal feed. The

European Union recently decided to phase out the use of all growth-promoting antibiotics for livestock. Until the United States catches up, look for meat raised without antibiotics. You won't see the label "antibiotic-free" on meat packages because the U.S. Department of Agriculture (USDA) considers that label unapprovable. But you may see labels claiming "no antibiotics administered" or "raised without antibiotics." Either of these makes a healthy choice for ensuring that antibiotics keep working to treat human illnesses.

Beef Raised without Growth Hormones

Federal regulations specifically prohibit the use of hormones on hog farms. So you needn't worry about those drugs showing up in your pork chops. However, beef cattle are typically raised with growth promoters and synthetic hormones in order to boost the producer's profit margin.

To understand the impact of growth hormones on the beef industry, consider this: In the early 1930s, it took about 5 years for a cow raised on pasture to reach a size and weight suitable for slaughter. Today, beef cattle are fattened up for slaughter in just over 1 year. This accelerated growth comes directly from the modern cow's high-calorie diet of corn and protein supplements, as well as growth-promoting hormones.

The Food and Drug Administration has approved six steroid hormones for use in food production, including estradiol and progesterone (natural female sex hormones) and testosterone (the natural male sex hormone). These are usually injected into the back of a cow's ear or added directly to cattle feed. Eventually, these hormones make their way from the manure into nearby waterways and contribute to the disruption of sex hormones in fish and other wildlife. They also make their way into humans through milk and meat from hormone-treated cows.

While research into the human health impact of current hormone use in livestock is in its early stages, some scientists have explored a possible link between synthetic estrogens and the early onset of puberty in girls, as well as a subsequent increase in breast cancer risk. One Italian study targeted hormone-treated beef in school lunches as the cause of breast enlargement in very young girls and boys. However, the study was not conclusive. There simply haven't been enough long-term studies in this area to draw a clear link. The fact is, children are exposed to so many different sources of hormones and hormonally active chemicals—from the rBGH in milk to hormone-disrupting pesticides to residues of birth control pills in drinking water—that it is extremely difficult to attribute any single adverse effect to a specific cause. Nonetheless, research shows that prolonged exposure to *natural* estrogen at elevated levels increases breast cancer risk in women. And some scientists speculate that the same may be true of the synthetic estrogens in our cattle.

The European Union has determined that the practice of feeding growth hormones to livestock is questionable enough to ban it altogether. For those in America, why risk disease if you don't have to? Other choices are readily available. A growing number of U.S. beef producers, such as Niman Ranch, do not use hormones in their beef. As consumer demand grows, more and more producers are beginning to follow suit. Look in your supermarket for beef labeled "no hormones administered," which means that the meat is free from any added hormones over the lifetime of the animal. Or check the list of food sources on page 276.

Free-Range Beef and Pork

The term "free-range" seems to refer to cows and hogs freely roaming among rangeland for all of their lives. However, the current USDA definition of free-range means only that animals are "given access to the outdoors" for an unspecified period of time. In other words, meat labeled "free-range" could still come from animals raised indoors or in crowded feedlots, rendering the label fairly meaningless.

In the spring of 2003, the USDA proposed a new definition of free-range for beef and pork. If passed, free-range beef may soon be defined as meat from cattle raised with "unrestricted access to the outdoors and never confined to a feedlot." That's a good thing. For pigs, however, the proposed definition allows hogs to be confined to a feedlot for 20 percent of their lives—a significant loophole. Hopefully, enough public comment will encourage the USDA to make the definitions for free-range beef and pork identical. Otherwise, the "free-range" label on pork will remain misleading to consumers.

Labeling issues aside, free-range meat generally makes a good choice for the environment. That's mostly because free-range animals, when raised in the true sense of the word, are not kept in crowded, often unsanitary feedlots, which avoids many of the soil and water pollution problems associated with CAFOs.

While you might also expect free-range meat to be more nutritious as well, that's only the case if the animals graze on pasture. If you're looking for more nutritious meat, find out whether your free-range producer raises the animals on pasture or grass, instead of on a diet of grain. Or, better yet, look for meat labeled "grass-fed" or "pasture-raised." See the sources on page 276 for these types of meat.

Grass-Fed or Pasture-Raised Beef

Organic regulations for beef production don't require that cattle be raised on pasture or grass, even though grass is the cow's natural food. Like other ruminant animals, cows have a special internal organ—the rumen—that turns grass into an efficient source of protein, carbohydrates, vitamins, and other essential nutrients. Grass is simply the healthiest food for the cow, and it makes grass-fed or pasture-raised beef a top choice for your health and the environment.

When calves are born, almost all start out eating grass. But after just 5 or 6 months, most cows are shipped to feedlots, where they are switched to a diet of corn, growth hormones, and antibiotics. This rich diet fattens up the cow fast but eventually takes a serious toll on its health. While ruminants efficiently digest grass, cows—especially young ones—have a hard time with corn. This grain is so much higher in starch than grass that it can lead to life-threatening bloating in the animal's stomach. Corn can also trigger a type of severe animal heartburn called acidosis, which can lead to ulcers, liver disease, and a weakened immune system that makes it difficult for cattle to fight off the infections common on crowded feedlots. That's one reason why low doses of antibiotics are mixed right into the feed. Veterinarians say that a feedlot diet is so rich that it would kill a cow after about a year and a half. But on a diet of grass and natural forage, cows thrive for 7 years or more.

A Nation of Cows

According to the U.S. Department of Agriculture's latest figures, livestock and dairy operations account for 41 percent of our nation's land use in the contiguous 48 states. That's more than agriculture crops, which use 31 percent of our land. Beef cattle production accounts for the majority of land use, farms, and ranch operators, with 100 million head of cattle on the ground at any given time.

Grass-feeding is healthier for the environment, too. Grass takes relatively few resources to grow, and grazing cows responsibly has been shown to improve soil health and biodiversity. Most grass-feed ranchers periodically rotate their livestock to different pastures, which deposits manure over a large area of grassland. The manure naturally fertilizes the soil, improving its overall health. Researchers from Colorado State University found that this sort of rotational grazing can encourage diverse plant life. Over a 55-year period, the researchers studied plant life on Colorado rangelands that had been either ungrazed by cattle or grazed lightly, moderately, or heavily. The most diverse plant life was found on the moderately grazed rangeland. Even the heavily grazed pasture had more types of plant life than the ungrazed areas, which were overrun with a single species of prickly pear cactus.

Raising cattle on pasture results in healthier meat, too. A serving of sirloin steak from a grass-fed steer has 100 fewer calories and nearly half the fat of a similar cut from a corn-fed feedlot steer. That healthy savings makes the fat content of grass-fed beef similar to that of skinless chicken. Grass-fed beef also has about four times more omega-3 fatty acids than grain-fed beef, making it a better choice for heart health. And it's higher in another beneficial fat called conjugated linoleic acid (or CLA), which may play an important role in warding off cancer.

Pasture-raised cattle do take longer to reach slaughter weight, and the meat needs to age to make it juicy, so grass-fed beef is more expensive than grain-fed. But keep in mind that as demand for grass-fed beef goes up, price will come down. And while more and more grocers are choosing to carry pastured-raised beef, the quality varies greatly. The keys to good-tasting grass-fed beef are high-quality breeds, such as Black Angus and Hereford, well-managed grassland, and careful aging of the meat.

If you've never tasted grass-fed beef, be prepared for something a little lighter than well-marbled corn-fed beef. While corn-fed beef often tastes rich and assertive, grass-fed beef is generally milder, juicier, smoother, and less gristly. After all, it is lower in fat. The cow's diet of grass also results in meat with more subtle aromas and flavors, which many health-conscious diners prefer. Look for a well-known brand of grass-fed beef, such as Niman Ranch, or see other sources on page 276.

Pasture-Raised Pork

As with beef, USDA regulations don't require hogs to be raised on pasture or a natural diet of forage. But studies show that pasture-raised pork has environmental benefits similar to those of pasture-raised beef.

Waste management is the biggest obstacle facing intensive pork producers. Nearly 100 million hogs are raised in the United States every year, and most are kept in crowded enclosed facilities that produce vast amounts of manure. The sheer volume of decomposing manure inside these facilities, combined with bacterial toxins and dust, creates toxic levels of gases such as hydrogen sulfide and ammonia. Research shows that 60 percent of hog farm workers suffer impaired breathing from inhaling these gases. Once the waste is removed, it is usually stored on or near the hog farm in manure lagoons. These giant cesspools of untreated hog sewage can create hazardous waste spills and water contamination from excessive nitrogen in the waste runoff. And it happens more than it should, often due to unavoidable weather problems such as hurricanes.

North Carolina, one of the country's largest pork producers, suffered the most devastating manure spill on record in 1995. A staggering 25 million gallons of hog manure spilled from a concentrated storage lagoon, killing about 10 million fish and closing more than 350,000 acres of coastal wetlands to shell fishing. Living near such concentrated amounts of waste can be hazardous to local residents. In the early 1990s in the LaGrange County farming region of Indiana, three women who lived near hog farms suffered multiple miscarriages due to unsafe levels of nitrates in their drinking water wells. According to the Centers for Disease Control and Prevention, when the women changed their drinking water source, they all gave birth without trouble.

Hogs raised on pasture tend to cause fewer soil and water quality problems than those raised on confined factory farms. Of course, pasture-raised hogs create manure, but pasture farms tend to be smaller than concentrated animal feeding operations. And most pasture farmers practice rotational pasturing, which deposits the manure over a large area, naturally fertilizing the soil. Pasturing takes more careful management on the part of the farmer, but this extra care results in better meat and a safer environment. Studies also show that the bacterial count on pastured pork is usually lower than that of feedlot pork. That's partly because the pastured hogs are in better health. And it's partly because cuts of feedlot pork are usually misted with water to prevent them from drying out, which speeds up bacterial growth during processing and shipping.

Look for pasture-raised pork in your grocery store or call the meat manager and ask him or her to carry it. If that fails, you can buy pasture-raised pork through the sources on page 276.

Kosher Beef

This meat makes a good alternative if you're concerned about bacteria-contaminated beef. Principles of cleanliness and purity are woven right into the production process for kosher-certified meat. For instance, to ensure humane slaughter, a trained specialist uses an extremely sharp knife at the throat, which results in a clean, painless death. After slaughter, the organs are inspected for evidence of prior disease. If the meat shows signs of contamination, it is not sold as kosher. Kosher processing also minimizes bacterial growth by using cold water throughout the butchering. You can find kosher beef in many grocery stores, but you'll never find kosher pork, which is forbidden according to Jewish dietary law. Keep in mind that koshering refers only to the way the animals are processed—not produced. No restrictions are placed on cattle feed or the use of hormones or antibiotics in production.

Organic Beef and Pork

Organic meat makes a good overall choice for your health and the health of our soil and water. The main benefit to your health comes from reduced antibiotic use. The current overuse of antibiotics in conventional livestock production is contributing to the growing public health problem of antibiotic-resistant bacteria. These microbes are so inured to antibiotics from repeated exposure that they can resist their effects. As a result, certain classes of antibiotics have become less effective in treating humans. Choose organic meat and you will help to ensure that antibiotics continue to heal our illnesses.

The primary environmental benefit of organic meat comes from the organic—rather than conventional—production of vast quantities of corn, the main food source for America's 100 million head of cattle in production. More than 80 million acres of feed corn are planted in the United States, and this crop requires more chemical herbicides and synthetic fertilizers than any other. Research from the Center for Science in the Public Interest shows that the chemicals applied to conventional feed grain cause five times more toxic water pollution than the chemicals applied to conventional rice grown for human consumption.

Organic meat producers also use only the healthiest feeding practices. For instance, until a recent ban was enacted, conventionally raised cattle were often fed chicken manure as a cheap source of protein. Feather meal and by-products from pigs and fish were also permitted in conventional cattle feed. Fortunately, these practices were stopped due to concerns about the spread of *bovine spongiform encephalopathy* (mad cow disease). But there were other signs that these disturbing feeding practices caused health problems for cows. In 1999, for example, research into a fatal outbreak of copper poisoning in a cattle feedlot traced the copper back to chicken manure in the cattle feed. The chickens that produced the manure had been treated with copper sulfate to avoid a common disease of intensive poultry production known as *aspergillosis*. That excess copper in the cattle feed ended up killing almost 150 cows in the affected feedlot.

By choosing organic meat, you can be sure that the beef and pork you're eating come from healthy, well-managed cows and pigs fed only organic feed. In response to consumer demand, supermarkets are carrying more and more cuts of organic meat. And it often tastes better. If you can't find any in your local market, ask the meat manager to stock organic meat or go to the sources listed on page 276.

Lean Cuts of Beef and Pork

In the past 30 years, numerous studies have shown that the saturated fat and cholesterol in meat can increase your risk for heart disease, the number one cause of death in America. Researchers at Cornell University also looked at 10 different studies and concluded that eating beef may be associated with increased risk of breast cancer. But that doesn't mean you have to swear off meat altogether. Meat provides key nutrients like vitamin B$_{12}$, zinc, and iron.

When you eat beef and pork, choose lean cuts to reduce health risks in two important ways. First, lean cuts are lower in saturated fat, so eating them instead of higher-fat cuts can help to reduce heart disease risk. The leanest cuts usually come from the round and loin sections of the animal. Look for beef tenderloin, top loin, sirloin, top round, eye of round, tip, flank steak, and extra-lean ground beef. For pork, choose tenderloin, sirloin, lean boneless ham, and Canadian bacon.

Second, choosing these lean cuts will reduce your exposure to harmful environmental contaminants known as dioxins. For the most part, these toxins are produced by trash incinerators, coal-fired power plants, and backyard trash burning, which

What Does the Irradiation Symbol Mean?

 Irradiation is a food technology first developed in the 1940s to help make food safer to eat. It works by restructuring the molecules of most food-borne pathogens, such as *E. coli*, salmonella, and campylobacter (the leading causes of food-borne illness), making them unable to reproduce. Irradiation doesn't make food radioactive. But it does affect the nutrients the food provides by killing some beneficial bacteria and enzymes, decreasing the amount of some antioxidant vitamins, and increasing the number of free radicals.

Some of the early irradiation studies done in the 1950s and 1960s showed that the technology may cause increased risk for cancer and birth defects. And in 1998, a study published in *Radiation Physics and Chemistry* found that when fatty foods such as meat are treated by ionizing radiation, a toxic chemical known as 2-DCB (2-dodecylcyclobutanone) is formed that may promote tumor growth. These concerns justify the further study of irradiation technology.

In light of conflicting evidence, the European Union has put the brakes on approving new foods for irradiation. In the United States, however, the list of foods approved for irradiation continues to grow. Wheat flour and white potatoes have been irradiated for more than 25 years. Spices, fruits, vegetables, pork, and poultry have been approved since 1985. The Food and Drug Administration (FDA) gave beef the green light for irradiation in 1997 and fresh eggs in 2000. The FDA requires that all irradiated foods (except minor ingredients such as spices) be labeled with a symbol called a radura, shown above. But restaurants are not required to disclose whether their foods are irradiated, so ask your server if you're concerned.

Clean Meat: Irradiation versus Sanitation

Irradiated meat is here. It looks and tastes a bit different than conventional fresh meat, but more supermarkets nationwide are carrying it. That's because of massive recalls in recent years caused by widespread bacterial contamination.

In theory, irradiation makes meat safer to eat because it reduces the risk of food poisoning. But consumers have concerns about its human health effects and whether irradiation is the best strategy for reducing bacteria on meat.

When it comes to irradiating beef, the technology is only a short-term solution that doesn't fix the underlying food safety problem in U.S. beef production. The fact is that our meat comes to market contaminated with excessive bacteria from crowded, unsanitary cattle feedlots and improper handling at meat processing plants. In 2002, the amount of total recalls in the beef industry reached a record high — 57 million pounds of meat.

In that same year, a report from the U.S. General Accounting Office, which keeps watch over government agencies, found that USDA food safety regulations went widely unenforced at meat-packing plants across the country. The report concludes that meat tainted with *E. coli* and salmonella is regularly shipped to supermarkets and restaurants. In light of these facts, better alternatives to irradiation might be found in changing the modern cow's diet to reduce the spread of disease, improving the production process in meat processing plants, and stepping up the enforcement of U.S. Department of Agriculture sanitation regulations.

In the meantime, here's what you can do as a consumer. Buy clean meat in the first place. Look for beef that is packaged at the meat processing plant rather than in your supermarket. Studies show that bacterial counts tend to be lower on plant-packaged beef. When you can, choose pasture-raised, organic, or kosher beef, all of which are less likely to contain excessive amounts of harmful bacteria. Or buy meat raised without antibiotics, which will be less likely to carry the strongest antibiotic-resistant strains of bacteria. If you can't find these locally, look to mail-order sources. No matter which type of beef you choose, all meat should be handled with care and cooked thoroughly to avoid food-borne illness.

release dioxins into the air. When they fall to the ground, they are absorbed into feed crops or eaten by grazing animals.

According to the EPA, more than 95 percent of our exposure to dioxins comes through the food we eat, particularly animal foods. And since dioxins tend to concentrate in animal fat, most of that exposure comes from eating meat, dairy products, and eggs with a high fat content. As for the health risks that exposure creates, dioxins are believed to be responsible for more than 3,800 cases of cancer every year, according to a 2000 EPA report. Dioxins are also linked to increased risk for diabetes, heart disease, endometriosis, learning disabilities, birth defects, immune system suppression, and lowered levels of the male hormone, testosterone. According to the EPA report, most Americans already have nearly the amount of dioxin in their bodies that causes health problems in lab animals, and some have already passed that threshold. Children are especially vulnerable because dioxin is a persistent chemical carcinogen that stays in the body and becomes a lifelong burden compounding other health risks.

Because dioxins concentrate in fatty tissues, choosing leaner cuts of meat and low-fat milk and cheese will help to reduce your exposure.

Locally Raised and Packed Beef and Pork

In the United States, food typically travels about 1,300 miles from farms to processors to supermarkets and restaurants. Meat raised and packed in your local region makes a sound environmental choice because it requires fewer resources to get to your table. It doesn't have to be refrigerated as long or shipped as far, which lowers the

What Makes Meat Organic?

According to the U.S. Department of Agriculture standards, certified organic beef and pork come from animals that are fed 100 percent organic feed. Organically raised animals are also given access to the outdoors and do not receive unnecessary animal drugs such as growth hormones, antibiotics, and synthetic antiparasitic drugs, all of which are routinely given to conventionally raised livestock. Under organic management, any sick animals that are given antibiotics must be removed from the herd and can no longer be sold as organic.

The mill and equipment that mix and deliver the organic feed, as well as the meat processing plant, also must meet organic standards. If organically raised cattle or pigs are given access to pasture, the land they forage on must be free of chemical applications for 3 years before the animals can be certified organic. The following practices are also prohibited from organic beef and pork production: irradiation, genetic engineering, the use of sewage sludge as fertilizer, and synthetic pesticides, including herbicides, fungicides, and chemical fertilizers.

Safe Meat Handling

To enjoy meat without risk, handle and cook it safely. When cooking, test meat for doneness by inserting an instant-read thermometer into the thickest part of the meat without touching bone to get an accurate reading. The U.S. Department of Agriculture recommends cooking beef and pork to the internal temperatures listed below. Don't eat meat cooked to less than 150°F (less than "medium") unless you know the source of the meat and trust its safety.

BEEF		PORK	
Ground	160°F, no longer pink	Chops, ribs	160°F, juices run clear
Steaks, roasts	145°F (medium-rare)	Roasts, tenderloin	155°F, juices run clear
	160°F (medium)	Country ham	160°F
	165°F (well-done)	Precooked ham	140°F
Pot roasts	160°F, fork-tender		
Cutlets	160°F, no longer pink		

impact of production and distribution on our air, water, and soil quality. In the case of ground beef, local meat is also less likely to be contaminated with harmful bacteria because it's probably not mixed with meat from hundreds of other cows. While buying locally produced beef and pork obviously helps support your local economy, it also helps you know where your food comes from, which is especially important if you are trying to avoid food from environmentally troubled areas. Look for locally produced beef and pork in the farmers' markets and grocery stores in your area.

To help consumers make informed choices when buying locally, the USDA will soon regulate the definition of labels such as "Raised in Nebraska," which you might see on packages of beef or pork.

Game Meats

If you're a meat lover concerned about the safety of beef and pork, try game meats like elk, bison, venison, or yak. These lower-fat meats usually come from smaller producers who raise free-range animals responsibly and humanely.

Chili Beef Nachos

Turn to this munchie whenever you want to crunch something warm and yummy—after work or school or when you have friends over.

1 pound pasture-raised or organic lean ground beef

1 organic jalapeño pepper, seeded and chopped

1 clove garlic, minced

1 teaspoon chili powder

1 teaspoon dried oregano

½ teaspoon ground cumin

1 cup chunky salsa

3 ounces organic reduced-fat cream cheese

8 ounces organic tortilla chips

8 ounces organic reduced-fat Cheddar or Monterey Jack cheese, shredded (about 2 cups)

1½ cups cooked or canned small red beans

Choice Advice: While organic, grass-fed, and pasture-raised meats make good choices for your health and the environment, organic poultry makes an even better choice because the meat is leaner and producing it takes less of a toll on our soil and water. Substitute ground turkey in this dish if you wish.

Heat a medium skillet over medium heat. Add the beef, pepper, garlic, chili powder, oregano, and cumin. Cook, stirring occasionally and breaking up the meat, until the beef is no longer pink, about 5 minutes. Drain any juice from the salsa into the pan, stirring into the meat. Cook until most of the liquid is evaporated. Stir in the cream cheese until incorporated and remove from the heat.

Preheat the oven to 350°F.

Spread a layer of chips in a shallow 2-quart casserole or deep-dish pie plate. Sprinkle on one-fourth of the Cheddar or Monterey Jack. Scatter one-third of the beef mixture, one-third of the salsa, and one-third of the beans over top. Make two more layers of chips, cheese, beef, salsa, and beans. Top with the remaining cheese and bake until the cheese melts all the way through, 15 to 20 minutes.

Makes 10 appetizer servings

Helping Hand: To make tortilla chips at home, cut a stack of 5 corn tortillas into 8 wedges like a pizza. You'll end up with 40 wedges. Arrange the wedges on baking sheets and coat with cooking spray. Sprinkle on a little salt and bake at 350°F until crisp, about 10 minutes.

Grilled Beef Satay

This Indonesian dish has become an American favorite. Strips of marinated beef are skewered, grilled, and served with a spicy peanut sauce. It makes a great appetizer or even a modest main dish served with rice and a salad.

2½ pounds pasture-raised or organic beef top round, about 1½" thick

3 tablespoons organic tamari or soy sauce

2 tablespoons rice vinegar

1 tablespoon honey

3 tablespoons chopped fresh ginger

2 scallions, chopped

2 cloves garlic, minced

2 teaspoons toasted sesame oil

1½ teaspoons crushed red pepper flakes

½ cup peanut butter

1 cup pasture-raised or organic chicken broth

Put the beef in the freezer for 30 minutes to make it easier to cut.

Meanwhile, mix together the tamari or soy sauce, rice vinegar, and honey in a medium microwaveable bowl. Pour ¼ cup of this marinade into a large, shallow dish or resealable plastic bag. Stir the ginger, scallions, garlic, sesame oil, and ¾ teaspoon pepper flakes into the dish or bag. Reserve the remaining marinade in the bowl.

Cut the cold beef crosswise (against the grain) into ¼"-thick slices. Put the slices in the dish or bag with the seasoned marinade. Cover or seal and refrigerate for 30 minutes or up to 8 hours for more flavor.

Preheat the grill to medium. Soak bamboo skewers in water for at least 30 minutes.

Thread the beef slices onto skewers, poking each slice at least twice. Spread out the slices on the skewers so that the beef lies flat, which helps it to cook evenly. Grill the skewers, turning once and basting with the marinade occasionally, until the meat is no longer pink, about 5 minutes per side.

Add the peanut butter, broth, and the remaining ¾ teaspoon pepper flakes to the reserved marinade. Microwave on medium until hot, stirring occasionally, about 2 minutes. Serve the sauce with the beef skewers.

Makes 10 appetizer servings

Orange Ginger Beef with Broccoli

If your family doesn't like broccoli, serve it to them this way: smothered with sweet-and-sour sauce in a simple beef stir-fry. Add cooked rice and halved slices of fresh orange to complete the meal.

1 pound pasture-raised or organic beef flank steak

1 cup pasture-raised or organic beef broth

¼ cup organic tamari or soy sauce

¼ cup dry sherry or white wine

¼ cup organic orange marmalade

½ teaspoon crushed red pepper flakes

5 teaspoons cornstarch

1 tablespoon sesame seeds

2 tablespoons peanut oil or vegetable oil

1 pound broccoli (about 1 head), cut into florets

2 cloves garlic, minced

1½ teaspoons minced fresh ginger

2 teaspoons grated organic orange zest

Put the beef in the freezer for 30 minutes so it will be easier to cut.

Meanwhile, whisk together the beef broth, tamari or soy sauce, sherry or wine, marmalade, pepper flakes, and cornstarch. Set aside.

Heat a wok or large, deep skillet over medium heat. When hot, add the sesame seeds and cook, stirring frequently, until the seeds are fragrant and toasted, about 2 minutes. Remove to a plate.

Cut the cold beef lengthwise down the center and then crosswise (against the grain) into ¼"-thick slices. Add 1 tablespoon oil to the wok or skillet and heat over medium-high heat. When very hot, add the beef slices in batches and cook, stirring frequently, until no longer pink, about 3 minutes per batch. Transfer to a plate and cover to keep warm.

Heat the remaining 1 tablespoon oil in the pan over medium-high heat. When hot, add the broccoli and toss to coat with the oil for 30 seconds. Add 1 tablespoon water and cover the pan. Cook, shaking the pan frequently, until the broccoli turns bright green yet is still crisp and the water evaporates, 2 to 3 minutes. Add the garlic and ginger to the pan and stir-fry for 30 seconds. Add the cooked beef and orange zest and stir-fry for 15 seconds. Push the meat and vegetables to the sides of the pan to leave the center open. Briefly rewhisk the broth mixture and then pour into the center of the pan. Stir until thickened and bubbly, cooking for at least 1 minute. Stir the meat and vegetables into the sauce until well coated. Divide among plates and sprinkle with the toasted sesame seeds.

Makes 4 to 6 servings

Helping Hand: Broccoli reaches peak flavor in the cooler months, from late fall through early spring. Make this dish in the winter for best results.

Hot Dogs or Not Dogs?

Before the advent of mechanical refrigeration in the early 1900s, smoking and salting were necessary to cure meat or preserve it to keep it safe to eat. Of course, cured meats like hot dogs taste great, too. And that's why most people eat them. But today's commercially cured meats also contain nitrites and nitrates as preservatives, which researchers have linked to increased risk for diabetes and cancer.

When the International Agency for Research on Cancer (an arm of the World Health Organization) looked at the diets of nearly half a million Europeans, they found that those who ate more cured meats like hot dogs, sausage, salami, bacon, bologna, and deli meats had a 50 percent increase in colon cancer risk. In the United States, Cornell University researchers looked at 12 different studies and concluded that eating processed meats can increase breast cancer risk. And a recent study from the Harvard School of Public Health found that eating too much processed meat may increase risk for type 2 diabetes. Nitrites are the suspected culprit, as previous studies have already linked nitrites to increased risk for type 1 diabetes, the kind that most often afflicts children.

To reduce risk of these illnesses, try to eat fewer processed meats—two meals or less per week. Look for nitrite-free hot dogs and other nitrite-free processed meats. Meatless versions of these foods make another good option. Many grocery stores carry veggie versions of hot dogs, pepperoni, and sliced bologna and ham that hold their own when sandwiched between some good-quality cheese and bread. An added bonus: These products are also lower in fat and sodium than meat versions.

Rick Bayless's Spicy Jalapeño Beef Tips

Right from the start of this recipe, your kitchen will be filled with the head-swirling aromas of fresh-roasted tomatoes, jalapeños, and garlic. These form the basis of a simple salsa that transforms beef cubes into something magical.

1 pound (2 medium-large round or 6 to 8 plum) ripe red tomatoes

2 large organic jalapeño peppers

3 cloves garlic, unpeeled

Salt

½ small white onion, finely chopped

About 1½ teaspoons cider vinegar

2 tablespoons extra-virgin olive oil

1½ pounds pasture-raised or organic boneless beef (sirloin, strip steak, rib eye, or tenderloin), cut into 1" cubes and patted dry

1 tablespoon Worcestershire sauce (optional)

⅓ cup chopped fresh cilantro

Roast the tomatoes on a baking sheet 4" below a very hot broiler until soft and blackened, about 6 minutes per side. Cool and peel, collecting all the juices with the tomatoes. While the tomatoes are roasting, roast the peppers and garlic directly on an ungreased griddle or heavy skillet over medium heat, turning occasionally, until soft (they'll blacken in spots): 5 to 10 minutes for the peppers and about 15 minutes for the garlic. Cool, then pull the stems from the peppers and peel the garlic.

In a large mortar (or food processor), pound (or whir) the peppers, garlic, and ½ teaspoon salt into a coarse-textured puree. Add the tomatoes and their juices (a few at a time, if using a mortar) and work into a coarse, rich-textured salsa. Scoop the onion into a strainer, rinse under cold water, shake off the excess moisture, and add to the salsa, along with the vinegar and 3 tablespoons water. Taste and season highly with additional salt if necessary.

In a large heavy skillet, heat the oil over medium-high heat. Sprinkle the meat with salt. Lay the meat in the hot skillet in an uncrowded layer and quick-fry, stirring and turning the pieces regularly, until browned, about 4 minutes. Add the salsa, Worcestershire sauce (if using), and cilantro. Continue to cook, stirring regularly, until the salsa has reduced enough to lightly coat the meat, about 2 to 3 minutes.

Makes 4 servings

Braised Beef Short Ribs with Cabbage

Some recipes turn up on family tables again and again over the years. This one comes from Rochelle Davis's family. She adapted the recipe from Dorothy Zimmermann and uses a slow cooker for effortless braising. If you can't find beef short ribs, use flanken, a strip of beef that comes from the chuck end of short ribs. Like most stews, this one tastes better when reheated the next day.

1½ pounds pasture-raised or organic beef short ribs (about 4 ribs) or flanken on the bones

½ head cabbage, shredded

1 can (28 ounces) chopped tomatoes

1 small onion, sliced

3 tablespoons sugar

4 teaspoons lemon juice

1½ teaspoons salt

¼ teaspoon ground black pepper

Choice Advice: Cruciferous vegetables like cabbage consistently rank low in pesticide residues when grown by conventional methods.

Put the beef, cabbage, tomatoes (with juice), onion, sugar, lemon juice, salt, and pepper in a 4-quart slow cooker. Add water to cover the meat. Cover and cook until the meat is fork-tender, on low for 10 hours or on high for 4 to 5 hours. Remove to deep soup plates, spooning generous amounts of the sauce over and around the beef.

Makes 4 servings

Slow-Cooked Beef Stew

Sundays were made for stews. Throw all the ingredients in a pot and let them cook for hours. This stew cooks completely unattended so you can come home to dinner already prepared. Serve with crusty bread.

2 pounds pasture-raised or organic lean stew beef

¼ cup unbleached all-purpose flour

¾ teaspoon salt

¾ teaspoon ground black pepper

2 large onions, chopped

2 cloves garlic, minced

3 medium organic baking potatoes, peeled and finely chopped

4 carrots, quartered

3 organic celery ribs, quartered

2 cups pasture-raised or organic beef broth

1 tablespoon Worcestershire sauce

1 tablespoon ketchup

Place the beef in a 4-quart slow cooker. Mix together the flour, salt, and pepper. Toss with the beef in the cooker. Add the onions, garlic, potatoes, carrots, celery, broth, Worcestershire sauce, and ketchup. Mix well. Cook until the meat is fork-tender, on low for 8 hours or on high for 4 to 5 hours.

Makes 8 servings

Food Lore: In the late 1970s, annual U.S. beef consumption hit an all-time high of 90 pounds per person. Today, we eat a little less, but we're still holding steady at about 65 pounds per person. Americans simply love to eat beef.

Jesse Cool's Steak with Fruit Sauce

Here's a winning recipe from chef Jesse Cool, owner of three California restaurants that serve sustainable cuisine (see page 138). The combination of figs, blue cheese, and balsamic raspberry sauce over steak is truly inspired.

½ pint organic red raspberries

3 tablespoons sugar

2 tablespoons balsamic vinegar

1 tablespoon extra-virgin olive oil

1 small red onion, thinly sliced

8 large or 16 small fresh figs, quartered

2 ounces ham, chopped (optional)

1 teaspoon finely chopped fresh rosemary

¾ teaspoon garam masala

¾ teaspoon ground black pepper

¾ teaspoon salt

8 pasture-raised or organic boneless rib-eye or beef tenderloin steaks (about 2½ pounds)

6 ounces imported blue cheese, crumbled

Preheat the grill or broiler. Lightly oil the grill rack or broiler pan.

In a small saucepan, combine the raspberries, sugar, and vinegar. Simmer over medium heat until the liquid is reduced by half, about 10 minutes. Set aside.

Meanwhile, heat the oil in a medium skillet over medium heat. Add the onion and cook until soft, about 5 minutes. Add the figs, ham (if using), rosemary, garam masala, and ¼ teaspoon pepper. Cook until the figs are very soft, about 5 minutes. Set aside and cover to keep warm.

Sprinkle the salt and the remaining ½ teaspoon pepper over the steaks. Grill or broil, turning once, until an instant-read thermometer inserted in the center registers 145°F (medium-rare) or 160°F (medium).

Put each steak on a plate. Crumble the cheese evenly over the steaks and top with some of the fig mixture. Drizzle the raspberry sauce on top. Serve the remaining fig mixture on the side.

Makes 8 servings

Another Plus for Lean Meat

When fatty meats are grilled, the melted fat drips onto the hot coals or fire, causing flare-ups. Researchers have found that flare-ups create two cancer-causing compounds: heterocyclic amines and polycyclic aromatic hydrocarbons. These carcinogens are carried back to the food via the smoke. To grill safely, choose less fatty cuts of meat or, if you're grilling fattier cuts, trim all visible fat before grilling. It also helps to keep a spray bottle of water nearby to cut short any flare-ups.

Spicy Italian Pork Chops

Salad dressing can be used for so much more than salad. It makes an easy marinade for roasted meat or poultry. Here, it also forms the basis for a simple pan sauce. This dish comes together really fast—about 15 minutes from start to finish.

¼ cup drained oil-packed or soft sun-dried tomatoes

1 cup bottled Italian salad dressing

4 pasture-raised or organic center-cut pork loin chops, ¾" thick

1 teaspoon salt

1 teaspoon ground black pepper

1 tablespoon extra-virgin olive oil

½ cup dry white wine

2 tablespoons mild pepper sauce (such as Frank's)

1 tablespoon chopped fresh basil or parsley

In a food processor, puree the sun-dried tomatoes with the Italian dressing. Set aside.

Season the chops with the salt and pepper. Heat the oil in a large skillet over medium-high heat. When hot, add the chops and brown on both sides, about 3 minutes per side. Add the wine and bring to a simmer.

Pour the dressing mixture over the pork. Reduce the heat to medium, cover, and simmer until the pork registers 160°F on an instant-read thermometer and the juices run clear, about 10 minutes. Stir in the pepper sauce and return to a boil. Serve the chops topped with the sauce. Garnish with the basil or parsley.

Makes 4 servings

Helping Hand: Serve with rice pilaf or couscous and a side of steamed broccoli tossed with pressed garlic, olive oil, lemon juice, and black pepper.

Make It Kosher: Replace the pork with turkey breast tenderloins or cutlets. Cook until no longer pink in the center.

Jamaican Pork Chops with Pineapple Black Bean Salsa

Despite the fancy name, this recipe is ready from start to finish in about 20 minutes. Look for Jamaican jerk seasoning in the spice aisle of your supermarket. If you like your food really spicy, add some chopped habanero peppers or habanero hot sauce along with the bell peppers.

2 tablespoons peanut oil or extra-virgin olive oil

2 tablespoons unbleached all-purpose flour

2 tablespoons Jamaican jerk seasoning

4 pasture-raised or organic center-cut pork loin chops, ¾" thick

2 tablespoons brown sugar

2 tablespoons cider vinegar

1 can (8 ounces) crushed pineapple

1½ cups cooked or canned black beans

½ organic red bell pepper, seeded and chopped

Heat the oil in a large, deep skillet over medium-high heat.

Mix together the flour and jerk seasoning in a shallow dish. Dredge the chops in the flour mixture to coat evenly, shaking off any excess. Cook in the hot pan until browned on both sides, about 3 minutes per side. Remove to a plate and cover with foil to keep warm.

Stir the brown sugar, vinegar, and any remaining flour mixture into the pan. Bring to a boil over high heat. Stir in the pineapple (with juice), beans, and pepper. Add the chops back to the pan. Reduce the heat to low, cover, and simmer until the chops register 160°F on an instant-read thermometer and the juices run clear, about 10 minutes.

Makes 4 servings

Nutrient Boost: Garnish with chopped scallions and serve with mashed sweet potatoes.

Slow-Cooked Pork with Apple Cider

It doesn't get much simpler than this. Just put all the ingredients in a pot, turn it on, and forget about it for the rest of the day. Great for weekend days when you're out and about but want to come home to a nice meal. If the pork roast comes with netting, leave it on during cooking and remove it before slicing and serving.

3 tablespoons unbleached all-purpose flour

½ teaspoon salt

¼ teaspoon ground black pepper

1 pasture-raised or organic boneless sirloin pork roast (about 3 pounds)

1 cup organic apple cider

½ cup dry white wine

1 small onion, chopped

1 clove garlic, minced

2 teaspoons dried thyme

Mix together the flour, salt, and pepper in a cup. Sprinkle evenly over the pork roast and place in a 4-quart slow cooker. Pour in the cider, wine, onion, garlic, and thyme. Cover and cook until the meat registers 155°F on an instant-read thermometer and the juices run clear, on low about 8 hours or on high for 5 hours.

Let stand 10 minutes before slicing. Spoon the sauce over the slices.

Makes 8 servings

Nutrient Boost: To complete the meal, serve this with mashed potatoes and steamed green beans, which add fiber and vitamin C.

Pork Medallions
with Plum Port Sauce

Plums and port wine add a deep, sweet note to the versatile flavor of pork tenderloin. Save this recipe for a special occasion—even if on a weeknight. It comes together really fast, tastes fabulous, and has good looks to boot.

1 pasture-raised or organic pork tenderloin (about 1¼ pounds)

2 tablespoons organic butter or extra-virgin olive oil

1 cup ruby port

½ cup pasture-raised or organic chicken broth

2 tablespoons brown sugar

1 tablespoon Dijon mustard

¼ teaspoon ground cinnamon

¼ teaspoon ground cloves

¼ teaspoon ground black pepper

3–4 ripe plums, cut into ½" wedges

Choice Advice: Unlike other stone fruits like peaches, plums rank low among all fruits for insecticide residues.

Slice the pork crosswise into ¾"-thick medallions.

Melt the butter or heat the oil in a large, deep skillet over medium-high heat. Add the pork (in batches if necessary) and cook, turning once, until the pork registers 160°F on an instant-read thermometer and the juices run clear, about 2 minutes per side. Transfer the pork to a platter and cover with foil to keep warm.

Add the port, broth, brown sugar, mustard, cinnamon, cloves, and pepper to the skillet. Boil over medium-high heat until the liquid reduces slightly and thickens enough to coat a spoon, 8 to 10 minutes. After about 5 minutes, add any pork juices that have collected on the platter. One minute later, add the plums, reduce the heat to medium, and cook just until the plums are softened, 3 to 4 minutes. Spoon the sauce over the pork and serve.

Makes 4 servings

Cinnamon Chipotle-Crusted Pork Tenderloin

Perfect for a dinner party, this roast cooks unattended and tastes fabulous. Make it the centerpiece of a Mexican menu with sides of cumin-scented black beans and Mexican rice. If you have chile-heads at the table, they'll love it. This one is hot, hot, hot!

4 cloves garlic

3 seeded chipotle chile peppers in adobo sauce

3/4 teaspoon dried sage

1 teaspoon ground cinnamon

2 teaspoons extra-virgin olive oil

2 teaspoons red wine vinegar

1 pasture-raised or organic boneless pork loin roast (3 pounds)

1/2 cup pasture-raised or organic chicken broth

In a small food processor or large mortar and pestle, combine the garlic, peppers, sage, cinnamon, oil, and vinegar. Puree until smooth. Spread over the surface of the pork. Set in a small roasting pan, cover, and refrigerate for at least 2 hours or up to 12 hours.

Remove the roast from the refrigerator 1 hour before roasting. (Room temperature meat roasts and browns better than cold meat. If you let it sit, covered, the food-poisoning risks are pretty low if cooked within 2 hours of coming out of the fridge.)

Preheat the oven to 450°F. Roast for 30 minutes, turning halfway through cooking. Reduce the oven temperature to 325°F and pour the broth into the bottom of the pan. Roast until the pork registers 155°F on an instant-read thermometer and the juices run clear, about 55 minutes. Let stand 10 minutes before slicing.

Makes 10 to 12 servings

Helping Hand: Chipotle chile peppers in adobo are smoked jalapeño chiles packed in a spicy sauce. It's a popular Mexican canned item. Look for the 5-ounce cans in the international aisle of your supermarket or at Mexican groceries. Refrigerate unused chipotles in their sauce in an airtight container for up to 6 months. Chop them and toss into chili or burrito fillings to add a spicy, smoky flavor.

JAN SCHAKOWSKY
Stepping into the Food Fight

To those who know Illinois Congresswoman Jan Schakowsky, her name is synonymous with fighting for the underdog. For decades, she has battled tenaciously for safer food and stronger consumer protection laws.

Back in 1969, before her political career began, Jan was a homemaker pushing her toddlers through a supermarket in a grocery cart. One day in her local market, she heard yelling in the distance: "If you don't like it, I'll throw you out on your fanny, you geeks!" Wheeling over, Jan found a red-faced butcher scolding a group of women for questioning the age of some meat. It was something she herself had done just the week before. In no time, Jan joined the group (called National Consumers United) and resolved to crack the freshness codes, which told grocery employees when to rotate the stock on the shelf.

With pens, clipboards, and children in tow, this group of women inspected grocery stores, questioned managers and stockboys, and met with industry representatives. Over time, they deciphered hundreds of freshness codes and published them in a little book. They searched shelves for outdated food, loaded it into carts, and challenged grocers to remove it. These informed shoppers generated media attention to the food freshness issue. Eventually, they won their fight for freshness information. Jewel Food Stores announced a plan to print freshness dates on their house brand. Soon after, packaged meat giant Oscar Mayer followed suit. Today, virtually every product in grocery stores is stamped with a "sell by" date.

This fight launched Jan's career as a political activist. "While freshness labeling didn't change the world in a dramatic way," she explains, "it changed my life. It showed me that anyone can make a difference when they join forces with other people." For this very reason, Jan encourages people concerned with policy reform to get involved by joining organizations like Generation Green.

As a state representative in the early 1990s, Jan took on the food industry again, sponsoring a landmark pesticide disclosure bill. Jan's bill would have required food labels to list the pesticides used in production. Predictably, the agriculture and chemical industries, as well as business trade associations, all united to kill her bill.

Although Jan's bill didn't make it into law, the Food Quality Protection Act did. Jan is a champion of this act, as it will help to reduce the pesticides, additives, and environmental toxins in our food—especially what we feed to our children. And she still fights for full-disclosure food labeling as a congresswoman and a member of Generation Green's sponsoring board. As Jan puts it: "The American people have a right to put healthy food on the table—and not worry that their food could jeopardize their lives."

Milk, Cheese, and Eggs

Despite the frequent and sometimes contradictory headlines about the health and environmental issues surrounding milk and eggs, there are plenty of good reasons to keep these foods on the menu. Milk products are particularly high in calcium, which is crucial for helping children to develop strong bones. Milk may even help to reduce the risk of diabetes in children and young adults, according to researchers at the Harvard Medical School and Children's Hospital in Boston. For adults, especially older women, the calcium in milk and other dairy products can help ward off osteoporosis, lower blood pressure, and reduce cholesterol.

As for eggs, they have been called everything from the perfect food to the perfect food for a heart attack. Once and for all, lay your worries aside and know that there's nothing to fear in the humble egg. It's got almost everything in it a chick needs to grow, which means it's got plenty of good stuff for you, too. Eggs are a great source of protein and vitamin B_{12}, both of which help strengthen your blood, muscles, and nervous system. They're also pretty high in vitamin A, folate, and iron, all of which improve the health of your skin, eyes, and blood. The one thing you might not need as much as a soon-to-be chick is an egg's cholesterol. One regular egg yolk contains 213 milligrams of cholesterol, about 70 percent of the dietary cholesterol that most adults should get in an entire day. The American Heart Association recommends that if you have risk factors for heart disease or if you like to eat whole eggs frequently, you should try to limit your other sources of dietary cholesterol such as meats, seafood, and dairy products.

Dependable Dairy Choices

While the issues surrounding modern dairy farming are admittedly complicated, the good news is that in the dairy case, as with most things in our country, American consumers have lots of choices. The bad news is that it's not always easy to decide what's the right choice for you and your family. You have to know what you're deciding on before you can make a good pick. Here's a rundown of options and some help choosing food you can feel good about.

Milk and Dairy Products from Grass-Fed Cows

Federal organic standards have helped to improve the quality and ecofriendliness of dairy products. But current organic regulations don't require milk producers to raise their cattle on grass, despite the fact that grass is the most natural food for the cow. Cattle are ruminant animals that aren't accustomed to the corn and soy feed now common on most modern dairy farms. For this reason, dairy products from grass-fed cows make an excellent alternative both for health and the environment.

Research shows that milk, cheese, yogurt, and other dairy products from grass-fed cows are higher in important nutrients like heart-healthy omega-3 fatty acids and cancer-preventing conjugated linoleic acid (more commonly known as CLA). Compared with grain, grass is simply a richer source of these nutrients, which get passed along to you when you eat milk, cheese, and other products from grass-fed dairy cows.

Moderate grazing practices also improve soil health, encourage a diversity of plants, and help avoid many of the other environmental problems associated with large-scale livestock operations. If you can't find organic dairy products—or even if you can—look for milk, cheese, and other milk-based products from cows raised on grass.

rBGH-free Milk and Dairy Products

For health and animal welfare reasons, milk labeled "rBGH-free" or "no growth hormones" makes a great choice in the dairy department.

DOES rBGH CAUSE PREMATURE PUBERTY?

Girls today are hitting puberty earlier than girls did about 40 years ago. This conclusion was reached in a landmark study of 17,000 girls published in the journal *Pediatrics* and conducted by Marcia Herman-Giddens, a researcher at the University of North Carolina School of Public Health. The study found that, on average, puberty in Caucasian girls now begins just before age 10 and in African-American girls just before age 9. That's about 1 year earlier than previous studies indicated. The study also found that girls as young as age 6 have developed pubic hair and breast buds. One concern with this trend is that early puberty in girls has been associated with increased risk for breast cancer.

Some scientists have linked rBGH-milk to premature puberty, suggesting that the growth hormones in cow's milk are passed on to humans, unnaturally simulating human enzymes and growth hormones. Other research points at the increase in childhood obesity, explaining how overweight girls have a tendency to reach puberty earlier. And still other scientists hypothesize that environmental toxins, stress in the family, and even sexual images on television may be causing girls to hit puberty earlier. To date, no studies have provided a conclusive explanation.

In the meantime, it's troubling that milk containing rBGH isn't required to be labeled as such. Generation Green promotes better labeling with clear and detailed regulations that are enforceable. But for now, parents should play it safe. Until further research is conducted on growth hormones, it makes good sense to give children organic or rBGH-free dairy products and meats. To stay informed, sign up to receive *The Fresh Choices Quarterly* at freshchoices@generationgreen.org or call 800-652-0827.

Recombinant bovine growth hormone (rBGH) is a genetically engineered product that was first marketed by the Monsanto chemical company in 1993. Avoiding the word "hormone," Monsanto calls their product recombinant bovine somatotropin (rBST) and markets it under the trade name Posilac. When injected into cows, it triggers the release of another naturally occurring hormone called insulin-like growth factor 1 (IGF-1) that speeds up a cow's metabolism so that it produces an estimated 25 percent more milk. Monsanto's promise to farmers is that with increased milk production comes increased profits. According to Monsanto's current estimates, nearly a third of all U.S. dairy cows, about 3 million, are given rBGH every 2 weeks.

However, this genetically engineered product has led to several unforeseen problems. One basic concern is that while farmers may envision a more competitive profit margin, the extra milk is not really needed in the marketplace. Annual milk production in the United States is now about 170 billion pounds, a 13 percent increase since 1993 and an estimated yearly surplus of about a quarter million tons. Surplus milk is turned into powdered milk, bought by the government at taxpayers' expense, and then stored for use in various domestic and overseas programs.

Another concern related to human health is that because IGF-1 survives pasteurization and digestion, the human body absorbs it into the bloodstream. A number of studies, including one important 90-day laboratory study conducted by Monsanto, have shown that elevated blood levels of IGF-1 may increase risk for prostate, colon, and breast cancers. IGF-1 has also been linked to osteogenic sarcoma, the most common bone cancer in children, according to Phil Landrigan, M.D., director of the Center for Children's Health and the Environment at the Mount Sinai School of Medicine in New York City.

As for the cows, researchers at Health Canada (the Canadian equivalent of the Food and Drug Administration) studied the physical effects of rBGH for 9 years. They found that using rBGH can cause 50 percent more lameness (leg and hoof problems), 25 percent more mastitis (udder infections), and increased reproductive problems such as infertility, cystic ovaries, and fetal loss. According to the Center for Food Safety, a Washington, D.C.–based nonprofit advocacy organization, many farmers have suffered big financial losses because their cows injected with rBGH have become too ill to produce milk.

To combat the health effects of cows growing too quickly, dairy farmers often give their cows additional antibiotics, which also end up in the milk and meat. The concern here is that the widespread use of antibiotics is increasing the number of antibiotic-resistant bacteria, effectively weakening the strength of antibiotics. The Center for Science in the Public Interest (CSPI) recently began a public education campaign to combat unnecessary antibiotic use in agriculture. According to CSPI, nearly half of all antibiotics in the United States are used in livestock production.

Both Canada and the European Union have found the potential animal and human health risks associated with rBGH great enough to ban its use. The Codex Alimentarius Commission, the United Nations food safety agency representing 101 nations worldwide, has also put a moratorium on rBGH. In the United States, however, the Food and Drug Administration maintains that rBGH is safe, despite the preliminary clinical evidence and expert consensus of many of the world's industrialized nations.

Further clouding the issues for the consumer, milk from cows injected with rBGH is not required to be labeled as such. Most dairy farms send their milk to large

The Raw Deal

As a teenager living in Florida one summer, I ate my first raw oysters. A squeeze of fresh lemon and a few drops of hot sauce magically transformed their slippery texture into a truly sublime eating experience. Now our oceans and lakes are less clean than they once were, and the pleasure of eating raw shellfish comes with a certain risk. Most health officials recommend avoiding raw foods of animal origin (like oysters on the half shell) because these are the top sources of food-borne illness. But if you trust the source, you may be more willing to accept that risk, and the risk may indeed be lower.

This same principle applies to raw milk. The Food and Drug Administration (FDA) suggests avoiding raw milk and even raw milk cheeses. But you may find that the flavor of raw milk and raw milk products is richer and more complex than pasteurized milk and its products. If you trust the dairy farm where the milk came from, you may be inclined to continue eating those foods.

Due to public health concerns, the FDA is considering mandatory pasteurization for all milk used in cheesemaking. Cheese lovers argue that a better idea would be to enforce sanitation regulations at dairy farms. The fact is, raw milk has been used to make cheese for thousands of years with relatively few outbreaks of food-borne illness. Food scientists argue that current milk-producing conditions are unlikely to change and that protecting public health is the number one priority.

To enjoy raw milk cheeses without worry, keep in mind that aged cheeses made from raw milk, such as Parmigiano-Reggiano and English Cheddar, are less risky than soft raw milk cheeses like Camembert and Roquefort. Young children, pregnant women, the elderly, and those with weakened immune systems are most at risk. If you're a cheese lover in one of those categories, buy raw milk cheeses only from a cheesemaker you know and trust. Ask questions about the cheesemaker's source for milk and how the milk is handled. It's safest if the milk comes from a single source. When it comes to imported cheese, look for AOC or Appellation d'Origine Contrôlée on the label. The AOC seal guarantees strict quality controls to ensure that the cheese has been produced in a specific region according to traditional methods.

processing plants where the milk is commingled in bulk tanks. So there's really no way to tell if the conventional milk you buy contains rBGH. Researchers estimate that 80 to 90 percent of the dairy products that Americans consume—including milk, butter, cheese, yogurt, ice cream, and other milk products—contains at least trace amounts of rBGH.

Look for the "rBGH-free" or "no growth hormones" label on milk containers. This label is not federally regulated, but several states require milk producers to sign affidavits guaranteeing that their cows are not injected with growth hormones, that separate trucks are used to haul the milk, and that the milk is assigned to specifically identified storage tanks at the processing facility.

While rBGH-free milk and dairy products are a great choice, keep in mind that rBGH-free doesn't mean organic. To carry an organic label, milk producers must use a whole host of ecologically sound practices that are not required for labeling milk rBGH-free (see "The Skinny on Organic Milk" on page 186).

Goat's Milk and Sheep's Milk Cheeses

Recombinant bovine growth hormone is given only to cows, not goats or sheep. If you skip cow's milk altogether, you'll avoid rBGH without necessarily buying organic. Look for goat's milk cheeses, or chèvre, such as Montrachet, banon, and Bûcheron. At least some variety of goat cheese is available in most supermarkets today. Try the Sun-Dried Tomato, Spinach, and Goat Cheese Soufflé on page 206. Or look for sheep's milk cheese like Greek feta or French Roquefort. Even buffalo milk cheese such as buffalo mozzarella will be free of rBGH. When buying any of these cheeses, check the label to be sure the cheese doesn't contain cow's milk. Although traditional feta cheese is made with sheep's milk or goat's milk, many U.S. cheesemakers use cow's milk instead.

Imported Cheese

Canada, Australia, New Zealand, and the entire European Union have banned rBGH. Buy imported cheese from these countries and you'll sidestep rBGH by default. Imported cheese is a great option if you can't find organic. Look for traditional Italian cheeses such as Parmigiano-Reggiano, Gorgonzola, and fontina; English cheeses like Cheddar and Stilton; Swiss cheeses such as Gruyère and Emmental; and French cheeses such as Brie and Camembert. Keep in mind that these varieties of cheese are sometimes made in the United States. To skip the rBGH, be sure the label says that the cheese was imported.

Locally Produced Organic Milk and Milk Products

For health and environmental friendliness, organic milk and dairy products make a top choice. This milk comes from animals that are not given growth hormones, antibiotics, or feed laden with synthetic pesticides. And if you buy locally, your food dollars help support small family-run farms.

Even if you can't find local or regional organic milk, a national brand of organic milk makes a good second choice. Since 1993, the year that bovine growth hormones were approved for sale, total sales of organic milk have skyrocketed to more than

The Skinny on Organic Milk

According to the U.S. Department of Agriculture, certified organic milk, cheese, yogurt, sour cream, and other dairy products are produced from animals that are raised under continuous organic production practices. The animals are not given growth hormones, such as the genetically engineered recombinant bovine growth hormone (rBGH). Organic milk is also produced without the use of antibiotics. Any sick animal is treated but removed from the herd, and the milk is not sold as organic. This measure helps to ensure that the animals are raised in a healthy environment rather than given antibiotics to compensate for unhealthy living conditions.

The animals that produce organic milk are given access to the outdoors and fed organically grown feed. The land they graze on, as well as the land used to grow their feed, must be free of chemical applications for 3 years before they can be certified organic. These dietary regulations help to ensure that the cows' food is grown in an ecologically sound and environmentally sustainable way. The following practices are also prohibited from the production of organic milk and dairy products: irradiation, the use of sewage sludge as fertilizer, and synthetic pesticides, including herbicides, fungicides, and chemical fertilizers.

$200 million annually, a 500 percent increase. In the United Kingdom, where organic foods are firmly embraced, even large chains like McDonald's have switched to serving organic milk. Look for organic milk, butter, cheese, yogurt, ice cream, and other dairy products in your grocery store or farmers' market. While a little more expensive, organic dairy products often taste richer and more interesting. Besides, as demand goes up and supply goes up, price will come down. See the resources on page 276 for some of the most available brands of organic milk, cheese, and yogurt.

Reduced-Fat Milk and Dairy Products

Cow's milk and dairy products made with a lower amount of milk fat are great sources of nutrition, especially compared with their full-fat counterparts.

Full-fat dairy products like cheese and sour cream are high in saturated fat, which may increase heart disease risk. For example, the amount of regular cream cheese that usually gets slathered on a bagel (about 2 ounces) has almost 20 grams of fat, more than half of it saturated. Plus, environmental contaminants like dioxins and polychlorinated biphenyls (PCBs) make their way up the food chain from plants to animals, where they tend to concentrate in animal fats, including milk.

According to the U.S. Environmental Protection Agency (EPA), more than 95 percent of our exposure to these potentially carcinogenic contaminants comes through our diet, with fatty animal foods being the most frequent source of exposure. The EPA recommends eating fewer full-fat dairy products to reduce your exposure to these environmental contaminants.

Until environmental cleanup efforts improve, choose reduced-fat varieties to get the health benefits of dairy without the drawbacks. Reduced-fat (2 percent) and low-fat (1 percent) milk, light cream cheese, part-skim mozzarella, and reduced-fat sharp Cheddar are all widely available. These taste remarkably good (much better than fat-free versions) and work well in the kitchen with no adjustments to recipes. You can even find organic reduced-fat milk and cheese in many supermarkets. When you can't find reduced-fat cheese, put the emphasis on strong-flavored cheeses that are naturally lower in fat, such as Parmesan and feta. For sandwiches, choose sliced provolone, which is naturally lower in fat than both American and Muenster cheeses.

Soymilk

If you're lactose-intolerant, looking for an alternative to cow's milk, or just want to boost your health, give soymilk a try. It can be used cup for cup instead of cow's milk in almost any recipe. It may also help prevent heart disease and reduce risk of breast and prostate cancers due to its powerful plant compounds called isoflavones. Plus, most brands of soymilk are fortified with calcium and vitamin D, so you still get many of the nutritional benefits associated with cow's milk. For my money, the best-tasting brands of soymilk are sold in the refrigerated dairy case right next to the cow's milk. And the best news? Most soymilk is 100 percent certified organic. See page 215 for more on the health benefits of soymilk and other soy foods.

The Chicken and the Egg

Not too long ago, the only thing you had to decide about buying eggs was the size: medium, large, or extra-large. If you were lucky, you might have been able to choose between brown and white eggs. Today, you have your choice of organic, free-range, omega-3-enhanced, low saturated fat, and even vegetarian eggs in sizes ranging from peewee to jumbo. Some eggs include two or more of these labels, such as "organic free-range vegetarian eggs." Fortunately, egg-laying hens are never given feed containing hormones, so you needn't worry about running across the same labeling issues you face in the dairy case. But to help navigate the many available choices, here's how to find a good egg at your market.

Free-Range Eggs

By definition, free-range eggs should come from hens raised outside or hens that have unlimited daily access to the outdoors. But in reality, few commercial egg-laying hens are actually raised this way—even those whose eggs are labeled free-range. You can blame loose labeling laws for this oversight.

Three government agencies set the rules for egg production, and they often compete for jurisdiction, disagreeing on the details of terms like "free-range." According to the U.S. Department of Agriculture (USDA) Food Safety and Inspection Service, the definition of free-range or free-roaming is simply this: "Poultry must be allowed access to the outside." The USDA does not regulate this term as it applies to egg production. As a result, many large egg farms are indoor floor operations with tens of thousands of birds that have limited access to the outdoors through a small opening. But that doesn't prohibit these operations from using a free-range or free-roaming egg label.

To make sure you're getting eggs from hens that are truly free-range, call the egg farm and ask a few questions.

- How do they define free-range?
- Do the hens typically roam and forage on pasture for most of the day?
- How many birds live together in the same containment system? Fewer than 150 birds per flock is ideal, even if there are dozens of flocks in a single operation. That way, the chickens can still establish a natural chicken society or pecking order within each flock.

Until federal regulations for free-range become more detailed, there's no other way to know how your eggs have been produced short of asking questions.

Eggs from Pasture-Raised Chickens

In the best-case scenario, free-range chickens have been raised on pasture and get much of their food by foraging on grass and seeds. Eggs from these birds may be labeled pasture-raised, so if you find them, buy them. Either way, both free-range and pasture-raised eggs do have one thing in common: They both come from hens that are most likely not kept in cages. For the animals' sake, that's a breath of fresh air.

Most modern egg-laying facilities use a battery cage system because it increases egg production and is easier to keep clean. These small wire cages are stacked and lined up together in huge warehouses. The USDA recommends 4 inches of feeding space for each hen; crammed into such close quarters, caged hens often can't stretch their wings and suffer bruises and feather loss from rubbing against the wire cages and each other. Most caged birds also have at least some of their beaks removed to prevent injuries from excessive pecking.

According to the American Egg Board, there are about 280 egg-producing companies with large flocks of *at least* 75,000 hens in cages (some flocks are half a million or more). These 280 companies represent about 95 percent of all the laying hens

Making the Grade

Most supermarket eggs are labeled "Grade A." The U.S. Department of Agriculture sets standards for egg quality with three grades: AA, A, and B. There is no nutritional difference among the different grades.

The eggs are examined inside and out by a process called candling. In the old days, the examiner held a candle up to the egg to help see through it. Today, eggs move along rollers over intense light. The examiner looks for a smooth egg shape and clean, unbroken shells with no thin spots or stubbly areas.

Inside the egg, the examiner checks for a thick, clear white and a plump yolk with no blemishes on it. By looking through the shell, the examiner can also check the size of the air pocket that forms at the top (large end) of the egg. The smaller the air pocket, the higher the grade. Airheads don't get good grades.

What else does an egg have to do to get an A or A-plus? According to the American Egg Board, here's what good eggs should look like when broken out.

Grade AA. The whole egg covers a small surface area and has a lot of thick, firm white that props up a plump, round yolk.

Grade A. The whole egg spreads out a little more and has a fair amount of thick, firm white and some thinner white. The yolk is round and stands up tall.

Grade B. The whole egg spreads out to cover a fairly wide area and has a lot of thin, watery white with almost no thick white. The yolk is wider and flatter. Grade B eggs rarely make it to egg cartons for retail sale. They usually end up in prepared egg products or go to bakeries or institutional food service operations.

in the United States. This means that most of the eggs we eat come from caged hens.

This all makes a pretty good case for choosing free-range or pasture-raised eggs. Plus, these eggs usually taste better than conventional eggs, and they may be more nutritious. Studies show that eggs from hens raised on pasture can have as much as 20 percent more omega-3 fatty acids and 30 percent more vitamin E than eggs from factory-farmed hens. That's largely because pasture-raised hens eat grass and grains that are richer in omega-3s and vitamin E. For this reason, moderate consumption of pasture-raised eggs may help protect you against heart disease.

Vegetarian Eggs

The feed given to commercial egg-laying hens usually contains meat and seafood by-products. Vegetarian eggs, on the other hand, come from hens fed only plant-based foods. A vegetarian diet results in eggs that have a deep-colored yolk and more pronounced egg flavor. But vegetarian eggs offer no guarantees on whether the plant foods are organic or whether the hens are raised on pasture.

Omega-3 Eggs

Hens given a diet that includes flaxseed produce eggs that are higher in omega-3s, the same heart-protecting fatty acids found in coldwater fish such as salmon. That's because flaxseeds are one of the plant foods highest in omega-3s. If you eat a lot of eggs, omega-3 eggs make a great choice because they may help offset the artery-clogging effects of the saturated fat and cholesterol found in the yolk of an egg.

You can also find eggs labeled "low saturated fat" and "low cholesterol," among other nutritional claims. Generally, these eggs result from plant-based feed rather than the commercial chicken feed that includes meat and seafood by-products. They're also great choices for heart health.

Another way to reduce saturated fat and cholesterol from good old-fashioned eggs is to replace one whole egg with two egg whites in recipes, since an egg's fat

Handle with Care

It used to be fairly safe to enjoy raw cookie dough. Not so anymore. According to the Centers for Disease Control and Prevention, raw foods of animal origin such as eggs are the most likely to cause food-borne illness (food poisoning). Due to modern factory farming methods, the salmonella bacteria that can make you sick from raw eggs are now harbored right inside the ovaries of thousands of chickens. From there, salmonella internally contaminates about one in 20,000 eggs in the United States.

The best way to reduce your risk of getting sick is to heat eggs to at least 160°F (enough to coagulate or "set" the eggs), which eliminates harmful bacteria. You can also heat the eggs to 140°F and hold them there for 3½ minutes to eliminate the bacteria. I use this method to make Chocolate Hazelnut Tiramisu (page 208). Of course, safe food handling can also reduce your risk of getting sick. Here's how to handle eggs with confidence.

- Keep eggs cold until cooking. If a recipe calls for eggs "at room temperature," crack the eggs into a warm metal or glass bowl and then set the bowl in another bowl of warm water for 5 minutes.
- When shopping, buy only refrigerated eggs and buy them last, along with other perishable refrigerated foods like milk, meat, and seafood.
- Refrigerate eggs in their carton in the coldest section of your fridge, usually one of the bottom shelves. Avoid storing them on the door, which is one of the warmest places.
- Discard any cracked eggs.
- Use eggs within 3 weeks of purchase.
- When separating eggs, use an inexpensive egg separator rather than the broken eggshell halves. The next best method is to wash your hands in hot, soapy water and use them to separate the eggs, letting the whites run through your nearly-closed fingers. If you need to remove any bits of eggshell, use a clean utensil rather than a broken eggshell half.
- Use hot, soapy water to wash any equipment or surfaces that have raw egg on them.
- Avoid eating raw eggs. Foods that may contain raw eggs include raw cookie dough, hollandaise and béarnaise sauces, stuffing, Caesar salad dressing, tiramisu, mousses, and homemade eggnog. In commercial versions of these foods, such as eggnog, check the ingredients list to make sure that pasteurized eggs are used instead of raw eggs.
- If you're eating out, ask whether the food includes pasteurized eggs or if the raw eggs have been thoroughly cooked.
- To eliminate harmful bacteria, cook eggs to 160°F (until the eggs are set) or cook to 140°F and hold them at that temperature for 3½ minutes. That means cooking fried eggs until the yolks are nearly firm. If you like drippy eggs, just be aware of the risks. For uncooked meringues or custards (as in tiramisu), you can heat eggs without coagulating them by whisking the eggs in a heatproof bowl over a pan of simmering water for 4 to 5 minutes.
- Serve egg dishes such as quiche promptly or keep them refrigerated. Avoid letting egg dishes sit at room temperature for more than an hour or two.

and cholesterol are all in the yolk. Egg whites are fat-free and have all the binding and leavening properties of whole eggs. Of course, omitting the fatty yolk will affect the richness and texture of a baked dish. To get good texture, especially in baking, I avoid replacing more than half of a recipe's whole eggs with egg whites.

Locally Produced Eggs

Go local if you can. Supporting local farmers bolsters your local economy and puts your food dollars toward a variety of smaller family farms rather than a few giant factory farms. Buying locally also helps to reduce the environmental burden caused by long-distance shipping and mass-scale factory farming. Some local chicken farmers sell eggs right at the farm. In my area, I often see farms with signs advertising brown eggs for sale.

By the way, if you've ever wondered about the difference between brown and white eggs, just remember that the only difference is the color of the shell. Brown eggs are not healthier or more flavorful; they simply come from a different breed of chicken. Hens with reddish brown feathers and reddish brown earlobes lay brown eggs. Hens with white feathers and white earlobes lay white eggs. It's that simple.

Organic Eggs

Eggs labeled organic are increasingly available in grocery stores nationwide, and they make a healthy and ecologically sound option. According to the USDA, certified organic eggs must come from hens fed rations that were grown without pesticides, fungicides, herbicides, or commercial fertilizers. Most organic eggs come from hens fed a combination of organic grains and legumes, such as corn and soy and maybe even wheat, peas, lentils, sunflower seeds, or flaxseeds. This plant-based diet is close to the chicken's natural diet, giving organic eggs a richer and "eggier" taste than eggs that come from commercial laying hens, which are often fed inexpensive meat and seafood by-products. Plant foods are also likely to make the eggs higher in key nutrients like vitamin A, vitamin E, and omega-3 fatty acids. There's a good chance that organic eggs come from free-range chickens, too, although this is not strictly regulated.

Organic eggs have higher production costs and a lower volume per farm, so they cost more than eggs from hens fed conventional feed. But that price difference is invaluable for its contribution to healthy soil, healthy people, and sustainable food production methods. Many consumers recognize this value. According to the Organic Trade Association, organic eggs and dairy saw the most growth of any organic food category throughout the 1990s.

Keep in mind that federal regulations for organic eggs place no restrictions on the type of facility in which the birds are kept. Most producers of organic eggs (especially the smaller ones) give their chickens free range to roam outside, but organic eggs could conceivably come from chickens that are kept indoors in cages or on the floor of a huge, automated egg facility. If the carton doesn't specify and you're concerned, call the egg company to find how the chickens are raised. Ask them the questions that appear on page 189 in the section on free-range eggs.

Baked Eggs with Tomatoes and Feta

When you need to warm up the kitchen on cool mornings, turn to this effortless method of cooking eggs. These make a nice presentation for brunch as well. Just put some vegetables, eggs, and seasonings in ramekins and bake. That simple. If you prefer, you can bake everything in a 1-quart baking dish; increase the baking time by a few minutes.

1 teaspoon extra-virgin olive oil

1 tomato, cut into 4 thick slices

2 scallions, thinly sliced

2 teaspoons chopped fresh oregano

½ cup crumbled sheep's milk feta cheese

4 pasture-raised or organic eggs

½ teaspoon salt

½ teaspoon ground black pepper

Preheat the oven to 350°F. Coat 4 small ramekins or custard cups (about 4 ounces) with the oil and put on a baking sheet. Lay a slice of tomato in each ramekin. Sprinkle half of the scallions, half of the oregano, and half of the feta evenly over the tomatoes. Break an egg into each ramekin right over the tomato, taking care not to break the yolk. Sprinkle evenly with the salt, pepper, and the remaining scallions, oregano, and feta.

Cover each ramekin with foil and bake the whole sheet of ramekins until the egg yolks are almost set (they will turn brighter yellow, beginning at the edges), 10 to 12 minutes. Remove from the oven when the egg yolks are not yet completely firm, because the heat retained by the ramekins will continue to cook them for a few minutes out of the oven. Let cool slightly and then serve.

Makes 4 servings

Scrambled Eggs with Tarragon, Chives, and Cheddar

On dewy spring mornings, I snip fresh wild chives from my backyard (I know they're safe because I don't use chemicals on my lawn). I love them simply mixed into scrambled eggs with fresh tarragon and sharp Cheddar cheese. This flavor combination gently opens my sleepy eyes like no other breakfast can. This low-heat method takes longer, but the moist, tender results are worth it.

2 teaspoons extra-virgin olive oil or organic butter

4 pasture-raised or organic eggs

1½ tablespoons water

3 tablespoons shredded organic extra-sharp Cheddar cheese

1½ tablespoons chopped fresh chives

2 teaspoons chopped fresh tarragon or ½ teaspoon dried

½ teaspoon salt

A few grindings of black pepper

Heat a medium nonstick sauté pan or skillet over medium-low heat. Add the oil or butter and let it warm up about 3 minutes.

Put the eggs and water in a medium bowl. Using a fork, beat vigorously until well mixed and a little bubbly. Beat in the cheese, chives, tarragon, salt, and pepper.

Using a spoon or pancake turner (spatula), spread the oil or butter evenly over the pan. Pour in the egg mixture and let cook undisturbed until the eggs just begin to set on the bottom, 2 to 3 minutes. Gently scrape the eggs from the edges toward the center and vice versa until the eggs are just set yet still moist, 8 to 10 minutes. Serve immediately.

Makes 2 servings

Helping Hands: The addition of water helps to make soft, melt-in-your-mouth scrambled eggs. The water steams the eggs as they cook. Gentle heat also helps to keep the eggs from cooking too quickly and turning rubbery.

Smoked salmon makes a nice addition. Coarsely chop an ounce or two of cold-smoked salmon (Nova Scotia or Scottish) and sprinkle with a light squeeze of fresh lemon. Scatter over the eggs when you begin to scrape the eggs in the pan.

Sausage and Red Pepper Frittata

Essentially an open-faced omelet, a frittata is incredibly easy to make and open to countless variations. It's great for feeding a crowd on a weekend morning. Just sauté your favorite ingredients, add eggs, and cook. A final browning under the broiler heightens the flavor.

4 vegetarian breakfast sausage links

½ organic red bell pepper, seeded and chopped

6 pasture-raised or organic eggs

2 pasture-raised or organic egg whites

¼ cup organic 2% milk

1 teaspoon fresh thyme or ½ teaspoon dried

¼ teaspoon salt

⅛ teaspoon ground black pepper

½ cup shredded organic extra-sharp Cheddar cheese

Choice Advice: Red bell peppers are higher in pesticide residues than many other vegetables, but they're so good it's hard to avoid them. The solution is to buy organic bell peppers whenever possible. Or buy locally grown peppers and ask if they are sprayed; they may be sprayed less than peppers that are shipped from thousands of miles away.

Coat a large nonstick skillet with cooking spray and heat over medium heat. Add the sausages and cook until heated through and browned, about 5 minutes. Remove to a plate to cool. Slice into thick coins.

Meanwhile, add the bell pepper to the skillet and cook, stirring often, until soft, about 5 minutes.

In a medium bowl, lightly beat the eggs, egg whites, milk, thyme, salt, and pepper just until blended. Stir in ¼ cup cheese.

Preheat the broiler and set an oven rack to the top third of the oven.

Add the sausage back to the skillet and pour the egg mixture over top. Reduce the heat to medium-low and cook for 2 minutes, gently scraping the bottom of the pan to loosen the eggs. Cook until the eggs are almost set but the top is still wet, another 8 minutes. Scatter the remaining cheese over the top and transfer the pan to the broiler. Broil until the top is set, puffed, and lightly browned, about 1 minute. Cut into wedges and serve.

Makes 4 to 6 servings

Helping Hand: Look for vegetarian breakfast sausages in the frozen meat or breakfast section of your supermarket. Most brands have less than half the fat, none of the cholesterol, and more important, none of the antibiotics found in pork sausages. And they taste great in this frittata. My favorites are Morningstar Farms Breakfast Links and Boca Breakfast Links. Both are made with soy protein that's not genetically modified, but I prefer the flavor of the Morningstar Farms links. Try them both to find your favorite.

Strata with Celery Root, Chard, and Gruyère

Strata is one of the best brunch dishes I know. It's a layered casserole of beaten eggs, bread, and usually some type of vegetable filling. I like to make stratas in the fall when cooler temperatures inspire me to bake in the kitchen. I use fall vegetables for the filling, but let your own taste buds guide you. A simple sauté of mushrooms and peppers also makes a great filling. The best part is that you can assemble the whole thing the night before and then pop it into the oven the next morning.

1 celery root (about 1 pound), peeled and thinly sliced

4 cups organic 2% milk

1 cup vegetable broth

1 bunch green chard, stems and leaves separated, each chopped

1 large clove garlic, minced

A few sprigs of fresh thyme

¾ teaspoon salt

¾ teaspoon ground black pepper

6 pasture-raised or organic eggs

2 teaspoons Dijon mustard

Pinch of grated nutmeg

12 slices sourdough or firm white sandwich bread

2 cups grated Gruyère cheese

Put the celery root, 1 cup milk, the stock, chard stems, garlic, and thyme in a deep, wide sauté pan. Simmer over medium heat, stirring occasionally, until the celery root is fork-tender, about 20 minutes. Remove the thyme stems (the leaves should have cooked into the vegetables). Stir in the chard leaves and cook until wilted and most of the liquid evaporates, 3 to 5 minutes. Add ¼ teaspoon salt and ¼ teaspoon pepper (taste and add more salt if necessary, depending upon the saltiness of the stock used).

Preheat the oven to 350°F. In a large bowl, whisk together the eggs, mustard, nutmeg, and the remaining 3 cups milk, ½ teaspoon salt, and ½ teaspoon pepper.

Line the bottom of a shallow 3½ to 4-quart baking dish (such as a 15" × 10" dish) with 6 bread slices. Pour just enough of the egg mixture over the bread to cover, spreading it out to coat the bread completely. Spread the chard filling evenly over top. Sprinkle with half of the cheese. Layer with the remaining 6 bread slices. Pour the remaining eggs over the top, pushing on the bread to thoroughly saturate it. Sprinkle the remaining cheese on top. Bake until the eggs are set and the cheese is slightly browned on top, 45 to 50 minutes.

Makes 10 to 12 servings

Helping Hand: Celery root (also called celeriac) is a gnarled root vegetable that comes from a type of celery grown only for its short, squat root. Look for it in the fall. It has a celery-like taste and potato-like texture. It's great boiled along with potatoes and mashed into a puree. Celery root browns like an apple when cut and exposed to air for more than 5 minutes or so. Prevent the browning by tossing the cut pieces into a bowl of water with a few squeezes of lemon juice as you work. Remove from the water and pat dry before using.

My Lucky 7 Cheeses

I love cheese. With hundreds of varieties, there's plenty to explore, and I try new types whenever I can. But seven fairly common varieties have become regulars in my kitchen. I use these cheeses in more dishes than any other type, and they've never steered me wrong. If I were to add one more to the list, it would be goat cheese. Yum!

CHEESE VARIETY	A FEW USES
Extra-sharp Cheddar (full-fat and reduced-fat)	Cheese and crackers, egg dishes, sandwiches
Fontina (imported)	Pizza, pasta tosses, lasagna
Gorgonzola (imported)	Salads, pizza, bruschetta, sauces
Gruyère (imported)	Hot sandwiches, gratins, egg dishes
Mozzarella (fresh and part-skim)	Salads, pizza, pasta
Parmigiano-Reggiano (imported)	Pasta, pesto, on a cheese plate, on vegetables
Pepper Jack (reduced-fat)	Burritos, nachos, almost anything Mexican or Southwestern

Berry-Stuffed French Toast

Some days are meant for luxuriating in the unplanned expanse of the morning. French toast is tailor-made for those days. Assemble the dish the night before and you'll be ready for a leisurely morning meal whenever it suits you. For the bread, choose a rather wide loaf so there's plenty of room to cut a pocket and spoon in the sweetened cream cheese filling. I usually make this with dried fruit in the fall, but if fresh fruits are available, by all means use them.

1 loaf Italian or French bread

8 ounces organic reduced-fat cream cheese, at room temperature

4 tablespoons confectioners' sugar

½ teaspoon almond extract

⅓ cup dried blueberries

⅓ cup dried cranberries

4 pasture-raised or organic eggs

2 pasture-raised or organic egg whites

1½ cups organic 2% milk

1 teaspoon vanilla extract

Pinch of salt

Cut off and discard a small diagonal slice from each end of the bread. Cut the bread on a diagonal into about ten 1"-thick slices. Cut a slit through the top crust of each slice to form a deep pocket.

In a medium bowl, mix together the cream cheese, 3 tablespoons sugar, and the almond extract. Stir in the blueberries and cranberries. Spoon the filling equally into the bread pockets and lay the stuffed slices of bread in a shallow 4-quart baking dish, such as a 15" × 10" dish.

Clean and dry the bowl and then use it to whisk together the eggs, egg whites, milk, vanilla extract, salt, and the remaining 1 tablespoon sugar. Pour the mixture evenly over the bread. Turn the slices to coat completely. Let stand for 5 minutes or cover and refrigerate up to 8 hours (overnight).

Coat a nonstick griddle or skillet with cooking spray and heat over medium heat. When hot, cook the bread in batches until browned on each side, about 4 minutes per side. Serve immediately.

Makes 4 servings

Helping Hands: For a simple blueberry syrup, toss about ¼ cup fresh blueberries into a small microwaveable pitcher with ¼ teaspoon ground cinnamon and ½ cup pure maple syrup. Microwave on high until heated through, 30 to 45 seconds. Or top the toasts with blueberry jam instead.

You can make this with sliced sandwich bread instead of French bread. Spread the filling over one slice, then top with another to make a sort of sandwich. You'll need about eight slices total.

Banana Cinnamon Dutch Baby

Kids love to watch this pancake puff up in the oven. And it's so quick to put together. Just be sure everyone's seated at the table if you want to make a puffy presentation. The pancake begins to deflate as soon as it cools. Also known as a German pancake, this dish has a light and eggy texture, sort of like a pancake soufflé. I add sautéed fruit for more flavor and nutrients. Use blueberries or sliced organic apples if you don't have bananas.

¾ cup unbleached all-purpose flour or whole-grain pastry flour

½ teaspoon salt

4 pasture-raised or organic eggs

⅔ cup organic 2% milk

2 tablespoons organic butter, melted

1 large or 2 small bananas, peeled and sliced

2 tablespoons brown sugar

½ teaspoon ground cinnamon

Preheat the oven to 450°F.

In a medium bowl, whisk together the flour, salt, eggs, milk, and 1 tablespoon butter.

Heat the remaining 1 tablespoon butter over medium heat in a 10" ovenproof skillet (cast-iron pans work great). Add the bananas and 1 tablespoon brown sugar. Cook, stirring occasionally, just until heated through and the sugar melts, about 2 minutes. Stir in the cinnamon.

Rewhisk the batter and then pour into the pan, stirring briefly to scrape the fruit from the bottom. Transfer to the oven and bake until the pancake begins to puff around the edges, about 10 minutes. Sprinkle evenly with the remaining 1 tablespoon brown sugar and bake until very puffed and golden brown, about 5 minutes more. Serve immediately and cut into wedges.

Makes 3 or 4 servings

GARY HIRSHBERG
On a Mission with Stonyfield Farm Yogurt

Spending a few minutes with Gary Hirshberg is like eating ice cream on a hot day. He's pure refreshment. And 100 percent organic. A longtime environmentalist, Hirshberg happened upon a great yogurt recipe back in 1983 at a friend's small organic farming school in New Hampshire. His coup as an entrepreneur was turning that recipe into a $150 million company that could fulfill his deeper mission: environmental education. Take a look at the lid of any Stonyfield Farm yogurt container and you'll see a clever environmental message like "Let's Put a Lid on Global Warming" or "Make Your Voice 'Cow'nt' for Organic Standards."

An ardent supporter of sustainable agriculture, Hirshberg believes one of his company's most tangible accomplishments to date is helping to convert 100 farms from conventional to organic farming. Another of his objectives is to inspire huge multinational corporations to follow his lead. "I want to show them that you can make more money by incorporating environmentally responsible practices into the fabric of what you do," he says. This is why Stonyfield recently partnered with $12.7 billion conglomerate Group Danone, makers of Dannon yogurt and other well-known brands. The partnership expands Stonyfield's environmental mission.

Hirshberg also knows that the future of the planet is in the hands of our children. "Kids don't necessarily choose food for its organic attributes," he admits. "But if it's delicious, then there's no compromise. And we can help them understand that as an organic producer, there's a whole range of things we do that is kinder to animals and the planet than conventional producers." Hirshberg's broad vision inspired Stonyfield's Yo Baby and other yogurt products specifically for children. "We can help children to have a greater appreciation earlier," he says, "which will allow greater change to happen in their lifetimes, even greater than what's happened in ours."

Hirshberg's environmental message is definitely getting across. His company is now the number one producer of organic yogurt in the United States. Stonyfield Farm is fast becoming the number three yogurt brand overall, hot on the heels of leaders Dannon and Yoplait.

Yogurt Waffles

Inspired by Gary Hirshberg, founder of Stonyfield Farm, I came up with this recipe one morning when I was almost out of milk. I had some Stonyfield Yo Baby yogurt in the fridge and thought to myself, "What is yogurt but cultured milk anyway?" The yogurt made deliciously crisp waffles with a moist, fluffy interior. My 4-year-old gobbled them up faster than I could make them.

1¾ cups unbleached all-purpose flour or whole-grain pastry flour

1 tablespoon baking powder

½ teaspoon salt

2 pasture-raised or organic eggs

1 cup organic 2% milk

¾ cup organic vanilla yogurt

½ cup vegetable oil

1 tablespoon sugar

Preheat a waffle iron.

In a big bowl, mix the flour, baking powder, and salt.

Separate the eggs, putting the whites into a small bowl and the yolks into another small bowl. Whisk the milk, yogurt, and oil into the yolks. Stir the milk mixture into the flour mixture until moist but still a little lumpy.

Beat the egg whites with a mixer on medium speed for 2 minutes. Increase to high, add the sugar, and beat until stiff peaks form when the beaters are lifted, about 5 minutes. Fold the egg whites into the batter just until the whites are almost incorporated (fold gently to avoid deflating the whipped whites).

Coat the waffle iron with cooking spray and scoop about one-quarter of the batter onto the grids, spreading gently. Close the lid and cook until the steam is almost gone and the tops are golden. Lift the waffle from the iron with a fork. Oil the grids and repeat with the remaining batter.

Makes about four 8" waffles

Helping Hands: For richer waffles, use ¼ cup oil and ¼ cup melted butter in place of the ½ cup oil.

For crispier waffles, use 1 cup flour and ¾ cup cornmeal, mixing the cornmeal in with the other dry ingredients.

To keep waffles warm, set your oven to 225°F and place the waffles directly on the oven rack. If you have leftover waffles, cool them completely and then freeze in a heavy-duty plastic bag for up to 6 months. Reheat in a toaster or in a 325°F oven.

KELLY PRESTON
Safeguarding the Home

Actor Kelly Preston was always outdoors when growing up in Hawaii. She knew the benefits of an active lifestyle. She considered herself environmentally aware. And she prepared food for her family that was full of fresh fruits and vegetables. Kelly was doing all the right things. Or so she thought.

To help manage her son's allergies, Kelly plunged into research about allergy causes, treatments, and prevention. She found that the probable causes ranged from the ingredients in his food to the chemicals in the cleaning solution used by their professional carpet cleaners. Kelly was shocked to find that the compounds in many of the household cleaners she used were linked to rising rates of asthma, allergies, learning disabilities, and even cancer.

"Like so many other new mothers," she says, "I just didn't know. What do you mean that detergent has a little bit of unrefined gasoline in it? No wonder it gets the stain out!" Quickly, Kelly removed all chlorine-based and petroleum-based cleaning products from her home. Today, she uses only natural cleansers, has banned pesticides from the premises, and insists on completing any home repairs toxin-free.

Her personal experience motivated Kelly to teach other parents about safeguarding their homes. One unforgettable night, she volunteered to read a poem at a fund-raiser for the Children's Health Environmental Coalition (CHEC). She read the poem with a child suffering from a nongenetic form of cancer, likely caused by environmental exposure. That experience was more than heartbreaking; it made her want to get more active. "You realize that you have to do something," she says, "as a duty and a person on this planet."

Kelly is now CHEC's national spokesperson and has lent her acting talents to a new educational video. *Not under My Roof* is part of CHEC's national childproofing campaign. It shows families how to "safe-point" their homes against environmental toxins. The film is distributed to hospital maternity wards, where it reaches millions of new parents.

Kelly's husband, John Travolta, and their two children, Jett and Ella, remain a daily inspiration. She is convinced that, joined with others, people can have an impact. She urges all parents to educate themselves about the environment. "Talk with friends," she says, "join an organization, or ask your legislators to stop the misuse of toxins such as pesticides." Her advice is simple and specific: "Get angry and then get active."

Grilled Fontina and Mushroom Sandwiches

Who says grilled cheese has to be made with white bread and orange cheese? In this simple spin on the American classic, rich fontina cheese melts deliciously with sautéed mushrooms and pesto on crisp sourdough bread. Treat yourself to a grown-up grilled cheese sandwich. Adventurous kids may want one, too!

1 tablespoon organic butter

4 large button or cremini mushrooms, sliced

4 large slices sourdough bread

¼ cup prepared pesto

4 ounces fontina cheese, sliced

Pinch of salt

A few grindings of black pepper

Heat the butter in a large nonstick skillet over medium heat. Add the mushrooms and cook until soft, about 5 minutes.

Meanwhile, spread the top of 2 bread slices with the pesto. Arrange the cheese and cooked mushrooms over the pesto. Sprinkle with salt and pepper and cover with the remaining 2 bread slices. Cook in the same skillet until the cheese melts and the bread is golden, 3 to 4 minutes per side.

Makes 2 sandwiches

Helping Hand: Prepared pesto is available in jars in most grocery stores. To make your own, see the recipe for Basic Basil Pesto on page 77. Make mounds of it in the summer when the herb is plentiful and freeze it in airtight containers. Use a melon baller to scoop out just what you need during the off-season.

Holy Cow!

The average person living in the United States consumes more than 600 pounds of dairy products every year, including about 420 pounds of fluid milk and cream, 70 pounds of various milk-based fats and oils, 30 pounds of cheese, and 17 pounds of ice cream.

Sun-Dried Tomato, Spinach, and Goat Cheese Soufflé

Don't be scared off by the word "soufflé." This dish is pretty easy to make. It's perfect for special occasions in early spring like an Earth Day dinner or Mother's Day brunch (hint, hint to dads and kids reading this!). Serve the soufflé as soon as it comes out of the oven. After that, the poofy drama begins to deflate. (For less fat, you could omit one or two egg yolks.)

10 ounces organic baby spinach leaves, rinsed

4 tablespoons extra-virgin olive oil

1 tablespoon plain dry bread crumbs

½ small onion, finely chopped

¼ cup unbleached all-purpose flour

1½ cups organic 2% milk, heated

6 pasture-raised or organic eggs, separated

¾ cup finely crumbled goat cheese

½ cup drained oil-packed or soft sun-dried tomatoes, finely chopped

2 tablespoons chopped fresh oregano or parsley

1 teaspoon Dijon mustard or ½ teaspoon dry mustard

½ teaspoon salt

¼ teaspoon ground black pepper

Pinch of grated nutmeg

Pinch of cream of tartar

Shake excess water off the spinach and place in a medium saucepan. Cover and cook over medium heat, stirring occasionally, until just wilted, about 3 minutes. Transfer to a colander to drain and cool.

Preheat the oven to 400°F. Coat a 2-quart soufflé dish or deep baking dish with 1 teaspoon of the oil, spreading thoroughly with a paper towel. Sprinkle with the bread crumbs and rotate the pan until all the crumbs have clung evenly to the oil.

Heat the remaining oil in the same saucepan over medium heat. Add the onion and cook, stirring occasionally, until tender, about 3 minutes. Whisk in the flour and cook for 2 minutes. Gradually whisk in the hot milk and cook, whisking frequently, until thickened, about 3 minutes. Remove from the heat and stir in the egg yolks, cheese, tomatoes, oregano or parsley, mustard, salt, pepper, and nutmeg. Stir in the spinach.

Choice Advice: Be sure to buy organic spinach for this dish. According to the Environmental Working Group, spinach is among the vegetables with the highest pesticide residues. Replace the spinach with chard if you like—tests confirm it ranks among those with the lowest residues.

Put the egg whites and cream of tartar in a clean large bowl. Beat with clean beaters on medium speed until soft peaks form when the beaters are lifted, about 5 minutes. Stir about ½ cup egg whites into the spinach mixture to lighten it. Gently fold in the remaining egg whites, being careful not to deflate the egg whites.

Gently scrape into the prepared dish and bake until puffed and browned on top, 30 to 35 minutes. A skewer inserted into the center should come out slightly moist but not wet.

Makes 6 servings

Helping Hands: Soufflé is simple to make, but keep a few things in mind. There should be no yolks in the egg whites, because even a speck of fat can keep the whites from expanding to their full volume. Make sure the bowl and beaters are perfectly clean and dry. Let the whites come to room temperature before beating so they whip up fully (set the bowl of whites in a larger bowl containing warm water for a few minutes to warm them). To fold in the egg whites, use a gentle lifting and rolling motion with a rubber spatula to turn the two mixtures over and over one another, rather than stirring or mixing them together. This helps to keep the whipped egg whites from deflating.

For individual servings, replace the soufflé dish with six 1½-cup ramekins and start checking for doneness after about 20 minutes.

I like to use oil-packed or soft sun-dried tomatoes because they don't need rehydrating like dry-pack ones do. For less fat, use the soft ones, which are packed in tubs without oil and are available in many markets.

Chocolate Hazelnut Tiramisu

This dessert takes a bit of assembly but is truly fabulous. Mascarpone, a triple-cream Italian cream cheese made from cow's milk, makes all the flavor difference. I reduced the fat a bit by mixing the mascarpone with reduced-fat cream cheese. I also used a fat-free egg-white meringue instead of an egg yolk custard in the filling. No one will miss the fat, believe me. You'll be lucky if this dessert sticks around for more than a day.

3 pasture-raised or organic egg whites, at room temperature

1 cup sugar

1 tablespoon cold water

¼ teaspoon cream of tartar

4 ounces mascarpone cheese

4 ounces organic reduced-fat cream cheese

½ cup hazelnut spread (such as Nutella)

1 cup brewed espresso or strong coffee, at room temperature

¼ cup Frangelico hazelnut liqueur

6 ounces ladyfingers (about 24), split

1½ teaspoons unsweetened cocoa powder

Bring about 2" of water to a simmer in a large saucepan over medium heat. In a medium heatproof bowl that will rest over the saucepan, combine the egg whites, sugar, water, and cream of tartar. Put the bowl over the saucepan. Using an electric mixer, beat the mixture on low speed for 5 minutes. Increase the speed to high and beat until the mixture begins to thicken, about 3 minutes more. Remove the bowl from the saucepan and beat on high until the mixture is thick and fluffy, another 4 to 5 minutes.

Put the mascarpone and cream cheese in a big bowl. Using the same mixer, beat on medium speed until blended and creamy. Remove about one-third of the cream cheese mixture to a medium bowl. Beat the hazelnut spread into that bowl. Gradually beat about one-third of the egg white mixture into the same bowl, scraping the sides of the bowl as necessary.

Rinse the beaters and then beat the remaining two-thirds of the egg white mixture into the other bowl of cream cheese mixture.

Line the bottom of an 8" × 8" baking dish with a double-layer of foil, leaving enough foil to hang over opposite sides. Combine the espresso or coffee and liqueur in a cup.

Put a few of the split ladyfingers in your hand and brush with the espresso mixture. Invert into the pan and brush the top sides thoroughly with the espresso. Repeat to make a layer of soaked ladyfingers in the bottom of the pan. Spread half of the white filling evenly over the layer of ladyfingers. Put ½ teaspoon cocoa into a sifter or small strainer and sift or shake evenly over the filling. Use the espresso and ladyfingers to make another layer. Spread all of the dark filling evenly over the layer. Sprinkle with another ½ teaspoon of cocoa. Repeat the layering one more time, using all of the ladyfingers, espresso, and the remaining white filling. Sprinkle with the remaining cocoa.

Cover and refrigerate for at least 4 hours or up to 2 days before serving. To serve, carefully lift the entire dessert out of the pan using the foil as a sling. Cut into squares and serve.

Makes 9 servings

Helping Hands: If you don't have an espresso machine at home, pick up an extra-large espresso at the local gourmet coffee shop. Or, if all else fails, mix 1 cup boiling water with 2 tablespoons instant espresso powder, which many grocery stores carry in the coffee or baking aisle.

Nutella is a hazelnut spread made with skim milk, cocoa, and ground hazelnuts. Most supermarkets carry it near the peanut butter. Or look for it in an Italian market.

Ladyfingers, a delicate type of sponge cake in the shape of long, thick fingers, are traditional here. But you can use thinly sliced pieces of sponge cake instead.

Why are the egg whites partially cooked here? Traditional versions of this dish use raw eggs in the custard. But I like to play it safe. The egg white mixture is heated over simmering water long enough for it to reach at least 160°F. According to the U.S. Department of Agriculture, this brief heating eliminates any harmful bacteria and makes the eggs safe to eat.

Frozen Chocolate Pudding Pops

When the kids ask for ice cream on a hot summer day, pull these out of the freezer. You might want one, too! If you have a set of plastic frozen dessert cups and sticks (sold in most grocery stores), use those instead of the paper drinking cups and spoons. I cut down on fat a bit by using just one egg in the pudding and using a combination of cocoa powder and solid chocolate.

½ cup sugar

¼ cup unsweetened cocoa powder

4 tablespoons cornstarch

1 pasture-raised or organic egg

3 cups organic 2% milk

2 ounces bittersweet or semisweet chocolate, broken into pieces (about ⅓ cup)

1 tablespoon organic butter

1 teaspoon vanilla extract

In a medium saucepan, whisk together the sugar, cocoa powder, and cornstarch. Whisk in the egg until fully incorporated (the mixture will be very thick). Gradually whisk in the milk. Put the pan over medium heat and cook, whisking frequently, until the mixture bubbles and thickens, about 10 minutes. Cook 1 minute longer. Remove from the heat and stir in the chocolate, butter, and vanilla until the chocolate is completely melted.

Cool slightly and then pour into eight ⅓-cup (3-ounce) plastic or paper drinking cups. Cool further and insert wooden craft sticks or small metal spoons, holding the sticks or spoons briefly until they stand upright as the pudding cools. Cover with plastic wrap, poking the wrap right through the stick or spoon, and freeze until solid, about 8 hours or up to 2 weeks.

To unmold, hold by the stick or spoon and run warm water over the outside of the cup just until the dessert can be loosened free.

Makes 8 servings

Helping Hand: For Frozen Mocha Pudding Pops, replace 1 cup of the milk with 1 cup brewed strong coffee.

For Frozen Chocolate Orange Pudding Pops, add 1 teaspoon grated orange zest along with the chocolate.

For Frozen Chocolate Mint Pudding Pops, add ½ teaspoon mint extract along with the vanilla.

Orange Walnut Meringues

These sweet, crunchy cookies have almost no fat. Aromatic allure and fantastic flavor come from orange zest, vanilla, and toasted walnuts. For a nice touch, sprinkle the meringues with ground cardamom before baking.

½ cup walnuts

3 pasture-raised or organic egg whites, at room temperature

Pinch of cream of tartar

½ cup sugar

1 tablespoon grated organic orange zest

½ teaspoon vanilla extract

Choice Advice: Oranges tend to be heavily sprayed with pesticides, so buy organic if you can, especially for recipes like this one where you'll be using the zest. If you can't find organic oranges, buy tangerines and use the zest from them instead.

Preheat the oven to 350°F. Put the walnuts on a baking sheet and toast in the oven, shaking the pan once or twice, until the walnuts smell fragrant, about 5 minutes. Cool and finely chop.

Reduce the oven temperature to 200°F. Line the baking sheet used for the walnuts as well as another baking sheet with parchment paper or foil.

Put the egg whites and cream of tartar in a clean and dry large bowl, preferably copper or glass. Using an electric mixer, beat on medium speed until the whites form soft peaks when the beaters are lifted, 3 to 5 minutes. Gradually add the sugar, beating until the whites resemble shaving cream and hold stiff peaks when the beaters are lifted, 3 to 5 more minutes. Fold in the walnuts, orange zest, and vanilla.

Spoon the meringue into a large gallon-size resealable plastic bag, cut off a small bit of the corner, and squeeze the meringue into 1½" rounds on the baking sheets.

Bake without opening the oven door for 1 hour and 15 minutes. Turn off the oven and let the meringues sit in the closed oven until cool, at least another hour (you can even turn off the oven just before you go to bed and let them cool in there until morning). Serve immediately or store in an airtight container for about a day.

Makes about 60 cookies

Beans, Nuts, and Grains

All beans are not created equal. There are some, I must confess, that I like better than others. Cocoa beans, for instance. The sweet, lip-luscious caress of high-quality chocolate melting slowly around my tongue gives me much more pleasure than eating bean curd does.

But I realize that eating isn't all about pleasure. It's also about satisfaction and nourishment. I've come to understand what nutritionists mean when they say "eat a balanced diet." For me, it means enjoying both chocolate and tofu for what they are. Chocolate gives instant gratification on the tongue. Tofu gives long-lasting nourishment to both body and soul. I enjoy eating both foods but for different reasons.

Part of the enjoyment I get from eating tofu comes from tasting the food itself—when it's well prepared. Another part comes from knowing that soy foods are some of the healthiest foods we can eat, both for our bodies and for the planet. Soy foods like tofu and soymilk are high in good-quality protein. They contain special plant compounds called isoflavones that help protect against cancer. And on the farm, soybeans grow easily with relatively few chemical inputs. In fact, the soybean plant actually enriches soil rather than depleting it. That's probably why soy foods have been a dietary staple of the world's oldest civilizations, such as China and Japan, for thousands of years.

Good-for-You Beans and Grains

As a group, beans and whole grains are some of the most nutritious foods available to us. They can be extremely satisfying and comforting when made into, say, a bowl of creamy red lentil soup. The only concern with these foods is that new varieties have made them more problematic as food choices. Certain beans and grains, such as most soy and corn grown in the United States, contain genetically engineered organisms that have introduced potential health hazards to our soil and ourselves. Fortunately, there are ways to keep these foods working for your health. Take a look at the smart options among beans and grains below.

Soy Foods Made without Genetically Modified Organisms (GMOs)

Soy food consumption in the United States has more than tripled in the past decade. According to Soyatech, a soy information clearinghouse, retail sales of soy foods grew from less than $1 billion in 1992 to more than $3.6 billion in 2002. Growth has been driven by strong sales of soymilk, veggie burgers and other meat alternatives, cold cereals made with soy, and energy bars made with soy protein. And according to industry estimates, the upward trend is expected to continue.

It's hardly surprising that soy sales are on the rise, given the many health benefits soy offers. While there is some question about whether soy can help reduce hot flashes in menopausal women, research shows that it may help prevent osteoporosis and lower the risk of certain cancers—particularly breast cancer in women. Among the many studies that have established soy's cancer-protective effects, one recent study of 406 Chinese women found that those who ate the most soy foods were 60 percent less likely to have "high risk" breast tissue than women who ate the least soy foods.

In addition, experts say there's little doubt that eating soy can strengthen your heart. Several major health organizations, including the American Heart Association, agree that the soy protein in soymilk and other soy foods can lower your blood cholesterol, which reduces your risk of heart disease. In 1999, based on a review of 50 clinical trials, the Food and Drug Administration (FDA) approved the following health

What Is a Genetically Modified Food?

Genetic engineering. Biotechnology. Transgenics. These are all buzzwords for the current revolution in agriculture. According to the U.S. Food and Drug Administration (FDA), biotechnology involves "techniques that allow scientists to modify DNA." You may have learned about this in science class, but here's a quick refresher: DNA forms the molecular basis of heredity in all living organisms, including plants and animals. DNA is like the blueprint that every plant and animal inherits. Specific segments of this blueprint, the genes, control specific traits or functions of the plant or animal. In your DNA, for instance, specific genes determine things like what color your eyes are as well as the color of your children's eyes.

Genetic engineering is the process of *manually* transferring a gene from one organism to another to create a new, genetically modified organism (GMO). Scientists use this technology to produce specific traits in the new organism.

Tomatoes make a good example of GMOs that are eaten as food. Tomatoes are sensitive to frost, which gives them a relatively short growing season. Fish, on the other hand, thrive in cold water, a desirable trait for the tomatoes. Scientists identified the particular gene that enables fish to resist cold temperatures. By transferring this "antifreeze" gene into the tomato, scientists created GM or "transgenic" tomatoes that are able to withstand frost and have a longer growing season.

This biotechnology has exciting potential for creating new types of plants and animals. The troubling part is that GMOs, as they are currently produced, step over the boundaries of natural crossbreeding. In nature, it's obvious that a fish would never mate with a tomato to create a new organism. This may help to explain why some GMOs have had undesirable effects, such as increased allergenicity in humans and increased toxicity to insects such as butterflies.

There is enough evidence about human health effects to be concerned about the safety of GMOs. But federal regulatory agencies permitted their use based on a single assumption: that GMOs are "substantially equivalent" to natural hybrid plants and animals. For regulatory purposes, the Environmental Protection Agency, FDA, and U.S. Department of Agriculture don't consider GM foods to be any different from other foods, despite the fact that most GM foods would never occur in nature.

Even more troubling, many studies of GMOs are not conducted on the GM plant proteins. Rather, researchers usually test genetically modified "surrogate proteins" derived from bacteria. This means that the foods farmers are growing and people are eating have not actually been tested for safety. According to recent estimates, about 70 percent of foods sold in American supermarkets contain genetically modified ingredients.

claim that now appears on many soy foods: "Diets low in saturated fat and cholesterol that include 25 grams of soy protein a day may reduce the risk of heart disease." Twenty-five grams is roughly equivalent to the amount of soy in a typical Asian diet.

While it seems self-evident that any food that can help prevent heart disease and cancer is certainly worth eating, some new varieties of soybeans are casting a gray shadow over soy's sterling health profile. Researchers have found that genetically modified (GM) soy may lead to some human health problems and negative environmental impacts.

The most common type of GM soy, comprising more than half the world's total soybean crop (more than 90 million acres in 2002), has been genetically engineered to withstand the direct application of an herbicide known as glyphosate. As a result, farmers can spray the weed killer directly onto the GM soy, killing undesirable weeds without killing the desired crop.

While herbicide-resistant soy has certainly made it easier for farmers to manage weeds, it has also led to increased use of herbicides because there is little threat of these pesticides harming the crops. In 2001, Dr. Charles Benbrook, a pest management expert at the Northwest Science and Environmental Policy Center in Sandpoint, Idaho, analyzed 4 years of U.S. Department of Agriculture (USDA) data for the six major soy-producing states. Dr. Benbrook found about 30 percent more total herbicides were used on GM soy crops than on conventional soy crops. These additional pesticides eventually make their way into the soy foods (and other foods) we eat and may aggravate existing health conditions, particularly for children.

Another human health concern about genetically modified soy relates to the increasing problem of antibiotic-resistant bacteria. In 2002, British researchers found that when we eat genetically modified soy, the herbicide-resistance gene it contains is expressed in our gut bacteria. That fact alone doesn't present a significant problem, but these findings have led many scientists to question whether other genetically modified organisms, such as those with antibiotic-resistance genes, may also be transferred to humans. While the answers aren't clear yet, the British Medical Association has recommended an outright ban on the use of antibiotic-resistant genes in GM foods, based on the available evidence.

To help keep soy foods healthy on all fronts, choose those made without GMOs when you can. Look for labels like "GMO-free" and "made with non-GMO soy."

Fortunately, many of the widely available soy foods, like soymilk, are almost always made from organic soybeans, which are non-GMO by default. But watch those veggie burgers and meat alternatives—products that contain GM soy aren't required to say so. And because GM and conventional soy crops are often mixed during processing, some manufacturers are reluctant to promise their products are GMO-free, even if they routinely avoid GM soy. Of the three major brands on the market—Boca, Morningstar Farms, and Gardenburger—only one (Morningstar Farms) could assure me in writing that their soy foods do not contain GMOs. To find GMO-free brands of soy foods, check with Mothers for Natural Law, an organization with a terrific listing at www.safe-food.org.

Organic Dried Beans, Legumes, and Nuts

Like soybeans, other legumes—such as lentils, black beans, chickpeas, and great Northern beans—have outstanding health benefits. Plus, they taste good and fill you up fast. Nutritionists say Americans aren't eating enough beans. These foods are high in protein, relatively low in fat, and good sources of potassium, calcium, iron, and B vitamins. Their high fiber content can also help lower blood cholesterol and stabilize blood sugar. They're even packed with phytochemicals that have been shown to ward off certain cancers.

Nuts, too, boost your health. Sure, nuts are a little higher in fat than beans, but most of that fat is the healthy monounsaturated type that strengthens your heart. Here's some strong evidence. The long-running Nurses' Health Study tracked the diets of more than 86,000 women for 14 years. Researchers concluded that women who ate 5 or more ounces of nuts a week (just a little more than ½ cup) reduced their risk of death from heart attacks by 35 percent. That's good health insurance in a tasty little package. So bring on the nuts! Snack on Sesame Curried Walnuts (page 229). Add pine nuts to pasta dishes, almonds or pecans to salads, and walnuts to cereal or oatmeal.

Don't forget peanuts. Even though they're technically legumes, they have the benefits of nuts. Make a meal out of Grilled Beef Satay on page 165. And see the kid-friendly recipes for Warm Peanut Noodles (page 257) and Peanut Butter Banana Spirals (page 228).

If you can get organic beans, legumes, and nuts, they're the top choice. Organic regulations prohibit genetic modification and the use of synthetic pesticides, two measures that help to keep these foods healthy for us as well as the planet.

Most natural food stores and some large supermarkets carry organic beans. You can also check out the list of producers on page 276. But don't drive yourself crazy if you can't find them. Even if you eat conventionally grown beans and nuts, the many health benefits of these foods outweigh any potential risk from pesticide exposure or genetic modification.

Corn and Corn Products Made without GMOs

Corn is among the top four crops that comprise almost all of the 101 million acres of genetically engineered crops in the United States today (soy, canola, and cotton are the other three). GM corn is used to make everything from breakfast cereals and tortilla chips to the corn syrup in soda and the corn oil in margarine. GM corn shows up in so many foods that when you choose a brand that's non-GMO, you're casting a strong vote for naturally grown foods that protect your health and the vitality of our soil and water.

GMOS AND THE LABEL DEBATE

Most of the world's policy makers agree that genetically modified (GM) foods are something different than conventionally grown foods. Based on this worldwide agreement, 35 countries, encompassing half the world's population, now require mandatory premarket safety approvals for GM foods. These countries include the European Union, Australia, New Zealand, India, China, Japan, Thailand, Indonesia, and Korea. As of 2004, all of these countries (except India) also require mandatory labeling of GM foods. Testing and labeling both help to ensure the safety of foods from these countries.

In the United States, however, neither safety testing nor labeling of GM foods is required. The reason? American policy makers assume that GM foods are "substantially equivalent" to plant or animal foods that occur in nature. They take the position that GM foods are essentially safe until proven otherwise.

Other countries take a more precautionary approach, using the idea of "substantial equivalence" only as a starting point for further study. In the European Union, before any GM food goes on the market, a government agency conducts safety assessments to ensure that the GM food contains no dangerous toxins or allergens. As of 2004, all commercial movement of GM foods in the international market will also be tracked so that buyers and sellers know where GM foods have come from and are going to.

This full-disclosure policy in foreign trade (which is a great step forward for consumers) has created some problems for U.S.-grown GM crops such as corn and soybeans. Europeans don't want to buy genetically engineered food that hasn't been safety-tested and isn't labeled. In the absence of any significant human health benefit, there's just no good reason to buy it or eat it. According to the U.S.-based National Family Farm Coalition, American corn producers have lost $200 million in annual sales to markets in the European Union because there is simply no market for U.S.-grown genetically modified corn.

In 2002, the U.S. National Academy of Sciences urged federal policy makers to label GM foods, saying that at the very least "there are reasons, beyond safety or nutrition, for a consumer to want labeling of food derived from genetically engineered plants or animals, including religious, ethical, right-to-know, or simple preference reasons." Most American consumers want the GM label, too. Over the past few years, polls consistently show that more than 80 percent of Americans think genetically engineered food should be labeled.

Meanwhile, federal policy makers have stood their ground, even in the face of mounting evidence that GM foods are "substantially *different*" from conventionally grown foods. If GM foods are still unlabeled by the time you read this and you'd like to voice your support for labeling, sign one of the many petitions available on the Internet.

Grown and revered for centuries, corn is one of nature's most versatile and healthy foods. Although fresh corn is often perceived as a vegetable, it's actually a grain. Like other grains, corn is packed with cholesterol-lowering fiber, thiamin, and other B vitamins. And when you eat fresh corn, you get the full health benefits of the whole grain, including the germ and bran, where most of the nutrients reside. Stone-ground cornmeal also preserves many of the nutrients of the whole grain.

Corn's many health and agricultural benefits have been somewhat compromised in GM versions. Scientists have found that GM corn may contribute to increased use of chemical pesticides in agriculture and that the plant itself may cause or aggravate allergic reactions in humans.

The most widely planted GM corn, known as BT corn, has been genetically engineered so that the plant itself resists pests by producing an insecticide as it grows. The insecticide, known as BT (*Bacillus thuringiensis*), is a naturally occurring soil bacterium that's long been used in powdered form on both organic and conventional crops to control European corn borers, common pests. To create BT corn, bioengineers insert the BT bacterium directly into corn DNA. As a result, every part of the plant is rendered pest-resistant—the corn contains the insecticide in its stalk, leaves, and pollen.

One problem with this innovation is that the plant generates these toxic effects over its entire life cycle, including decomposition. Researchers at New York University recently found that the BT toxin leaches into the soil and stays there for nearly a year. And with more BT in the soil, a big concern is that bugs will develop a resistance to it. Scientists say that corn borers will keep coming back every year and will eventually adapt to survive ingesting BT. This adaptability is a natural process that is expected to speed up with the widespread planting of genetically modified BT corn. When corn borers become resistant to BT, stronger toxins may be needed to control these insects. In the long run, that cause and effect could likely lead to more harmful toxins in our soil, water, and food. And pesticide-resistant bugs would pose a particular problem for organic corn farmers because BT is one of the few naturally occurring pesticides that organic growers can use to keep corn borers at bay.

Another concern with BT corn is that BT has been shown to cause allergic reactions in humans. A 1999 study of farm workers found that BT sprays caused allergic reactions such as itching, swelling, rash, and worsening of asthma. After reviewing laboratory studies that found similar results, scientific advisors at the Environmental Protection Agency (EPA) concluded that BT proteins could be allergenic and antigenic, meaning that when exposed to them, the body tries to fight them off because they pose some sort of health threat. Some researchers believe that GM foods such as BT corn may also play a role in the rise in allergic reactions among children. That's one reason why labeling of genetically modified foods has become so important. Without a label on GM foods, those suffering from food allergies have no way of knowing if the foods they buy contain allergenic GM corn and could cause an allergic reaction. And given the latest estimate that GM crops comprise 66 percent of total U.S. acreage, the odds are great that it could.

For this very reason, Starlink corn (a type of BT corn) was denied approval for human consumption in 1998 after tests showed that it might cause allergies in humans. However, the EPA did approve Starlink corn for use as animal feed. To prevent the two crops from mixing, farmers were to separate the GM corn for animals from the GM-free corn for humans. Nonetheless, the BT corn found its way into an estimated 50 percent of the U.S. corn supply by 2000, just 2 years after it was denied approval for human consumption. Unapproved BT corn was found in hundreds of pounds of Taco Bell taco shells and other consumer products in September 2000.

A widely publicized recall of these foods heated up the entire debate over genetic modification, particularly the issue of keeping GM foods separate from organic foods, which are specifically prohibited from including GMOs. Because they are so widely planted, GMOs naturally make their way into organic crops when pollinating insects, such as bees, carry GMO pollen to organic crops. More than one organic farmer has lost money because tests revealed that crops contained unacceptable levels of GMOs due to this natural process of "genetic drift."

In 2001, the EPA reapproved BT corn for 7 additional years, so BT corn won't come up for review again until 2008. Hopefully by that time, more studies will be made available to federal policy makers and will be thoroughly analyzed by regulatory agencies such as the EPA. Experts say that if the allergenicity of BT corn is reevaluated according to the new guidelines detailed in a report from the World Health Organization, it's unlikely that this GM crop would be reapproved for any commercial use.

In the meantime, you can skip the hazards altogether by buying corn and corn products that are labeled "GMO-free" or "made with non-GMO ingredients." Look for GMO-free fresh corn, frozen corn, popcorn, cornmeal, corn oil, corn-based breakfast cereals, tortilla chips, and taco shells. Buying these foods allows you to sidestep the GMOs and still enjoy the taste and health benefits of America's quintessential grain.

Whole, Unrefined Grains and Cereals

Whether GM-free, organic, or conventionally grown, whole grain foods make a tremendous choice for your health. Whole grains like steel-cut oats also tend to have better flavor and a more interesting texture than refined grains. That's because more of the original grain is left intact during processing.

All grains consist of three basic parts: germ, bran, and endosperm. The endosperm contains mostly starch and protein. The more elusive nutrients are in the germ and bran, which are rich in fiber, folate, vitamin E, B vitamins, and minerals. The refining process removes the fiber-rich germ and bran, stripping the grain of its key nutritional value.

The primary benefit of whole grains comes from their high fiber content. More than five major studies found that regular consumption of whole grains can reduce heart disease by an average of 30 percent. Foods like oatmeal are so rich in soluble fiber that, in 1997, the FDA approved the following health claim for oatmeal: "Soluble fiber from oatmeal, as part of a diet low in saturated fat and cholesterol, may reduce the risk of heart disease." You may have seen this claim on packages of oatmeal, oat-based breakfast cereals, oat bran, or oat flour.

Most Americans don't eat enough whole grains. According to current USDA figures, only 7 percent of us get the recommended three or more servings of whole grain foods a day. But it's not that hard a habit to get into. If you don't like waiting for regular brown rice to cook, try instant brown rice. Or if brown rice isn't your

Top Foods to Buy Non-GMO

Canola, corn, soybeans, and cotton account for nearly 99 percent of the genetically engineered crop acreage in the United States. Research into the long-term health effects of genetically modified (GM) foods is still in its early stages. But there is some evidence to suggest that GM foods may be less healthful in the long run than conventionally grown foods and organic foods. To avoid potential health and environmental drawbacks, look for non-GMO or organic versions of the following canola, corn, and soy foods when you can.

CANOLA
Canola oil
Chips, cookies, fried foods, margarine, and
    other foods made with canola oil
Salad dressings

CORN
Corn flour
Cereals made with corn or corn flour (such as
    cornflakes)
Corn oil
Chips, cookies, fried foods, margarine, and
    other foods made with corn oil
Cornstarch
Corn syrup
Candies, ice cream, soda, and other foods
    made with corn syrup

SOY
Soy flour
Soy formula for infants
Soymilk
Soy protein isolates and concentrates
Soy sauce and tamari
Soy-based veggie burgers, hot dogs, and
    other meatless foods
Soybean oil (often sold as "vegetable oil")
Breads, chips, cookies, crackers, salad dress-
    ings, and other foods made with soybean oil
Tofu

pleasure, try other whole grains that are minimally processed, like quinoa, oatmeal, and stone-ground cornmeal. Even popcorn is a whole grain. Check out the recipes throughout this chapter for ideas on how to make whole grain dishes that both kids and adults will love.

Canola Oil Produced without GMOs

Canola is one of the top three genetically modified food crops in the world. Technically, it's known as a seed plant, rapeseed, which is grown for the versatile rapeseed oil. What we know and use today is called canola, a contraction of "Canada oil," as credit to the Canadian growers who created a natural hybrid of the plant.

Despite urban legends to the contrary, canola is truly a nutritious oil. In fact, canola oil is lower in saturated fat than any other cooking oil and higher in heart-healthy monounsaturated fats than every other cooking oil, except olive oil. And canola contains some omega-3 fatty acids, which can benefit your heart.

The only drawback to this amazing oil is that an estimated 60 percent of North American canola crops are genetically modified. These GM crops suffer from some of the same issues as other GM crops, most notably that they are subject to wide-

Golden Rice Not Such a Treasure

Golden rice, the common name for a genetically engineered rice that is higher in vitamin A than conventional rice, has been promoted as a cure for malnourished children around the world. Bio-engineers created this grain by inserting two genes from daffodil DNA and one gene from a bacterium into a natural variety of japonica rice.

While the hope of alleviating malnutrition with science is, of course, a noble cause, critics argue that vitamin A-enriched rice won't solve the real problems that lead to malnutrition. Although rice-eating populations tend to have higher rates of malnutrition, rice consumption isn't the major cause. Rather, poverty, poor soil and water conditions, and disproportionate food distribution are more direct causes of malnutrition. And these basic problems, obviously, will never be solved by golden rice.

And despite its hoped-for potential, the reality is that golden rice isn't as high in vitamin A as many other foods. A normal-size serving of golden rice for preschool children—the most malnourished population—supplies only about 10 percent of the child's daily requirement for vitamin A. What's more, that vitamin A won't even be metabolized by the child's body unless fat and protein are also present in the diet. Yet, these two nutrients are severely low in the diets of most malnourished children.

Many health officials agree that a more effective way to fight vitamin A deficiency and malnutrition would be to make better use of the inexpensive and nutritious foods that are already available in rice-eating countries. Two forkfuls of mashed sweet potatoes, a half cup of dark green leafy vegetables, or the better part of a medium-size mango would meet the daily vitamin A requirements of preschool children just fine.

spread genetic drift. The GMOs in genetically modified canola can migrate to organic or conventionally grown crops via pollinating insects such as bees.

Farmers are directed to establish "buffer zones" between GM and other crops to prevent genetic drift. But studies show that these methods may not always work. For instance, in the United Kingdom, trials of GM crops are required to have buffer zones of about 55 to 220 yards. To test this requirement's effectiveness, researchers at the Scottish Crop Research Institute recently planted crops of male-sterile GM canola with buffer zone distances ranging from zero to nearly 2½ miles away from conventional canola crops. Since the GM plants were sterile, the researchers knew the GM crops could not produce seeds on their own and that the presence of any seeds would reflect the amount of cross-pollination that was occurring despite the buffer zones.

The U.K. study found that pollen was carried to all of the GM test crops, even the one 2½ miles away, where 5 percent of the GM plants produced seeds. In the test plants that were closest to the conventional crops, up to 90 percent of the GM plants produced seeds. These findings indicate that cross-pollination of conventional with GM crops—and vice versa—is not adequately controlled by buffer zones. If further studies continue to link GM crops with adverse health and environmental effects, it will be difficult to control the spread of GMOs due to cross-pollination. Not to mention the difficulty that organic farmers will have selling organic crops that test positive for genetically altered material.

If you use a lot of canola oil like I do, buy GMO-free when possible. It makes a sound choice for the environment—at least until we can adequately contain GM crops and until we know more about the long-term environmental and health effects of genetically modified foods. Alternatively, look to other cooking oils such as safflower oil and peanut oil.

Homemade Peanut Butter

Making peanut butter at home is incredibly easy. And fun for the kids! Use shelled roasted peanuts from a can or buy whole roasted peanuts and shell them yourself. Keep homemade peanut butter in the refrigerator, where it will stay fresh for about 4 months. If the oils rise to the top, just stir them back in.

1 cup shelled roasted peanuts

2 tablespoons safflower oil or another light salad oil

½ teaspoon salt (optional)

Put the nuts, oil, and salt (if using) into a blender or small food processor. Puree until chunky or creamy (your choice). Transfer to a jar, seal, and refrigerate until ready to use.

Makes about 1 cup

Helping Hand: This recipe can easily be doubled and may work better that way if you have a large food processor. If you've got cashews on hand, use the same recipe to make cashew butter. Yum!

Good News about GMOs

They're getting more strictly regulated. In July 2003, after 3 years of research and debate among food safety scientists worldwide, the United Nations Codex (an international regulatory body for food and agriculture) established tighter controls on safety testing and regulation for the global sale of genetically modified (GM) foods. Some of the biggest pluses of the U.N. ruling seem like common sense, but it's taken decades to establish some basic ground rules for producing and selling genetically modified foods. Hopefully, all major producers of GM foods will soon follow these rules. The Codex standard:

- Establishes a baseline that GMOs should be as safe as the conventional counterpart.
- Provides guidelines for assessing the safety of genetically engineered food plants, such as corn and soybeans.
- Provides detailed procedures for determining if a GM food contains new toxins or allergens, is altered nutritionally, or exhibits unexpected effects.
- Advises against using any antibiotic resistance marker genes in GMOs that create resistance to therapeutic or "clinically used" antibiotics. This measure is intended to curb the overuse of antibiotics and mitigate the growing problem of antibiotic resistance.

Peanut Butter Banana Spirals

Here's a healthy twist on Elvis's beloved peanut butter and banana sandwiches. I ditched the frying pan and used flour tortillas instead of sandwich bread. Yogurt adds creaminess, wheat germ adds crunch, and cinnamon bumps up the flavor. Kids love to see the spiral shape of these snacks.

½ cup creamy peanut butter

⅓ cup organic low-fat vanilla yogurt

2 large ripe bananas, sliced

1 tablespoon orange juice

4 flour tortillas (8" diameter), preferably whole wheat

¼ teaspoon ground cinnamon

2 tablespoons honey-flavored wheat germ

Choice Advice: Buy bananas labeled "Rainforest Alliance Certified" if you see them. While not strictly organic, these bananas are grown using responsible environmental practices you can feel good about.

In a small bowl, stir together the peanut butter and yogurt. In another small bowl, toss the bananas with the orange juice.

Spread the peanut butter mixture over the tortillas, leaving ½" border all around. Arrange the banana slices in a single layer over the top. Sprinkle with the cinnamon and wheat germ. Roll up and slice crosswise into pieces about 1" wide. Or wrap and refrigerate up to 2 hours before slicing.

Makes about 24 spirals (8 servings)

Sesame Curried Walnuts

I love to bring these snacks over to friends' houses. Put them in a bowl and watch them disappear! The sweet, salty, spicy combination of flavors is irresistible, and they're very easy to make. The recipe was inspired by Abby Duchin Dinces, a terrific food writer I worked with many moons ago. I've adapted the recipe over the years, but the basic idea remains the same.

1 tablespoon lemon juice

4 teaspoons water

¼ teaspoon hot pepper sauce

1 tablespoon toasted sesame oil

3½ cups walnut halves or large pieces

1 tablespoon sesame seeds

1 tablespoon curry powder

2½ teaspoons sugar

1½ teaspoons salt

In a small bowl, combine the lemon juice, water, and pepper sauce. Set aside.

Heat the oil in a wok or large skillet over medium heat. Add the walnuts and sesame seeds and cook, stirring frequently, until the walnuts smell fragrant, 4 to 5 minutes.

Scatter the curry powder, sugar, and salt over the nuts and then cook and stir until the curry powder starts to brown, 1 to 2 minutes.

Stir in the lemon juice mixture and remove from the heat. Stir the steaming nuts until the mixture begins to cool. Remove to a bowl to cool completely. When completely cool, cover or seal in an airtight container and refrigerate for 1 hour or up to 1 week. Bring to room temperature before serving.

Makes 10 to 12 snack-size servings

Honey Oatmeal with Spiced Pears and Pecans

Milk and honey make this oatmeal creamy and sweet—just the way kids like it (adults too!). The apple juice also adds sweetness, so if you like less-sweet oatmeal, replace some of the apple juice with water.

1½ cups organic apple juice

2 tablespoons honey

¾ teaspoon ground cinnamon

¼ teaspoon ground allspice

Pinch of salt

2 organic pears, peeled, cored, and chopped

1 cup raisins (optional)

1 cup steel-cut oats or old-fashioned rolled oats

½ cup organic 1% milk

3 tablespoons chopped pecans

Choice Advice: If you don't have organic pears, use organic apples or peaches instead.

Put the apple juice, honey, cinnamon, allspice, and salt in a medium saucepan. Bring to a boil over high heat. Reduce the heat to medium and add the pears, raisins (if using), and oats. Simmer until thickened and the liquid is absorbed, about 25 minutes for steel-cut oats or 5 to 7 minutes for rolled oats. Remove from the heat and stir in the milk. Serve sprinkled with the pecans.

Makes 2 to 3 servings

Helping Hand: Steel-cut oats, also known as Scotch oats or Irish oatmeal, are oats that have been cut into a few coarse pieces rather than rolled flat like old-fashioned oatmeal. These oats take a bit longer to cook, but they have a pleasantly chewy texture and nuttier flavor than old-fashioned rolled oats. Many supermarkets carry steel-cut oats in the cereal aisle.

For Baby: Replace ¾ cup of the apple juice with water and use sugar instead of honey. Also, use old-fashioned rolled oats and omit the pecans.

Sausage and Cheese Grits Casserole

Grits or "hominy grits" are coarsely ground kernels of dried corn. Like polenta, grits can be served loose and wet, or they can be cooked until semifirm or firm, cut into squares, and fried or baked again. I tend to like casserole-style grits best. This version is mild enough for the kids, but if you like it spicy, splash on a little more pepper sauce at the table. Or for more bite, stir in a chopped scallion or two along with the cheese.

4 ounces vegetarian breakfast sausage links (such as Morningstar Farms)

2 cups water

1 cup organic milk

½ teaspoon dried thyme

½ teaspoon salt

1 cup old-fashioned grits, preferably organic or GMO-free

2 pasture-raised or organic eggs, slightly beaten

1 cup plus 2 tablespoons organic shredded sharp Cheddar cheese

2 tablespoons organic butter

½ teaspoon mild pepper sauce (such as Frank's)

Cook the sausage links in a nonstick skillet over medium heat until heated through and browned all over, about 10 minutes. Set on paper towels to cool and then slice ¼" to ½" thick. Set aside.

Meanwhile, put the water, milk, thyme, and salt in a large saucepan. Bring to a boil over high heat (watch carefully so that it doesn't boil over). Gradually whisk in the grits and reduce the heat to medium-low so that the mixture simmers gently. Cover and simmer, stirring frequently, until the grits cook through and thicken enough to pull away from the sides of the pan, 10 to 15 minutes.

Preheat the oven to 350°F. Coat a shallow 1½- to 2-quart baking dish with butter, oil, or cooking spray.

Remove the grits from the heat and stir in the eggs, 1 cup cheese, the sausage, butter, and pepper sauce. Scrape into the prepared baking dish and bake until the grits are almost set in the middle (moist but not wet and loose when tested with a knife), 30 to 35 minutes. Turn on the broiler and sprinkle the grits with the remaining 2 tablespoons cheese. Cook 4" to 5" from the broiler until the cheese is bubbly and begins to brown, 1 to 2 minutes.

Let cool for 5 minutes and then spoon onto plates.

Makes 6 servings

For Baby: Omit the sausage links and pepper sauce.

MICHAEL JACOBSON
Improving Public Health and Protecting the Environment

For more than 30 years, Michael Jacobson, Ph.D., has been educating the public and improving federal food policies through the Center for Science in the Public Interest (CSPI). It all started with an internship under Ralph Nader in Washington, D.C.

In 1970, Jacobson was one of three recent Ph.D.s serving as an intern for Nader's organization. He was tapped to write a book on food additives. In 1971, Jacobson and his fellow interns formed CSPI and spun off from Nader. Even though his two cofounders left in 1977, Jacobson and CSPI kept going.

Jacobson's resolve and determination led to many positive changes in food policy. CSPI helped to get the Nutrition Facts labels now seen on foods everywhere, and the organization pushed for tougher standards on health claims made on food packages. Also, thanks in large part to CSPI's efforts, thousands of restaurants—including fast-food restaurants—now have healthier options on their menus. Major fast-food chains have stopped frying with beef fat, and millions of people have learned about simple ways that they can improve their diets.

"Our major concern is that the food Americans eat contributes to hundreds of thousands of deaths a year, thanks to saturated fat, cholesterol, sugar, and sodium content," Jacobson says. "Some of the biggest problems in terms of food are fatty dairy products and meat. We are encouraging people to move in the direction of a vegetarian diet."

A plant-based diet is good for more than just personal health, though. As Jacobson explains, raising less livestock means less manure and problems related to manure disposal, reduced need for chemical fertilizer to grow grain feed, and other environmental benefits.

Though he clearly takes a "big picture" view, Jacobson admits that kids specifically have captured much of his attention, with many of his articles and books aimed squarely at the issue of children's nutrition and health.

"There's a hope that children who start eating healthfully will continue to do so, maybe with some interruptions in the teenage years," he says. "Parents can also exercise a significant amount of control over their children's diets. So can schools."

But it's never too late to make the right choices in nutrition. As he constantly learns more about nutrition issues, Jacobson has been inspired to modify his own diet over the years.

"Cutting out soda pop was the first change I made. It's just sugar water with added flavorings," he notes. "I also switched to brown rice, and I cut out hot dogs and lunch meats. I also use less salt when cooking now. My diet isn't perfect, I admit, and people shouldn't look at me as a paragon of virtue. But I have made gradual changes in my diet as a result of what I've learned from working with CSPI."

Michael Jacobson's Granola

Granola is another name for muesli, the cereal mixture first promoted as a healthy breakfast food by Swiss natural health practitioner Dr. Bircher-Benner. Michael Jacobson's high-fiber version includes vanilla and maple syrup for extra flavor.

4 cups old-fashioned rolled oats

⅔ cup unsweetened toasted wheat germ

2 tablespoons sesame seeds

1 ounce sunflower seeds

¼ cup chopped pecans

¼ cup slivered almonds (or pine nuts or peanuts)

½ cup maple syrup or packed brown sugar

¼ cup apple juice

1 tablespoon vanilla extract

1 cup raisins or chopped dates

In a large bowl, mix together the oats, wheat germ, sesame seeds, sunflower seeds, pecans, and almonds.

In a small bowl, combine the maple syrup or brown sugar, apple juice, and vanilla. Pour into the dry mixture and stir until well moistened.

Preheat the oven to 325°F.

Spread the mixture across the bottom of a large baking sheet (or two small ones) so that the layer of granola is no more than ½" thick.

Bake until the oats are toasted and golden, stirring every 5 minutes to prevent burning, about 20 minutes total. Remove and let cool slightly. Stir in the raisins or dates and then cool completely. Store in an airtight container.

Makes 6 servings

Helping Hand: Look for toasted wheat germ in the cereal aisle of your grocery store and store it in the refrigerator to maintain freshness.

Quinoa Pilaf with Golden Raisins and Almonds

Like rice, quinoa works tremendously well in pilafs, those grain side dishes in which the grain is first sautéed in butter or oil and then simmered in stock. If you've never cooked quinoa, don't be afraid. It cooks even faster than rice. Look for quinoa near the rice in natural food stores or in large supermarkets. If you don't have golden raisins (plump dried green grapes), you can use regular raisins.

2 cups uncooked quinoa

1 tablespoon peanut oil or GMO-free vegetable oil

½ teaspoon cumin seeds

1 onion, finely chopped

1 small carrot, finely chopped

½ small organic red bell pepper, finely chopped

2 tablespoons slivered almonds

1 clove garlic, minced

4 cups pasture-raised or organic chicken broth or vegetable broth

½ cup golden raisins

½ teaspoon salt

Put the quinoa in a mesh strainer and rinse under cool running water, shaking the strainer now and then, until the water runs clear. Set aside.

Put the oil and cumin seeds in a medium saucepan. Cook over medium-low heat until the seeds smell toasty and fragrant, 2 to 3 minutes. Raise the heat to medium. When the oil gets hot, add the onion, carrot, bell pepper, and almonds. Cook until the carrot is crisp-tender, about 5 minutes. Stir in the garlic and quinoa, cooking for 1 minute.

Add the broth or stock, raisins, and salt. Raise the heat to high and bring to a boil. Reduce the heat to low, cover, and simmer until the quinoa is tender (yet delicately crunchy) and the liquid is absorbed, about 15 minutes. Fluff with a fork before serving.

Makes 6 servings

Food Lore: Quinoa has been a South American staple food for thousands of years. It looks like little ivory-colored beads. When cooked, the beads become disk-shaped and nearly translucent, except for a tiny, white seed sprout inside. Compared with other grains, quinoa is higher in protein and lower in carbohydrates. It produces its own natural insect repellent called saponin, so it grows easily without chemical pesticides. Be sure to rinse quinoa before cooking to remove this naturally bitter coating. When rinsed and cooked, quinoa has a delightfully nutty taste and a subtly tender crunch.

NANCY AND JIM CHUDA
Keeping Children's Health in Check

Nancy and Jim Chuda had done everything possible to safe-guard the health of their young daughter Colette. She was even fed organic baby food produced by Nancy's own baby-food company, Baby's Choice. But at age 4, Colette was diagnosed with a rare cancer known as Wilms' tumor. Genetic testing showed that Colette's cancer was not inherited. The Chudas suspected environmental contamination, a hunch that was later given credence by a study associating Wilms' tumor with pesticide exposure.

When Colette died, the Chudas transformed their grief into action. They founded the Colette Chuda Environmental Fund (CCEF) and the Children's Health Environmental Coalition (CHEC), both dedicated to protecting children by eliminating environmental toxins. CHEC has since prompted a report from the Natural Resources Defense Council, *Handle with Care: Children and Their Exposure to Carcinogens*, and helped win a California state law—The Healthy Schools Act—to minimize pesticide use in schools.

According to Nancy, "Most parents don't even know there is a problem with pesticides." To help get the message out, CHEC created an educational video starring Olivia Newton John and Kelly Preston. *Not under My Roof* will be shown in clinics and hospitals around the country, teaching CHEC's "Recipe for Healthy Children." The recipe has five simple steps to help avoid pesticide exposure.

1. Shop smart: Buy organic or low-pesticide food. Wash and peel.
2. Ventilate: Indoor air can be worse than the air outside.
3. Clean with care: Look for nontoxic labeling because cleaners leave residues.
4. Renovate right: Caulk to eliminate bug holes where plumbing enters the home.
5. Keep it out: Avoid pesticides in and around the home because residues enter on shoes.

Coconut-Ginger Rice

Why stick with water for boiling rice? Milk, broth, or even tea can really punch up the flavor. Here, coconut milk and ginger make exotic-tasting rice that's equally at home with Indian and Caribbean dishes. It's especially good with Jamaican Pork Chops with Pineapple Black Bean Salsa (page 173) and Lentil Dal with Potatoes, Tomatoes, and Spinach (on the opposite page). Top with chopped cilantro and peanuts for more flair.

1 cup water

1 cup light coconut milk

1 tablespoon minced crystallized ginger

½ teaspoon salt

⅛ teaspoon ground allspice

1 cup uncooked white or brown rice

In a medium saucepan over high heat, combine the water, coconut milk, ginger, salt, and allspice. Bring to a boil and add the rice. Reduce the heat to low, cover, and simmer until the liquid is absorbed and the rice is tender, 12 to 15 minutes for white rice or 35 to 40 minutes for brown. Remove from the heat and let rest, covered, for 10 minutes. Fluff with a fork before serving.

Makes 4 servings

Helping Hand: You can make fresh coconut milk at home, but for something like a rice dish, I find that the convenience of canned outweighs the minor loss in flavor. Look for light coconut milk in the international or Asian section of your supermarket. It has less fat and calories than regular coconut milk.

For Baby: Serve as is.

Lentil Dal with Potatoes, Tomatoes, and Spinach

Dal is the Indian word for almost any simmered dish made with lentils. If you've never made Indian food at home, this simple dish is a great introduction. Don't be put off by the number of ingredients. They are mostly spices that are added in seconds. Look for the spices in an Indian grocery or in the international aisle of your supermarket.

1 teaspoon cumin seeds

1 teaspoon brown mustard seeds

½ teaspoon coriander seeds

1 tablespoon GMO-free or organic canola oil

1 onion, chopped

2 cloves garlic, minced

1 bay leaf

2 small whole dried chile peppers (such as cayenne) or ¼ teaspoon ground red pepper

1 teaspoon curry powder

½ teaspoon turmeric

4 large tomatoes, chopped (about 2 cups)

2 cups vegetable broth

1½ cups brown lentils

12 ounces organic Yukon gold potatoes, chopped (about 2¼ cups)

½ teaspoon salt

8 ounces organic spinach, coarsely chopped (about 5 cups)

Put the cumin seeds, mustard seeds, and coriander seeds in a large, deep skillet. Cook and stir over medium heat until toasty and fragrant, 3 to 4 minutes. Remove from the skillet and crush with a mortar and pestle, spice grinder, or a plastic bag and hammer.

Heat the oil in the same skillet over medium heat. When hot, add the onion and cook until soft, about 4 minutes. Stir in the garlic, bay leaf, pepper, curry powder, turmeric, and crushed spices. Cook for 2 minutes. Stir in the tomatoes, stock, lentils, potatoes, and salt. Bring to a boil over high heat. Reduce the heat to medium-low so that the mixture simmers very gently. Simmer until the lentils and potatoes are tender and the mixture is slightly thickened (mash some of the potatoes if it needs to thicken up more), about 25 minutes.

Gradually stir in the spinach and cook until wilted, about 5 minutes.

Makes 6 to 8 servings

Helping Hand: Like other beans, lentils are sometimes dusty or accompanied by the occasional tiny pebble. To clean them, spread them on a baking sheet or kitchen towel and pick out any debris or old-looking, shriveled lentils. Then pour the beans into a sieve or colander and rinse clean under cool water.

Food Lore: Used for centuries throughout the Middle East and India, lentils are among the oldest cultivated crops. They're fast-cooking and don't need soaking like most other legumes do. Brown lentils are the most common variety, but you can also find red, yellow, and tiny black lentils.

Polenta with Zucchini Marinara

Here's a quick dish for rushed evenings. To save time, I sometimes buy prepared polenta instead of making it at home. Frieda's makes an organic version sold in a cylinder shape in the refrigerated produce aisle of many supermarkets. Once you get the sauce started, you can just let it simmer for half an hour while you go do something else.

2 tablespoons extra-virgin olive oil

1 onion, chopped

4 medium-small zucchini

4 cloves garlic, minced

1 can (28 ounces) chopped tomatoes

2 tablespoons chopped fresh rosemary

½ teaspoon salt

¼ teaspoon ground black pepper

2 pounds prepared organic polenta

4 teaspoons pine nuts, toasted

3 tablespoons grated Parmesan Reggiano cheese

Choice Advice: By using an imported Parmesan cheese, you'll sidestep the issues surrounding rBGH.

Heat the oil in a large skillet or sauté pan over medium heat. When hot, add the onion. Cook, stirring occasionally, until the onion is almost tender, about 4 minutes.

Cut the zucchini lengthwise into quarters and then slice crosswise to make wedge-shaped slices. Add the zucchini and garlic to the skillet. Cook, stirring now and then, until the zucchini starts to become tender, 8 to 10 minutes. Add the tomatoes (with juice) and rosemary. When the mixture bubbles, reduce the heat to medium-low, cover, and simmer until the sauce is thick and the zucchini is fall-apart tender, 20 to 30 minutes. Add the salt and pepper.

Meanwhile, preheat the oven to 375°F. Coat a baking sheet with oil.

Slice the polenta crosswise into ½"-thick rounds and place on the baking sheet. Bake until slightly browned on the bottom, about 15 minutes. Transfer to plates and top with the zucchini sauce. Sprinkle with the pine nuts and Parmesan.

Makes 4 to 6 servings

Nutrient Boost: To add more protein, toss in 8 ounces cooked vegetarian dinner sausages (such as frozen Boca Italian sausage links). Cook the frozen links with a little water in a covered nonstick skillet until defrosted and then uncover, add a little oil, and cook until browned all over, about 10 minutes. Remove from the pan, slice, and add to the sauce along with the tomatoes.

Tofu Bites

My uncle Bill started bringing a bowl of these to the annual family gathering about 10 years ago. They were such a hit that the bowl grew bigger and bigger every year. No one wants to admit that they actually like these little bites of bean curd, but these are always the first nibbles to go. Kids especially love them. They're best at room temperature, so don't be afraid to pack them in a plastic container for lunches or road trips. And they're an excellent source of protein.

1 pound GMO-free or organic extra-firm tofu, drained

1 tablespoon peanut oil

2 tablespoons GMO-free or organic tamari or soy sauce

2 teaspoons rice vinegar

1 teaspoon toasted sesame oil

Cut the tofu into small cubes. Heat the peanut oil in a wok or large nonstick skillet over medium-high heat. When hot, add the tofu and toss to coat with the oil. Cook, flipping the pieces every few minutes, until lightly browned all over, 15 to 20 minutes. Remove from the heat and cool slightly.

Mix the tamari or soy sauce, vinegar, and sesame oil in a bowl or plastic container. Add the tofu, cover, and toss until the tofu is well coated. Uncover to release any steam. Cover and refrigerate for at least 1 hour or up to 3 days, tossing occasionally. Serve cold or at room temperature.

Makes 4 servings

Helping Hands: Double the recipe if you have a very large skillet or wok. These go so fast, you'll be glad you made extra.

To make tofu more firm-textured, drain it and then cut the block in half through the side to make two thinner slabs. Place the slabs side by side on a cutting board and prop the board up slightly near the sink. Cover the tofu with paper towels and put a heavy weight, such as a heavy pan, on it. Let stand for 30 minutes to drain. For a quicker press (but not quite as effective), wrap the tofu in a clean kitchen towel and place a weight on top for 5 minutes.

For Baby: If your baby or toddler has teeth, serve this as is.

Blackened Tofu

A few years ago, some vegetarian friends were having a Mardi Gras party. I wanted to make them a tofu dish reminiscent of Cajun blackened fish and came up with this recipe. It's got a kick, so adjust the ground red pepper to taste! To heighten the briny flavor, mix ½ teaspoon of crushed dulse sea vegetable flakes in with the blackening spices. Serve with cooked red beans and rice.

1 pound GMO-free or organic extra-firm tofu, drained

1¼ cups vegetable broth

1 tablespoon light miso

2 teaspoons Dijon mustard

1½ teaspoons lemon juice

2 tablespoons Cajun blackening seasoning

½ teaspoon dried oregano

½ teaspoon ground black pepper

¼–½ teaspoon ground red pepper

½ teaspoon salt

2 tablespoons peanut oil

Carefully cut the tofu through the side into four thin, rectangular slabs or "cutlets." Put the cutlets close to one another on a cutting board near the sink. Prop up the board so that liquid can drain into the sink. Cover the tofu with paper towels and put a wide heavy weight, such as a cast-iron pan or griddle, on it. Let stand for 10 to 15 minutes to remove excess water.

Meanwhile, mix together the stock, miso, mustard, and lemon juice in a large glass baking dish. Set aside.

Combine the blackening seasoning, oregano, black pepper, red pepper, and salt. Spread on a plate. Set aside.

Preheat the oven to 375°F. Put the tofu cutlets in the stock mixture, coating completely (take care not to break the cutlets). Bake until most of the liquid is absorbed, turning the cutlets with a spatula halfway through cooking, 20 to 25 minutes total.

Using a spatula, transfer the cooked tofu to the seasoning mixture and coat all over with the seasoning. Lay the cutlets on a plate as you coat them.

Heat about 1 tablespoon of oil in a large nonstick skillet over medium-high heat. When hot, add two of the cutlets and cook until slightly firm, about 3 minutes per side. Repeat with the remaining oil and cutlets.

Makes 2 or 3 servings

Helping Hand: This dish creates a little smoke. Open the vents or windows during cooking!

G.I. Joes

On busy weeknights, my family loves to put together sloppy joes. They're fun to eat because you have to get just enough pressure on the buns to keep the filling from squishing out as you chomp down. G.I. is short for Garden Imp, a reference to my son August, who loves to romp in the garden and watch our peppers and tomatoes grow. I made this dish for him after one of our late-summer harvests. If you like it spicy, splash on some Tabasco at the table.

2 tablespoons extra-virgin olive oil

1 onion, chopped

1 small organic red bell pepper, chopped

2 cloves garlic, chopped

1 bag (12 ounces) frozen meatless crumbles (such as Morningstar Farms)

1 can (28 ounces) crushed tomatoes

6 drained oil-packed or soft sun-dried tomatoes, chopped

1 tablespoon GMO-free or organic tamari or soy sauce

1 tablespoon balsamic vinegar

1 teaspoon sugar

1 teaspoon chili powder

1 teaspoon dried oregano

½ teaspoon ground cumin

½ teaspoon ground black pepper

¼ teaspoon salt

6 soft whole wheat Kaiser rolls or hamburger buns

Heat the oil in a large skillet over medium heat. When hot, add the onion, bell pepper, and garlic. Cook until the vegetables begin to soften, about 5 minutes. Stir in the crumbles and cook until heated through, another 5 minutes or so.

Stir in the crushed tomatoes, sun-dried tomatoes, tamari or soy sauce, vinegar, sugar, chili powder, oregano, cumin, black pepper, and salt. Reduce the heat to medium-low and cook until thick enough to sit on a bun without running, about 20 minutes. Serve on the rolls or buns.

Makes 6 servings

Helping Hand: For a richer, meatier flavor, add ½ cup chopped mushrooms along with the bell pepper. If using fresh tomatoes, you'll need about 3½ cups (peeled, cored, and whizzed in a food processor until just crushed but not fully pureed).

5-Minute Chickpea Salad

"We do a lot of fantasy games around eating," says Dr. Sandra Steingraber, mother of two. "For chickpeas, we pretend that we're chickens in the barnyard and say, 'Here, little chick, chick, chick.' Then we peck them up [with our fingers]." Here's a simple way to dress up chickpeas for both kids and adults. To get more fancy, add some chopped fresh parsley or dill. Or add a tablespoon or two of tahini (sesame paste), mash it all up, and call it hummus.

2 tablespoons lemon juice

3 tablespoons extra-virgin olive oil

½ teaspoon lemon-pepper seasoning

2 cups cooked or canned chickpeas, drained and rinsed

½ organic red bell pepper, finely chopped

Put the lemon juice in a medium serving bowl. Whisk in the oil in a slow, steady stream until fully incorporated, 1 to 2 minutes. Whisk in the seasoning and then add the chickpeas and pepper. Mix well and serve.

Makes 4 servings

Helping Hand: Kids under age 3 should eat chickpeas mashed, as the round, soft shape could plug up little airways.

What's Fair Is Fair

Not all beans are turned into soup or salad. Cocoa beans are transformed into one of life's supreme gustatory pleasures: chocolate. And coffee beans are brewed into the world's most popular beverage. These two types of beans tend to come from tropical growing regions in Latin America, Asia, and Africa—all areas where small-scale, family farmers produce most of the food and can be taken advantage of in the global marketplace. To help ensure fair commodity prices for small farmers of coffee and chocolate, an international consortium of 17 organizations began a labeling program known as "fair trade" in the mid 1990s. The nonprofit agency TransFair USA was created in 1996 and began certifying and labeling fair-trade foods in the United States in 1998. This label ensures that the products you buy are produced in a socially responsible way by small-scale family farmers who are encouraged (but not strictly required by law) to use organic production methods. The fair-trade label appears mostly on coffee but also on chocolate, tea, and bananas in stores like Starbucks, Dunkin Donuts, Kroger, Safeway, and other national chains.

If you're concerned about the decline of family farms, especially in less-developed nations, look for fair-trade foods. The cost is similar to organic and gives you the peace of mind that your money is going to help support the family farmer who grew and harvested your food.

Chickpea Tangerine Salad with Walnuts

Save this sunny-tasting salad for early spring or summer. It's wonderfully refreshing and satisfying enough for a light lunch.

3 tangerines

2 tablespoons lemon juice

¼ cup extra-virgin olive oil (or half olive oil and half walnut oil)

½ teaspoon Dijon mustard

¼ teaspoon salt

¼ teaspoon ground black pepper

1 tablespoon chopped fresh basil or parsley

1½ cups cooked or canned chickpeas, rinsed and drained

3 scallions, sliced

1 large carrot, shredded

⅓ cup walnut halves or pieces, toasted

Squeeze the juice from one of the tangerines into a medium bowl. Whisk in the lemon juice and then the oil in a slow, steady stream. When the oil is incorporated, whisk in the mustard, salt, pepper, and basil or parsley.

Add the chickpeas, scallions, carrot, and walnuts and toss to coat.

Makes 4 servings

Helping Hand: To make this dish more special, candy the walnuts instead of just toasting them. In a medium saucepan over medium heat, combine 2 tablespoons brown sugar, 1½ teaspoons water, a pinch of ground cinnamon, a dash of salt, and a dash of ground red pepper. Stir until the mixture boils. Boil until the liquid turns a deep amber color, 1 to 2 minutes more. Add the walnuts and stir until most of the liquid is absorbed, 1 to 2 minutes. Quickly pour onto a foil-covered baking sheet, spreading the nuts apart from one another. Let cool completely, about 5 minutes, then pull the nuts off the foil and sprinkle over each serving of salad.

Black Bean and Goat Cheese Burritos

Here is yet another busy weeknight meal. You have a lot of those with kids in the house! Both kids and adults like these little bundles of beans. The recipe makes a fairly mild but flavorful filling. To spice it up, add ¼ to ½ teaspoon ground red pepper along with the chili powder.

8 flour tortillas (8" diameter), preferably whole wheat

2 teaspoons GMO-free or organic canola oil

½ onion, finely chopped

½ organic red bell pepper, finely chopped

2 cloves garlic, minced

½ teaspoon chili powder

½ teaspoon ground cumin

½ teaspoon dried oregano

1½ cups cooked or canned black beans, rinsed and drained

½ cup Chunky Tomato Salsa (page 79) or prepared salsa

3 ounces goat cheese

2 scallions, chopped

1 cup shredded organic pepper Jack or Cheddar cheese (optional)

Preheat the oven to 325°F. Tightly wrap the stack of tortillas in foil and bake for 10 minutes to soften.

Meanwhile, heat the oil in a large, deep skillet over medium heat. Add the onion and pepper and cook until the vegetables are soft, about 5 minutes. Stir in the garlic, chili powder, cumin, and oregano. Cook for 2 minutes. Stir in the beans and salsa. Reduce the heat to medium-low and cook, occasionally stirring and mashing some of the beans with the back of a spoon, until the mixture thickens slightly, 10 to 15 minutes.

Stir in the goat cheese until it melts and is thoroughly incorporated.

To assemble, spoon about ⅓ cup filling in a column down the center of each tortilla. Sprinkle with the scallions and the cheese (if using). Fold the bottom end of the tortilla over the filling and then fold over the sides to enclose. Serve with additional salsa, if you like.

Makes 8 burritos

Italian Sausage and Barley Stew

Barley makes great beer and whiskey when it's malted. Unmalted "pearl" barley makes good stew. If you have both beer and pearl barley on hand, use the beer to replace up to 1 cup of the broth in this recipe. Or if the kids will be eating this one, you can just use all broth and drink the beer yourself. For a dash of extra flavor, pass grated Parmesan cheese and chopped fresh parsley for sprinkling on top.

8 ounces frozen vegetarian Italian sausage links (such as Boca)

2 tablespoons water

2 tablespoons extra-virgin olive oil

1 onion, chopped

2 carrots, sliced

2 ribs organic celery, sliced

2 cloves garlic, minced

1 can (14 ounces) Italian-style stewed tomatoes

2 cups vegetable broth or beef broth

1 teaspoon dried thyme

1 bay leaf

¾ cup uncooked pearl barley

½ teaspoon salt

¼ teaspoon ground black pepper

1 tablespoon balsamic vinegar

Put the sausage links and water in a large nonstick skillet. Cover and cook over medium heat for 5 minutes. Uncover and cook until the liquid evaporates. Add about 1 teaspoon oil and shake the pan to thoroughly coat the links. Cook, turning often, until browned all over, about 5 minutes. Transfer to paper towels. When cool, cut crosswise into ½"-thick slices.

Meanwhile, heat the remaining oil in a large soup pot over medium heat. When hot, add the onion, carrots, and celery. Cook, stirring occasionally, until the vegetables are almost tender, about 5 minutes. Add the garlic and cook 1 minute. Stir in the tomatoes (with juice), broth, thyme, and bay leaf. Bring to a boil over high heat. Stir in the barley and sliced sausage. Reduce the heat to low, cover, and simmer for 30 to 40 minutes to blend the flavors. Stir in the salt, pepper, and vinegar. Taste and add more vinegar, salt, or pepper as necessary. Remove the bay leaf before serving.

Makes 6 servings

Wheat Flour, Bread, and Pasta

On weekends, our family almost always bakes something. Muffins, biscuits, breads, scones, cookies, cakes, pies . . . you name it. If we don't bake these foods ourselves, we usually end up buying our favorite items at a bakery, bagel shop, diner, or grocery store.

We're not the only people eating a lot of baked goods. Americans eat more wheat in the form of breads, rolls, crackers, cookies, and cakes than any other type of food. If you count up all wheat foods, including pasta, Americans eat nearly 150 pounds of wheat per person per year.

Wheat foods are so integral to our national diet that we hardly think about them. Take the hamburger, for example. It's an American icon. But without the bun, it's nothing more than ground beef. Pizza is another perennial favorite. Take away the crust and it's just tomato sauce covered with cheese. Even relative newcomers like burritos rely on wheat tortillas to hold them together.

I suppose the high consumption of wheat foods in America should come as no surprise. Wheat is our most widely planted human food crop (corn and soybeans have more total acreage, but most of that goes to feeding livestock rather than humans). The United States is also the world's biggest exporter of wheat, selling more than half its supply (some 30,000 metric tons) overseas every year.

This quintessential grain is relatively easy to grow, can be used to make a variety of foods, and has a mild flavor that's easy to like.

Amber Waves of Grain

Given the importance of wheat to both the American diet and our economy, experts point to some recent developments that are troubling to health and hearth in two very different ways. First, nutritionists say that we're eating so many foods made from refined wheat that we're contributing to the rising rates of obesity, diabetes, and heart disease in this country. And second, there are concerns that new varieties of genetically modified wheat may threaten the vitality of this essential U.S. commodity, which would certainly create a wider economic impact.

Of course, none of us are about to give up our daily bread. The key is to choose wheat foods that are healthy for you, our soil, and our economy. Here's how.

Whole Grain Pasta, Bread, and Wheat Flour

Organic or not, whole grain foods make an outstanding choice for your health. In fact, making this one simple switch in your diet can have a greater effect on your overall health than almost any other food choice you can make. That's because we eat more grain foods than any other type of food, and most of these foods are made from refined grains, which have been stripped of valuable nutrients. According to U.S. Department of Agriculture (USDA) figures, white breads, white rice, and refined-grain baked goods and cookies account for more than 25 percent of the calories in our national diet. Many nutritionists point a finger at these low-nutrient, high-carbohydrate foods to help explain rising rates of obesity in America.

Whole grains, on the other hand, can help you lose weight and lower your health risks, because they are simply higher in health-protecting nutrients. For instance, compared with white flour, whole wheat flour provides 4 times more fiber, 6 times more magnesium, and 20 times more vitamin E, among other nutrients. You'll reap the benefits of these health boosters every time you choose foods made with whole wheat flour, such as whole wheat breakfast cereals, pastas, breads, pitas, and tortillas.

Fiber is the most important nutrient in whole grain foods. Several major studies have found that soluble fiber can help you lose weight and live longer. A recent study of women in Iowa, for example, found that those who ate about 5 grams of fiber a day from whole grains were 17 percent less likely to die of any cause than women who ate only about 1 gram of whole grain fiber a day. One theory: Fiber simply fills you up so you eat less of the foods that can cause health problems. If you're following a low-carbohydrate weight-loss plan, the fiber in whole-grain foods may help you stick with the program and maintain a healthy weight.

Whole wheat foods can also help ward off diabetes. A study from the University of Minnesota tracked the diets of 36,000 women and found that eating just three daily servings of whole grain foods cut the risk of adult-onset diabetes by 21 percent. Researchers concluded that the soluble fiber in whole grain foods appears to help prevent disease, particularly disease associated with excess weight.

If you're not used to eating whole grain foods, here's an easy way to start: Pick the two types of grain foods that you eat most often. For many people, that means breakfast cereals and breads. Put the emphasis on whole grain versions of these two foods and you'll do your health a huge favor.

When shopping for whole grain cereals, look for a high fiber content on the nutrition label. At least 5 grams of fiber per serving makes it a healthy choice. Some breakfast cereals with this amount of fiber include All-Bran, Fruit & Fibre, Grape-Nuts, Kashi GoLean Crunch, raisin bran, and shredded wheat.

The same rule applies when shopping for bread. Look for 3 to 5 grams of fiber per slice on the nutrition label. Don't assume labels that say "multigrain" or "100 percent wheat" provide the same benefits. These breads may actually contain very little whole grain and fiber. True whole wheat breads say "100 percent whole wheat" on the package and list "whole wheat flour" (not "enriched wheat" or "white wheat") as the first ingredient on the food label.

No matter what type of whole grain wheat food you're buying—be it cereal, bread, pasta, or flour—the easiest way to be sure that it's whole grain is to look for a high fiber content on the nutrition label.

GMO-Free Whole Wheat Products

If you see pasta, bread, and wheat flour without genetically modified organisms (GMOs) in your market, grab 'em. Currently, the "GMO-free" label isn't all that common on loaves of bread and boxes of pasta. That's because genetically modified wheat isn't on the market yet. But it's coming soon, and many farmers, environmentalists, and scientists say there's good reason to avoid it.

Genetically modified wheat will likely be planted in the United States by 2006 or so. Monsanto, the company that developed GM wheat, has engineered the plant to withstand the company's top-selling herbicide, glyphosate, known by the brand name Roundup. The primary benefit of Roundup Ready wheat is that it will allow farmers to use herbicides on the crop without the risk of killing the wheat, theoretically making it easier for farmers to grow the crop and increasing demand for more herbicides.

However, like most genetically modified foods, Roundup Ready wheat does not appear to offer any distinct human health benefits. What's more, it poses some significant environmental and economic drawbacks. Canada, a country that exports almost 70 percent of its wheat, has led the way in researching the negative impacts of GM wheat.

A 2003 report from the Canadian Wheat Board found that GM wheat would likely accelerate soil erosion as farmers increase the amount of land they till in order to seed and remove plants. This landmark Canadian study also showed that GM wheat may result in more harmful chemicals being used on wheat fields as weeds become more resistant to chemicals.

As far as the economic impact is concerned, farmers in the United States and Canada are particularly concerned that GM wheat could weaken global sales, because major overseas importers like Japan and Europe have insisted they won't buy wheat containing genetically modified organisms due to concern over the product's safety claims. In fact, a full two-thirds of international buyers do not want to buy wheat containing any GM material, according to Canadian Wheat Board estimates. And experience with other GM crops such as soy, corn, and canola shows that GM wheat will inevitably mix with conventional wheat so that all wheat supplies will contain some genetically altered material. Even if only a small amount of GM wheat is sown in the United States, many farmers fear the entire U.S. spring wheat supply would be subject to boycott by the top overseas markets.

To understand both the farmers' and the consumer groups' concerns, it's important to know why the regulatory process for genetically modified foods needs stricter controls. The U.S. Food and Drug Administration (FDA) has approved the use of several genetically modified crops such as corn and soy since the early 1990s. Their use is based on the assumption that GMOs are "substantially equivalent" to natural hybrid plants and animals, but that's hardly a guarantee that these foods are safe for human consumption.

In 2003, the Center for Science in the Public Interest (CSPI) reviewed the FDA's regulatory process for GM grains and found that biotechnology companies did not provide adequate data to ensure that their products are safe. According to current law, U.S. biotech companies are encouraged, but not required, to submit food safety tests for review. When CSPI analyzed FDA data, the group found that only half of the time did biotech companies supply scientific studies requested by the FDA, which completed its approvals without the necessary information.

Until these issues are resolved, many farmers are approaching GM crops cautiously. In addition, many food industry groups want to put the brakes on genetically modified wheat before it makes it to market. The National Association of Wheat Growers, the U.S. Wheat Associates, and the Canadian Wheat Board all agree that GM wheat should not be introduced unless issues of segregation and market acceptance are resolved.

Until GM wheat is more rigorously tested, regulated, and—at the very least— labeled, it makes sense for consumers to avoid foods made with it. To vote for a precautionary approach, choose GMO-free breads, bagels, cookies, pasta, baking mixes, and other wheat flour-based foods when you can't find 100 percent organic.

Organic Pasta, Bread, and Wheat Flour

For overall health and environmental safety, organic wheat foods make an outstanding choice. You will not only avoid GMOs but also reduce your exposure to potentially harmful pesticides and help support agricultural methods that enrich our soil rather than deplete it.

The most widely used pesticide on wheat crops is chlorpyrifos, an organophosphate that kills unwanted insects. Chlorpyrifos also gets sprayed onto fruits such as apples and in homes, schools, parks, and other public places to control bugs like termites and cockroaches. It works by poisoning the nervous systems of unwanted bugs. The downside: Substantial evidence from laboratory studies indicates that organophosphates may have similar effects on the developing nervous systems of children. Due to mounting evidence that continuous low-level exposure to chlorpyrifos may be harmful to kids, the Environmental Protection Agency (EPA) recently phased out the use of this pesticide in homes, schools, parks, and other places frequented by children. The EPA also set stricter tolerances for chlorpyrifos residues on apples and grapes.

However, there has been no revision of how much of this pesticide should be tolerated on wheat products, one of the most widely consumed food groups in the United States, especially among snack-loving American kids. Due to children's cumulative exposure to chlorpyrifos from multiple sources, researchers at the Center for Children's Health and the Environment at the Mount Sinai School of Medicine in New York City recommend stricter controls of chlorpyrifos than the EPA has currently set.

As we continue to learn more about the relationship between environmental toxins and illness in children, play it safe with your family by avoiding unnecessary exposures to chlorpyrifos. Look for organic wheat foods like bread, pasta, and flour when you can, because they are grown without chlorpyrifos and other harmful pesticides. If you can't find them locally, check the source list on page 276 to find out where you can buy organic wheat foods.

Protecting Children from Cancer

Cancer seems like one of those age-related diseases that won't affect you until late in life. But cancer can affect young adults and children, too. In fact, new research shows that young children may be more susceptible to cancer-causing agents because their cells are rapidly proliferating as they grow. Their protective detoxifying systems are also less developed than those of adults.

Since the 1970s, the incidence of childhood cancers such as leukemia and brain cancer has risen sharply, according to Dr. Phil Landrigan, director of the Center for Children's Health and the Environment at the Mount Sinai School of Medicine in New York City. National Cancer Institute (NCI) figures show that about 8,500 American children were diagnosed with cancer, and 1,700 died from the disease in 1998 (the latest figures available). While the causes of cancer are complex, NCI epidemiological studies indicate an association between exposure to pesticides and cancer in children. In the period from 1973 to 1995, 53 percent of brain tumors and other nervous-system cancers in children up to age 4 were associated with environmental exposures such as pesticides and radiation.

To help reduce your child's cancer risk, avoid using synthetic pesticides in and around your home. It also helps to put the emphasis on cancer-fighting foods such as fruits, vegetables, beans, and grains. These plant foods are the top sources of anticancer compounds such as beta-carotene, indoles, and sulforaphane. For the best cancer protection (and least exposure to pesticide residues), focus on cruciferous vegetables such as broccoli, brussels sprouts, cabbage, cauliflower, chard, kale, mustard greens, rutabagas, and turnips.

Pesto Gorgonzola Bruschetta

Gorgonzola, an Italian blue cheese, melts into a rich, bubbly layer of bold flavor on these easy appetizers. They come together in less than 15 minutes.

½ long loaf crusty Italian or French bread, preferably whole grain

½ cup Basic Basil Pesto (page 77) or prepared pesto

3 plum tomatoes, chopped

2 ounces Gorgonzola cheese, crumbled

Preheat the broiler.

Cut the bread in half lengthwise through the side to make two long pieces. Arrange with the cut sides up. Spread the pesto over each piece. Top with the tomatoes and cheese. Broil until golden and the cheese melts, 2 to 3 minutes. Cool slightly and cut crosswise into 1" slices.

Makes 24 pieces

Choice Advice: To avoid the issues surrounding rBGH, make sure your Gorgonzola is not a domestic brand. European countries have restricted the use of growth hormones in their dairy herds.

Couscous with Arugula, Cucumbers, and Mint

Like most pasta, couscous is made from semolina, a coarsely ground form of durum wheat. The mild taste of this tiny pasta makes a wonderful culinary canvas for juicy cucumbers, aromatic mint, and peppery arugula in a simple pasta salad. Look for couscous in the grain aisle of most supermarkets or in natural food stores.

1 lemon

5 tablespoons extra-virgin olive oil

¾ teaspoon salt

¼ teaspoon ground black pepper

2 cups gently packed arugula leaves

⅓ medium English cucumber, halved lengthwise and sliced

3 tablespoons chopped fresh mint

1¾ cups pasture-raised or organic chicken broth or vegetable broth

1 small shallot, minced

1 cup couscous, preferably whole wheat

3 tablespoons pine nuts, toasted (optional)

Squeeze the juice from the lemon into a medium bowl. Whisk in 4 tablespoons oil in a slow, steady stream until thoroughly blended. Whisk in ½ teaspoon salt and the pepper. Stir in the arugula, cucumber, and mint. Set aside.

Bring the broth to a boil in a small saucepan. Set aside.

Heat the remaining 1 tablespoon oil in a medium saucepan over medium heat. Add the shallot and cook for about 1 minute. Stir in the couscous, tossing until coated with the oil, about 1 minute. Add the hot broth and remaining ¼ teaspoon salt. Bring to a vigorous simmer, stirring frequently. Remove from the heat, cover, and let stand until the liquid is absorbed, about 8 minutes. Fluff with a fork and then stir into the arugula mixture. Cover and let stand until the arugula is slightly wilted, 2 to 3 minutes. Serve sprinkled with the pine nuts (if using).

Makes 4 to 6 servings

Helping Hands: To prepare arugula, cut off any thick stems from the bunch and then rinse and dry the leaves. Some arugula leaves are available prestemmed, rinsed, and dried. Others have quite a bit of grit on them and need thorough washing.

English or "hothouse" cucumbers are long, skinny, and usually wrapped in plastic in the produce aisle of grocery stores. They tend to have fewer seeds and a less bitter taste than regular cucumbers.

Warm Peanut Noodles

Peanut butter makes a great base for a quick Asian-style sauce. If you like cold sesame noodles from Chinese take-out restaurants, you'll crave this peanut-based version. Leave out the hot pepper sauce when making this for kids. For adults, garnish with chopped scallions and toasted sesame seeds or chopped peanuts.

8 ounces spaghetti or vermicelli, preferably whole grain

½ cup vegetable broth or pasture-raised or organic chicken broth

1 teaspoon sugar

½ cup creamy peanut butter

2 tablespoons organic tamari or soy sauce

1 tablespoon rice vinegar

1 teaspoon sesame oil

½–1 teaspoon hot pepper sauce (optional)

Cook the noodles in a pot of boiling salted water until tender yet slightly firm in the center, about 8 minutes.

Meanwhile, mix the broth and sugar in a small saucepan and stir over medium heat until hot and the sugar dissolves. Pour into a medium bowl and whisk in the peanut butter, tamari or soy sauce, vinegar, oil, and pepper sauce (if using).

Drain the noodles and add to the bowl. Mix thoroughly and serve warm.

Makes 4 small servings

Helping Hand: For a bit more flavor, replace the hot pepper sauce with Vietnamese chili-garlic sauce, which is widely available in Asian grocery stores. Add more to taste.

Penne with Fresh Tomato Sauce and Fontina

Here's the perfect pasta sauce for a lazy summer day. Just toss chopped tomatoes into a simple vinaigrette and let them marinate all day. No cooking! A final grating of Parmesan or Pecorino Romano cheese makes a nice touch.

2 tablespoons balsamic vinegar

¼ cup extra-virgin olive oil

½ teaspoon salt

¼ teaspoon ground black pepper

2 cloves garlic, minced

4 large ripe tomatoes, chopped

1 pound penne or other shaped pasta, preferably whole grain

8 ounces fontina cheese, cut into small cubes

⅓ cup chopped fresh basil

Pour the vinegar into a bowl large enough to hold the pasta. Gradually whisk in the oil in a slow, steady stream until fully incorporated. Whisk in the salt, pepper, and garlic. Stir in the tomatoes. Cover and let stand at room temperature for 4 to 6 hours.

When you're ready to eat, cook the pasta in a large pot of boiling salted water until just tender yet slightly firm in the center, 8 to 10 minutes. Drain and add to the tomatoes. Add the cheese and basil. Toss to mix. Taste and add more salt and pepper, if necessary.

Makes 4 to 6 servings

Choice Advice: A semifirm yet creamy Italian cheese, fontina has a mildly rich, almost nutty flavor. It's a superb melting cheese. And imported versions avoid health issues surrounding rBGH. If you can't find fontina, use cubes of good-quality organic or imported mozzarella.

Helping Hand: Grilled vegetables make a wonderful addition to the mix here. Try cutting zucchini into thick slabs, coating them with oil, salt, and pepper, and then grilling the slabs for about 5 minutes per side. Coarsely chop and add to the pasta along with the fontina.

Tortellini with Broccoli and Chickpeas

The king of cruciferous vegetables, broccoli is a good source of calcium and beta-carotene. It can help boost your immunity, fight off cancer, and protect against heart disease. No wonder broccoli is so low in pesticide residues. It can fight off pests naturally! Here, it stars along with chickpeas in a simple, flavorful pasta toss. There's a little white wine here, but don't worry. The alcohol boils off. Or you can replace it with vegetable broth.

12 ounces fresh or frozen cheese tortellini, preferably organic

1 tablespoon extra-virgin olive oil

½ large red onion, thinly sliced and quartered

4 cloves garlic, cut into matchsticks

2 heads broccoli, cut into florets (about 5 cups)

1¼ cups vegetable broth

1 can (15 ounces) chickpeas, rinsed and drained

½ teaspoon ground black pepper

½ teaspoon crushed red pepper flakes (optional)

½ cup dry white wine or vegetable broth

Salt

3 tablespoons organic butter

2 tablespoons chopped fresh parsley

⅓ cup grated imported Parmesan cheese

Cook the pasta in a large pot of boiling salted water until just tender, 4 to 8 minutes.

Meanwhile, heat the oil in a large skillet over medium heat. When hot, stir in the onion and garlic. Cook, stirring occasionally, until just softened, about 5 minutes. Add the broccoli and 2 tablespoons of the broth. Cover and cook, stirring once or twice, until the broccoli is bright green and just crisp-tender, 2 to 3 minutes. Uncover and stir in the chickpeas, black pepper, and pepper flakes (if using). Cook for 2 minutes. Remove to a serving bowl and keep warm.

Return the pan to high heat and pour in the remaining broth and the wine (or more broth). Boil, scraping the bottom of the pan occasionally, until the liquid is slightly reduced and begins to coat the back of a spoon, 3 to 5 minutes. Taste and add salt and pepper, if necessary (which will depend upon on the saltiness of the broth used). Remove from the heat and stir in the butter and parsley.

Drain the pasta and add to the broccoli along with the reduced sauce. Toss to mix. Serve sprinkled with Parmesan.

Makes 6 servings

Michael Jacobson's Linguine with Spinach, Mushrooms, and Tomatoes

Here's an old standby recipe from Dr. Michael Jacobson, executive director of the Center for Science in the Public Interest in Washington, D.C. It comes together quickly and gets a flavor boost from fresh tomatoes, mushrooms, and spinach. Look for whole wheat pasta right next to the regular pasta in your grocery store. It has more cholesterol-lowering fiber than regular pasta.

8 ounces whole wheat linguine or spaghetti

2½ cups jarred tomato-basil sauce

1 tablespoon extra-virgin olive oil

8 button mushrooms, quartered

2 tomatoes, coarsely chopped

1 clove garlic, minced

10 cups organic baby spinach leaves

¼ cup chopped fresh parsley

¼ cup grated imported Parmesan cheese

¼ teaspoon ground black pepper

Cook the pasta in a large pot of boiling salted water according to the package directions. Drain and divide among four dinner plates.

Meanwhile, warm the tomato sauce in a saucepan over medium-low heat.

Heat the olive oil in a large skillet over medium heat. When hot, add the mushrooms, tomatoes, and garlic. Cook until the mushrooms and tomatoes are soft and begin to give off liquid, about 8 minutes.

Rinse the spinach and place the wet leaves in a large saucepan over medium heat. Cover and cook until just wilted, about 5 minutes.

Spoon the warmed sauce over the pasta on each plate. Top with the spinach. Arrange the mushrooms and tomatoes around the edges of the plates. Sprinkle with the parsley, Parmesan, and black pepper.

Makes 4 servings

Helping Hand: If you time it right, you can wilt the spinach in the pasta pot right after draining the pasta. That way, you won't dirty another dish!

Thai Fettuccine Primavera

I first started making this Thai-meets-Italian dish about 15 years ago. I was crazy for everything Thai, eating in Thai restaurants and cooking familiar dishes with a Thai twist at home. Now that I've got little ones in the house to keep me busy, I make most Thai food with prepared curry mixes and canned coconut milk. Despite the shortcuts, this still has fabulous flavor. And quite a kick!

1 pound fettuccine, preferably whole grain

1 tablespoon peanut oil or GMO-free vegetable oil

2 heads broccoli, cut into florets (about 5 cups)

2 organic bell peppers (preferably red and yellow), cut into short strips

2 teaspoons minced fresh ginger

2 cloves garlic, minced

1 can (14 ounces) regular or reduced-fat coconut milk

2 tablespoons Thai red curry base

1 tablespoon brown sugar

¼ cup chopped peanuts

¼ cup chopped fresh cilantro or basil

Cook the fettuccine in a large pot of boiling salted water until just tender yet slightly firm in the center, about 8 minutes.

Meanwhile, heat the oil in a wok or large, deep skillet over medium-high heat. When hot, add the broccoli and stir-fry for 10 seconds. Add a tablespoon or two of the pasta water, cover, and steam until the broccoli is just bright green and barely tender, 1 to 2 minutes. Add the peppers and stir-fry for 1 minute. Add the ginger and garlic and stir-fry for 1 minute more. Remove to a bowl and cover to keep warm.

Add the coconut milk, curry base, and brown sugar to the pan and return to medium-high heat. Bring to a boil, whisking until thoroughly mixed. Reduce the heat to medium and simmer for 5 minutes.

Drain the pasta and put in a large bowl or return to the pasta pot. Mix in a few tablespoons of the curry sauce just to moisten the pasta. Stir the vegetables into the remaining sauce.

Divide the pasta among plates and top with the vegetables and sauce. Sprinkle with the peanuts and cilantro or basil.

Makes 4 to 6 servings

Helping Hand: Look for Thai red curry base in large packets in the international aisle of most grocery stores. You can also use the red curry paste that's available in small jars, but use about half as much because it's twice as potent.

Nutrient Boost: To add protein to the meal, stir in 1 cup Tofu Bites (page 239) along with the ginger and garlic.

Vegetarian Sausage and Chard Lasagna

Like most lasagnas, this one has three basic parts: the sauce, the noodles, and the cheese. I use only two pans here to help save on cleanup. Vegetarian sausage and sautéed green chard lend tremendous flavor and make this lasagna worthy of company. Or if it's for the family, the dish should provide a couple days' worth of dinners or lunches.

3 tablespoons extra-virgin olive oil

2 large onions, finely chopped

6 cloves garlic, minced

1 bunch green chard (about 1½ pounds), stems removed, leaves coarsely chopped

½ cup dry white wine

1½ cups part-skim ricotta cheese, preferably organic

1 pasture-raised or organic egg

¾ cup grated imported Parmesan cheese

⅓ cup finely chopped fresh parsley

1½ teaspoons salt

¾ teaspoon ground black pepper

1 pound frozen vegetarian sausage links (such as Boca Italian)

2 small carrots, finely chopped

2 cans (28 ounces each) whole tomatoes, drained

12 lasagna noodles, preferably whole grain

12 ounces shredded mozzarella cheese, preferably organic

Warm 1 tablespoon oil in a large, deep nonstick skillet over medium heat. Add 1 cup onion and 2 minced garlic cloves. Cook, stirring occasionally, just until the onion is soft, about 4 minutes. Add the chard and cook just until the chard is barely wilted, 2 to 3 minutes. Pour in the wine, cover, and cook for 3 minutes. Uncover and cook until the chard is soft and the liquid is mostly evaporated, 3 minutes. Transfer the mixture to a large bowl and let cool slightly. Stir in the ricotta, egg, ½ cup Parmesan, 2 tablespoons parsley, ½ teaspoon salt, and ¼ teaspoon pepper.

Return the skillet to medium heat. Add 3 tablespoons water and the frozen sausage links. Cover and cook until the sausage is defrosted, 4 to 5 minutes. Uncover and add 1 tablespoon of the remaining oil, turning to coat the sausage. Cook, turning the sausage occasionally, until browned all over, about 5 minutes. Transfer to a cutting board. When cool enough to handle, finely chop.

Return the skillet to medium heat and add the remaining 1 tablespoon oil. When hot, add the carrots and the remaining onion and garlic. Cook just until the onion is soft, about 4 minutes. Add the tomatoes, crushing them with the back of a spoon. Add the remaining 1 teaspoon salt and ½ teaspoon pepper. Simmer, crushing any large chunks with the spoon, until thick, 20 to 30 minutes. Stir in the remaining parsley.

Preheat the oven to 375°F. Lightly oil a 13" × 9" baking dish.

Cook the lasagna noodles in a large pot of boiling salted water until tender yet fairly firm in the center, about 10 minutes (the noodles will get more tender in the oven). Spread a thin layer of the tomato sauce in the bottom of the dish. Top with a layer of 3 noodles arranged lengthwise in the dish. Spread with one-third of the ricotta and one-quarter of the mozzarella. Top with about 1 cup of the tomato sauce and one-third of the sausage. Add another layer of noodles. Continue layering in the same manner until all the ingredients are used, ending with a top layer of noodles, tomato sauce, the remaining mozzarella and the remaining Parmesan (there should be a total of four layers of noodles).

Bake until the top is browned and bubbly, about 45 minutes. Let stand 15 minutes before serving.

Makes about 10 servings

Helping Hands: Sometimes canned tomatoes have rather tough cores. Check a few in the can you have. If they look tough at the stem end (where the brownish core is), cut off the core end. Or, if you're a hands-on person, pull the cores out: Hold each tomato over the skillet by the large end. Pinch off the stem end with your fingers and pull out the center core along with it, letting any juice fall into the skillet. This method removes more seeds and most of the core, leaving only the sweet tomato flesh.

If you find a brand of loose vegetarian sausage that you like, use that instead and skip the chopping step.

Reserve the chard stems for another use or serve alongside this dish. They're terrific sautéed or braised with a little chicken or vegetable broth, salt, and pepper.

Macaroni in Butternut Sauce

Here's one of my favorite fall casseroles. It has all the oven-baked comforts of macaroni and cheese, but the sauce is made with pureed butternut squash. Serve this with a side dish of warm stewed tomatoes.

12 ounces elbow macaroni, preferably whole grain

1 small butternut squash, peeled, seeded, and chopped (about 3 cups)

¼ cup nutritional yeast flakes

3 tablespoons light miso

2 tablespoons tahini (sesame paste)

2 teaspoons Dijon mustard

¼ teaspoon curry powder

¼ teaspoon salt

⅛ teaspoon ground black pepper

½–¾ cup organic 2% milk or soymilk

2 tablespoons seasoned dry bread crumbs

1 tablespoon organic butter, cut into small pieces (optional)

Cook the macaroni in a pot of boiling salted water until just tender yet slightly firm in the center, about 10 minutes.

Meanwhile, place the squash in a steamer basket set over simmering water. Cover and steam until the squash is very soft, about 15 minutes. Transfer to a food processor. Add the yeast flakes, miso, and tahini. Process until smooth. Add the mustard, curry powder, salt, and pepper and blend again. Blend in enough milk to make a sauce the consistency of very thick soup.

Preheat the oven to 375°F.

Drain the pasta and transfer to a large bowl. Pour the sauce over top. Mix thoroughly and then scrape into a 1½-quart baking dish. Sprinkle evenly with the bread crumbs and dot with the butter pieces (if using).

Bake until the top is lightly browned, 15 to 20 minutes. For an extra-crunchy topping, run the casserole under the broiler for a minute or two.

Makes 6 to 8 servings

Helping Hands: To easily peel butternut squash, prick it several times with a fork and microwave on high until the skin is tender, about 2 minutes.

Nutritional yeast flakes are available in most natural food stores. They melt into this sauce and lend it a cheeselike flavor. They also add a fair amount of protein, calcium, iron, and B vitamins.

For Baby: After pureeing the squash, nutritional yeast flakes, miso, and tahini, scoop out a few spoonfuls to feed your little one. Proceed with the recipe as directed.

JOHN PETERSON
Farming Biodynamically at Angelic Organics

By age 9, John Peterson was milking and feeding the cows on his family's farm in Caledonia, Illinois. This was a big promotion from the poultry chores he'd been doing since he was just old enough to wield a shovel.

The Peterson family farm expanded during the intensive agriculture boom of the 1950s and 1960s. The small farm had its financial ups and downs, nearly closing for good in the early 1980s. John took the remaining land and started over with a new approach. He wanted to farm in a way that would invigorate the soil rather than rely on crop chemicals and petroleum-based fertilizers.

In 1990, John started farming organically, but he prefers the term "biodynamic" to describe his 50-acre operation. "I don't like the word organic," he explains. "We were certified organic several years back, but now USDA certification is geared toward the bigger players in industrial agriculture." Focusing on quality rather than quantity, John's system of biodynamic agriculture goes beyond current U.S. Department of Agriculture standards for organic production. Rather than just avoid synthetic substances, he aims to stimulate the soil's biological activity with specially prepared compost.

John approaches his farm as a total system linking nature, food, and humans together in a dynamic cycle of production and consumption. With that in mind, he opened Angelic Organics in 1993 to help integrate his regional Illinois community into the farm. Today, Angelic Organics is one of the largest CSA (community supported agriculture) operations in the country, serving more than 1,000 members. Every week, the healthy, organic food from John's farm feeds nearly 3,000 people in the greater Chicago area.

As with other CSAs, members of Angelic Organics make a preseason payment and then receive a weekly box of farm-fresh food throughout the growing season. "It's pretty clear that people want this kind of personal connection to their food," says John. "We're 2 hours from Chicago, yet we regularly get 200 to 300 people at our open house events."

To help foster this connection, John established the CSA Learning Center, a clearinghouse of information that educates the public about local land and its food. In 1999, the King of Uganda and his prime minister visited the farm and Learning Center to find out more about biodynamic and organic agricultural methods. To access the Learning Center or learn more about Angelic Organics, go to the Learning Center's Web site at www.csalearningcenter.org or the Angelic Organics Web site at www.angelicorganics.com.

To find the nearest CSA in your area, see the Local Harvest Web site at www.localharvest.org.

Nell Newman's Spicy Raisin Walnut Bread

You'll be surprised how good this bread is without any eggs or butter. It makes a wonderful snack or breakfast bread. The aroma of cinnamon, nutmeg, cloves, and allspice (not to mention a little brewed coffee) are sure to open your sleepy eyes.

2 cups whole grain pastry flour or unbleached all-purpose flour

4 teaspoons baking powder

½ teaspoon salt

1 teaspoon ground cinnamon

½ teaspoon grated nutmeg

½ teaspoon ground cloves

½ teaspoon ground allspice

1 cup packed brown sugar

½ cup molasses

¾ cup organic 2% milk

¼ cup very strong brewed coffee

2 cups raisins

2 cups chopped walnuts

Preheat the oven to 350°F. Coat a 9" × 5" loaf pan with cooking spray.

In a large bowl, mix together the flour, baking powder, salt, cinnamon, nutmeg, cloves, and allspice.

In a small bowl, mix together the brown sugar, molasses, milk, and coffee. Stir into the flour mixture just until moistened. Stir in the raisins and walnuts.

Scrape into the prepared pan and bake until the top is browned and a toothpick inserted in the center comes out clean, about 45 to 50 minutes. Cool in the pan for 10 minutes. Remove from the pan and cool completely on a rack.

Makes 12 servings

Helping Hand: To save time, replace the spices with 2½ teaspoons apple pie spice or pumpkin pie spice. To make a vegan version of this cake (no animal products), use soymilk instead of cow's milk.

Whole Grain Banana Walnut Muffins

Perfect for the kids' lunch box or as an after-school treat, these moist mini muffins make good snacking anytime. Of course, they're delish at breakfast, too.

2 cups unbleached all-purpose flour or whole grain pastry flour

1 teaspoon baking powder

1 teaspoon baking soda

½ teaspoon salt

½ cup unsalted organic butter, at room temperature

½ cup packed brown sugar

2 pasture-raised or organic eggs

1⅓ cups mashed ripe bananas

¼ cup organic 2% milk

1½ teaspoons vanilla extract

1 cup chopped walnuts

Preheat the oven to 375°F. Coat thirty-six 1¾" muffin cups with cooking spray.

In a large bowl, mix the flour, baking powder, baking soda, and salt.

In another bowl, using an electric mixer, beat the butter and sugar until light and fluffy. Beat in the eggs. Stir in the bananas, milk, and vanilla. Add the dry ingredients and stir just to combine. Stir in the walnuts.

Spoon the batter into the prepared muffin cups. Bake until a toothpick inserted in a muffin comes out clean, about 15 minutes. Cool in the pans for 5 minutes. Transfer the muffins to racks to finish cooling.

Makes 36 mini muffins

Helping Hands: To make standard-size muffins, replace the mini-muffin pans with two 12-cup muffin pans and increase the baking slightly.

To freeze these muffins, cool completely and freeze in a resealable freezer bag. Reheat at 350°F for 10 minutes, or until heated through.

For Baby: Before stirring in the walnuts, fill a few muffin cups with the plain batter. Then stir the walnuts into the remaining batter. Let the baby nosh on the nut-free muffins.

Oatmeal Pecan Pancakes

My family tends to like hearty rather than fluffy pancakes. We toss in nuts, oats, fruit, or almost anything you'd put into trail mix. We've tried hundreds of pancakes over the years, and these are the all-time favorite. They're sweet and filling, and they fire you up for the day's activities.

1¼ cups unbleached all-purpose flour or whole grain pastry flour

1 cup old-fashioned rolled oats

¾ cup coarsely chopped pecans

⅓ cup packed brown sugar

1 tablespoon baking powder

1 teaspoon salt

1 pasture-raised or organic egg, slightly beaten

1½ cups organic milk or soymilk

1 tablespoon GMO-free canola oil

In a large bowl, whisk together the flour, oats, pecans, brown sugar, baking powder, and salt. Set aside.

In a medium bowl, whisk together the egg, milk, and oil. Pour into the dry ingredients and stir just until moistened, leaving a few lumps (the batter will thicken as it stands).

Coat a nonstick griddle with a little oil or cooking spray and heat over medium heat. When hot, drop the batter by half-cupfuls onto the griddle and cook until the edges begin to look dry and the bottom is golden, about 2 minutes. Flip and cook until golden on the other side, 1 to 2 minutes.

Makes nine 5" pancakes

Nutrient Boost: Serve these with fresh blueberry syrup to add a burst of flavor and cancer-fighting antioxidants. Put about ¼ cup fresh blueberries into a small gravy boat or bowl. Add ½ cup pure maple syrup and ⅛ teaspoon cinnamon. Microwave on high for 15 to 20 seconds, or just until warmed through.

Pineapple Orange Cookies

Simple and sunny-tasting, these cookies make good company with a cup of tea. If you prefer to replace the flavor extract with flavor essences, which are more concentrated, adjust the amount to ¼ to ½ teaspoon.

2⅔ cups unbleached all-purpose flour or whole grain pastry flour

½ teaspoon baking soda

½ teaspoon salt

½ cup unsalted organic butter, at room temperature

1⅔ cups sugar

2 pasture-raised or organic eggs

2 teaspoons orange extract

½ cup canned crushed pineapple

Preheat the oven to 350°F. Coat a baking sheet with cooking spray.

In a medium bowl, mix together the flour, baking soda, and salt.

In a large bowl, using an electric mixer, beat the butter and sugar on medium until light, 1 to 2 minutes. Beat in the eggs and orange extract. Stir in the pineapple (with juice). Stir in the flour mixture until moistened.

Drop by teaspoonfuls onto the prepared baking sheet. Bake until golden, 12 to 15 minutes. Cool slightly on the baking sheet, then transfer to racks to finish cooling.

Makes about 5 dozen

White Chocolate Cookies with Pistachios and Cardamom

Here's an unusual and crisp-outside, gooey-inside cookie with some panache. The method was inspired by a "brownie drop" recipe from Maida Heatter, the queen of cookies. Look for good-quality white chocolate made with cocoa butter, not vegetable shortening. The chocolate should be creamy white rather than stark white. French and Swiss brands tend to be of higher quality. Or use Ghirardelli brand, which is widely available in grocery stores.

¼ cup unbleached all-purpose flour or whole grain pastry flour

¼ teaspoon baking powder

¼ teaspoon ground cardamom

⅛ teaspoon salt

8 ounces good-quality white chocolate, broken into pieces

1 tablespoon organic butter

¾ cup shelled pistachios

2 pasture-raised or organic eggs

¾ cup sugar

½ teaspoon vanilla extract

Preheat the oven to 350°F. Line two cookie sheets with parchment or foil.

In a small bowl, mix the flour, baking powder, cardamom, and salt.

Put the chocolate and butter in the top of a double boiler or in a metal bowl set over barely simmering water. Cover and let stand until melted, about 2 minutes. Stir until smooth. Remove the pan or bowl from the water and set aside until lukewarm to the touch. Drop the pistachios into the hot water and simmer for 3 minutes. Drain and rub the nuts in a kitchen towel to remove the skins. Chop and set aside.

In a medium bowl, using an electric mixer, beat the eggs on high until light, 1 to 2 minutes. Add the sugar and beat until the batter forms a slowly dissolving ribbon when the beaters are lifted, 4 minutes. Beat in the vanilla.

Beat in the cooled chocolate on low speed just until smooth. Stir in the dry ingredients just until blended. Stir in the pistachios.

Drop the batter by rounded teaspoonfuls about 1½" apart on the prepared cookie sheets. Bake until the tops are firm to the touch and just beginning to brown, yet the centers are moist, 10 to 12 minutes. Cool on the baking sheets for 1 minute. Carefully transfer to racks to finish cooling (the cookies will be delicate).

Makes about 3½ dozen

Food Lore: Cardamom is an Indian spice that grows in green pods the size of large raisins, each containing about 20 small black seeds. Used in Scandinavian, East Indian, and South American cooking, cardamom's spicy-sweet flavor works equally well in savory dishes and desserts. It can be used almost anywhere you might use cinnamon—in a curry or in apple pie, for instance. As with most spices, the whole spice has more flavor, but ground cardamom is readily available in the spice aisle of grocery stores.

Helping Hand: If you don't want to bother peeling the pistachio nuts, skip the boiling step and leave the skins on (the cookies will have bits of skin throughout). Or use macadamia nuts instead. They're available already peeled in jars in the nut aisle of most grocery stores. You'll need about ¾ cup chopped.

Mocha Pudding Cake

This gooey mess of a cake is a surefire hit with kids of all ages. The hot chocolate pudding rests under a thick blanket of moist mocha cake. For total decadence, scoop it into bowls and serve drizzled with heavy cream (or milk).

1 cup unbleached all-purpose flour or whole grain pastry flour

1 cup sugar

½ cup unsweetened cocoa powder

2 teaspoons baking powder

½ teaspoon baking soda

¼ teaspoon salt

Pinch of ground cinnamon

½ cup organic 2% milk

¼ cup GMO-free or organic canola oil

1 teaspoon vanilla extract

½ cup packed brown sugar

1 cup hot brewed coffee

Preheat the oven to 350°F. Coat a 10" deep-dish pie plate with oil spray.

In a large bowl, mix the flour, ¾ cup sugar, ¼ cup cocoa, the baking powder, baking soda, salt, and cinnamon. Stir in the milk, oil, and vanilla (the batter will be thick).

Spread in the prepared pie plate and sprinkle with the brown sugar, remaining ¼ cup sugar, and remaining ¼ cup cocoa. Pour the hot coffee over top.

Bake until the cake is set on top and the pudding starts to bubble up through the cake, 30 minutes. Cool in the pan for 10 minutes. Use a spoon to serve.

Makes 8 servings

Helping Hand: Use decaffeinated coffee, if you prefer. Or make Chocolate Pudding Cake by omitting the hot coffee and using hot water instead.

LYNN GOLDMAN
Unafraid of Unpopular Issues

Growing up near Galveston, Texas, Lynn Goldman, M.D., M.P.H., witnessed the destructiveness of pesticides firsthand. DDT, a persistent toxic chemical that was sprayed in her area to control mosquitoes, also killed off pelicans in Galveston Bay.

As she continued her professional work, a brief job at the Berkeley Free Clinic convinced Lynn that environment and health are inextricably linked. "I became aware that the environments we live in have a direct effect on our health," she says. That realization prompted her to study with Richard Garcia, a pioneer of integrated pest management (IPM) techniques as an alternative to harmful pesticides. Under Garcia's direction, Lynn uncovered a trail of deception surrounding U.S. Department of Agriculture programs that drenched the South with pesticides to eradicate fire ants. This work helped the budding researcher to chart her own course in the science of environmental health, long before it was a recognized medical specialty.

Like her father, who was an early researcher on breast milk's role in childhood immunity, Lynn became a pediatrician. And she became fearless about tackling unpopular subjects. Eventually, her contributions brought her to the Environmental Protection Agency, where she expanded right-to-know laws and helped pass the landmark Food Quality Protection Act (FQPA). Lynn believes that the FQPA will eventually eliminate the worst pesticides from food production. Under FQPA, several harmful pesticides are already being phased out, such as chlorpyrifos (Dursban) and Diazinon, both used in homes and on lawns, as well as certain harmful chemicals used on apples, peaches, and apricots.

"FQPA will help us to move away from pesticides," says Lynn, "especially the ones that have more risks for children." As a scientist, Lynn links neurotoxic pesticides to several current health problems among children, including rising asthma rates, stunted growth, and impaired mental development. She also suspects that new research will continue to make the link between early exposure to pesticides and the development of cancer.

As cochair of Generation Green, Lynn focuses on what's doable for protecting children's health. She says that we can make choices to limit pesticide exposure, just as we can limit other threats. For instance, we can decide not to smoke. Likewise, we can reduce pesticide exposure by putting safe food on the table. "Most parents can't control the EPA," she admits, "but they can control the marketplace by making smart food choices. That's where parents have a lot of power." Lynn is currently professor of environmental health sciences at the Johns Hopkins Bloomberg School of Public Health in Baltimore. She also serves as chair of the Children's Environmental Health Network.

Lemon Herb Cornmeal Cake with Macerated Berries

Make this cake in the late spring or early summer, when fresh berries are in season. It's light, flavorful, and absolutely gorgeous with multicolored berries mounded in the center.

1½ cups cake flour

1 cup stone-ground organic yellow cornmeal

2 teaspoons baking powder

½ teaspoon salt

½ cup unsalted organic butter, at room temperature

2¼ cups sugar

2 pasture-raised or organic eggs

¼ cup chopped fresh basil

¼ cup chopped fresh mint

2 tablespoon grated organic lemon zest

2 teaspoons vanilla extract

1 cup organic buttermilk

¾ cup water

3 tablespoons raspberry vinegar

⅛ teaspoon ground cinnamon

3 pints mixed berries

2 tablespoons confectioners' sugar

Preheat the oven to 375°F. Generously butter an 8- to 9-cup tube pan or Bundt pan and lightly dust with flour.

In a medium bowl, mix together the flour, cornmeal, baking powder, and salt.

Put the butter and 1½ cups sugar in a large bowl. Using an electric mixer, beat on medium until light and fluffy, 3 to 4 minutes. Beat in the eggs, basil, mint, lemon zest, and vanilla. Beat in the flour mixture alternately with the buttermilk until the batter is smooth. Pour in the prepared pan and bake for 30 to 35 minutes, or until a toothpick inserted in the center comes out clean. Cool on a rack for 10 minutes. Invert onto the rack and shake the cake loose from the pan. Cool completely on the rack. When cool, carefully transfer to a cake plate.

Meanwhile, put the remaining ¾ cup sugar in a medium saucepan over medium-high heat. Stir in the water, vinegar, and cinnamon, stirring until the sugar is dissolved. Bring to a boil, then reduce the heat to medium and simmer until slightly thickened, 4 to 6 minutes. Remove from the heat and let cool to room temperature.

Put the berries in a medium bowl (hull any strawberries and quarter them if large). Pour the syrup over the berries, mix gently, and let macerate at room temperature for 1 to 2 hours.

Mound the berries in the center and around the sides of the cake. Sift the confectioners' sugar over the top of the cake. Serve drizzled with any remaining syrup.

Makes 12 servings

RECIPE FOR CHANGE

Healthy eating is not just a matter of making good personal choices. It also depends on policies set by government officials. These policies consider questions like: Should foods made with genetically modified organisms be labeled? Should schools be allowed to sell irradiated meat without informing parents? What should be the allowable level of pesticide residues on produce? And the list goes on. As a citizen, you have the right to be informed and involved as your government officials answer these questions and make decisions that will impact the healthfulness of the foods you and your family eat. Here's a recipe to help make sure you are a part of the decision-making process.

Several informed citizens

A few handfuls of collective power

One coordinated action

To have every opinion heard, informed citizens can take individual actions such as writing to your representatives in Congress.

To multiply that power, combine all of the above ingredients so that individual actions are heard collectively. When this happens, you are no longer a lone voice but part of a movement.

Joining an organization with the same concerns that you have can help to make sure that public policies represent your interests and meet your needs. Such organizations keep you informed about important issues at the critical times they need to be addressed. Such organizations pool the energies of their members so that companies and government decision makers have to listen.

Generation Green is one such organization—one that puts concerns for your family's health, especially your kids—first on the priority list. Generation Green is also allied with a number of environmental, children's health, and other organizations that may speak to your specific interests. To stay informed sign up to receive *Fresh Choices Quarterly* at freshchoices@generationgreen.org or call 800-652-0827.

Ecofriendly Food Sources

If your grocery store doesn't carry something you're looking for, talk to the department manager about getting it in. Point him or her in the direction of the suppliers listed below. Or have items shipped right to your door by contacting suppliers who take direct orders. For even more ecofriendly food sources, visit www.villageorganics.com/organicmarket.html.

FRUIT

Big B's
Hotchkiss, Colorado
800-348-0167
www.freshapplecider.com
Juices and ciders; available nationwide and via direct order

Boxed Greens
Tempe, Arizona
480-557-7060 or 888-588-8107
www.boxedgreens.com
Seasonal fruits; available via direct order

Diamond Organics
Freedom, California
888-674-2642
www.diamondorganics.com
Fresh and dried fruit; available nationwide and via direct order

Earthbound Farm
San Juan Bautista, California
800-690-3200
www.ebfarm.com
Fresh and dried fruit; available nationwide

Fiddler's Green Farm
800-729-7935
www.fiddlersgreenfarm.com
Dried fruit; available via direct order

Jerzy Boyz Farm
Chelan, Washington
509-682-6269
www.jerzyboyz.com
Apples, pears; available locally or nationwide via direct order

Lakewood
www.lakewoodjuices.com
Juice; available nationwide

Melissa's/World Variety Produce
Los Angeles, California
800-588-0151
www.melissas.com
Specialty fruits; available nationwide and via direct order

Organic Edibles
Brandon, Florida
813-654-4636
www.americanorganics.net
Citrus fruits; available via direct order

Rocky Mountain Fruit
Hotchkiss, Colorado
877-586-5417
www.rockymountainfruit.com
Apples, pears; available via direct order

S. Martinelli & Company
Watsonville, California
800-662-1868
www.martinellis.com
Juice; available nationwide and via direct order

Small Planet Foods
Sedro-Woolley, Washington
800-624-4123
www.muirglen.com
Frozen fruits, fruit spreads, juice concentrates; available nationwide

Walnut Acres
New Rochelle, New York
www.walnutacres.com
Juices, sauces, snacks; available nationwide

VEGETABLES

Amy's Kitchen
Petaluma, California
707-578-7188
www.amys.com
Bean chili, pasta sauce, soup, vegetable dishes, veggie burgers; available nationwide in stores and via direct order (Amy's itself does not sell direct to the consumer, but various other sites do sell the products)

Boxed Greens
Tempe, Arizona
480-557-7060 or 888-588-8107
www.boxedgreens.com
Seasonal vegetables; available via direct order

Diamond Organics
Freedom, California
888-674-2642
www.diamondorganics.com
Fresh and cultured vegetables, salad mix; available nationwide and via direct order

Earthbound Farm
San Juan Bautista, California
800-690-3200
www.ebfarm.com
Vegetables, salad mixes; available nationwide

Eden Foods
Clinton, Michigan
888-441-3336
www.edenfoods.com
Ginger, lentils, mushrooms, radishes, tomatoes; available nationwide

Hain-Celestial Group
Garden City, New York
www.hain-celestial.com
Soups, vegetable dishes,
vegetable chips, other vegetarian
products; brands available
nationwide

Maine Coast Sea Vegetables
Franklin, Maine
207-565-2907
www.seaveg.com
Ocean/sea vegetables; available
via direct order

Melissa's/World Variety
Produce
Los Angeles, California
800-588-0151
www.melissas.com
Specialty vegetables; available
nationwide and via direct order

Ready Pac Produce
Irwindale, California
800-800-7822
www.readypacproduce.com
Organic salad mixes; available
nationwide

Rocky Mountain Fruit
Hotchkiss, Colorado
877-586-5417
www.rockymountainfruit.com
Garlic; available via direct order

Small Planet Foods
Sedro-Woolley, Washington
800-624-4123
www.muirglen.com
Frozen vegetables,
tomatoes/tomato sauces;
available nationwide

Walnut Acres
New Rochelle, New York
www.walnutacres.com
Salsas, sauces, soups; available
nationwide

Whole Foods
Austin, Texas
512-477-4455
www.wholefoodsmarket.com
Canned, fresh, and frozen
vegetables; available via their
stores nationwide

Wild Oats
Boulder, Colorado
800-494-9453
www.wildoats.com
Canned, fresh, and frozen
vegetables; foods available via
their stores nationwide

FISH AND SHELLFISH

Alaska Wild Salmon Company
Juneau, Arkansas
866-463-3458
www.alaskawildsalmoncompany.com
Salmon; available nationwide via
direct order

Crown Prince
Petaluma, California
707-766-8575
www.crownprince.com
Abalone, anchovies, clams,
crabmeat, kippers, mackerel,
oysters, salmon, sardines, shrimp;
available worldwide

EcoFish
Portsmouth, New Hampshire
603-430-0101
www.ecofish.com
Bass, cod, crab, halibut, mahimahi, mussels, prawns, salmon,
scallops, trout, tuna; available
nationwide through distributors
to natural food stores,
restaurants, and caterers

Mary Lu Seafoods
Crescent City, California
707-458-9629
www.maryluseafoods.com
Albacore tuna; available in
California, Oregon, and Wisconsin
stores and via direct order

Permian Sea Shrimp Co.
Imperial, Texas
915-536-2216 or 915-536-2280
www.permianseashrimp.com
Shrimp; distributed primarily in
Texas but wholesale/retail and
shipping information are available

Raincoast Trading
British Columbia, Canada
604-582-8268
www.raincoasttrading.com
Salmon, tuna; available
nationwide and in Canada via
various distributors

Taku Wild Products
British Columbia, Canada
888-551-8258
www.takuwild.com
Salmon; available in the United
States via direct order

CHICKEN AND TURKEY

Eberly Poultry
Stevens, Pennsylvania
717-336-6440
www.eberlypoultry.com
Capon, chicken, cornish game hen,
duck, goose, guinea hen, partridge,
quail, turkey; available nationwide

Hills Foods
British Columbia, Canada
604-472-1500
www.hillsfoods.com
Canard, chicken, duck, goose,
ostrich/emu/rhea, partridge,
pheasant, quail, squab, turkey;
available worldwide

Homestead Healthy Food
Fredericksburg, Texas
888-861-5670
www.homesteadhealthyfoods.com
Chicken; available nationwide via
direct order

Oaklyn Plantation
Darlington, South Carolina
843-395-0793
www.freerangechicken.com
Chicken; available in South
Carolina and nationwide via
direct order

Organic Valley
LaFarge, Wisconsin
608-625-2600 or 888-444-6455
www.organicvalley.com
Chicken, turkey; available
nationwide

Petaluma Poultry
Petaluma, California
707-763-1904 or 800-556-6789
www.healthychickenchoices.com
Chicken; available nationwide

Shelton's Poultry
Pomona, California
909-623-4361
www.sheltons.com
Chicken, turkey; available
nationwide and some products
available via direct order

Stonewood Farm
Orwell, Vermont
802-948-2277
www.stonewoodfarm.com
Turkey; available year-round in
Vermont, New Hampshire, and
New York, in several other states
during Thanksgiving, and
nationwide via direct order

Van Wie Natural Foods
Hudson, New York
518-828-0533
www.vanwienaturalmeats.com
Chicken, duck, pheasant, turkey;
available nationwide via direct
order

Wise Kosher Natural Poultry
Brooklyn, New York
718-596-0400
http://wisekosher.com
Chicken, turkey; available in
several states and nationwide via
direct order

BEEF AND PORK

American Grass Fed Beef
Doniphan, Missouri
573-996-3716 or 866-255-5002
www.americangrassfedbeef.com
Beef; available nationwide via
direct order

American Pasturage
Marionville, Missouri
417-258-2394
http://americanpasturage.com
Beef/veal, lamb; available
nationwide via direct order

Coleman Natural Meats
Denver, Colorado
800-442-8666
www.colemannatural.com
Beef, lamb; available nationwide

Double Diamond Ranch
Baker City, Oregon
541-853-2352
Beef, lamb; available via mail
order

Earthwise Organic Beef
www.earthwiseorganicbeef.com
Beef; available nationwide and
via direct order

Green Circle Organics
Washington, Virginia
540-675-2627
www.greencircle.com
Beef; available nationwide
through network of ranchers

Hebrew National
Hudson, Wisconsin
800-275-5454
www.hebrewnational.com
Beef hot dogs; available
nationwide

Hills Foods
British Columbia, Canada
604-472-1500
www.hillsfoods.com
Alligator, beef, boar, buffalo,
caribou, elk, frog, muskox,
rabbit, rattlesnake, turtle,
venison; available worldwide

Laura's Lean Beef
Lexington, Kentucky
800-487-5326
www.laurasleanbeef.com
Beef; available nationwide

Maher Meats
Emmons, Minnesota
507-297-5097
Pork; available nationwide via
direct order

Maverick Ranch
Denver, Colorado
303-294-0146
www.maverickranch.com
Beef, buffalo, pork; available
nationwide

Montana Legend
Roberts, Montana
406-445-2700 or 800-838-5657
www.naturalmeatsmontana.com
Beef; available nationwide via
direct order and at selected stores

Morgan Ranch
Burwell, Nebraska
308-346-4394
www.morganranchinc.com
Beef; available nationwide and
via direct order

Mosher Products
Cheyenne, Wyoming
307-632-1492
www.wheatandgrain.com
Buffalo; available via direct order

Niman Ranch
Oakland, California
510-808-0330
www.nimanranch.com
Beef, lamb, pork; available
nationwide and via direct order

Organic Valley
LaFarge, Wisconsin
888-444-6455
www.organicvalley.com
Beef, pork; available nationwide

Rancher's Choice
Grand Prairie, Texas
972-606-1718 or 877-606-1718
www.rancherschoice
naturalmeats.com
Beef, pork; available nationwide
and via direct order

Roseland Organic Farms
West Cassopolis, Michigan
616-445-8769
www.roselandorganicfarms.com
Beef; available primarily in
Michigan and Indiana but also
available nationwide via direct
order

Tiensvold Farms
Rushville, Nebraska
308-327-3135
www.eatorganicbuffalo.com
Buffalo; available via direct order

Van Wie Natural Foods
Hudson, New York
518-828-0533
www.vanwienaturalmeats.com
Beef, buffalo, goat, lamb, pork,
rabbit; available nationwide via
direct order

Walnut Creek Organic Ranch
Deweese, Nebraska
402-262-2245
www.walnutcreekorganicranch.com
Beef; available nationwide via
direct order

MILK, CHEESE, AND EGGS

ORGANIC

Horizon Organic Dairy
Boulder, Colorado
888-494-3020
www.horizonorganic.com
Milk, chocolate milk, cream, whipped cream, yogurt, cheese, butter, sour cream, cottage cheese, cream cheese; available nationwide

Alta Dena Organics
City of Industry, California
800-MILK123 or 800-535-1369
Available nationwide

Morningland Dairy Cheese
Mountain View, Missouri
417-469-3817
Available nationwide and by mail order

Stonyfield Farms (organic line)
Londonderry, New Hampshire
603-437-4040
Yogurt and ice cream; available nationwide

Cascadian Farm
Sedro-Wooley, Washington
800-624-4123
www.cfarm.com/cfarm/default.asp
Frozen yogurt, ice cream; available nationwide

Organic Valley
LaFarge, Wisconsin
608-625-2600 or 888-444-6455
www.organicvalley.com
Milk, cheese, butter, cream cheese, cottage cheese, sour cream, cream, powdered milk; available nationwide

Wisconsin Organics
Bonduel, Wisconsin
715-758-2280
Milk, cheese, butter; available nationwide and at their own retail store in Bonduel

rBGH-FREE

Alta Dena
City of Industry, California
800-MILK123 or 800-535-1369
Milk, buttermilk, chocolate milk, eggnog, cream, sour cream, yogurt, natural select butter, ice cream, cottage cheese, and all cheeses except for cream cheese; available nationwide

Brown Cow Farm
Antioch, California
925-757-9209
www.browncowfarm.com
Yogurt and milk; available nationwide

Kate's Homemade Butter
Old Orchard Beach, Maine
207-934-5134
Available nationwide

Land O Lakes' Original
Arden Hills, Minnesota
651-481-2222 or 800-328-4155
Milk; available nationwide

Lifetime Dairy
Lifeline Food Co.
Seaside, California
831-899-5040
www.lifetimefatfree.com
Cheese; available nationwide

Stonyfield Farms
Londonderry, New Hampshire
800-PRO-COWS (776-2697)
www.stonyfield.com
Yogurt, frozen yogurt, ice cream; available nationwide

Biazzo Dairy Products
Riverfield, New Jersey
201-941-6800
www.biazzo.com
Cheese; available nationwide

Ben & Jerry's Ice Cream
S. Burlington, Vermont
802-846-1500
www.benjerry.com/ca/
Available nationwide

Franklin County Cheese
Enosburg Falls, Vermont
802-933-4338 or 800-933-6114
www.franklinfoods.com
Distributors of Bagel Factory, Shaw's, and Bruegger's Bagels cream cheese—available in eastern United States; All Seasons Kitchen and Lombardi's cream cheese and mascarpone and Vermont Butter and Cheese mascarpone—available nationwide

Crowley Cheese of Vermont
Healdville, Vermont
802-259-2340 or 800-683-2602
www.crowleycheese-vermont.com
Available nationwide and by mail order

Grafton Village Cheese
Grafton, Vermont
802-843-2221
www.graftonvillagecheese.com
Available nationwide and by mail order

Shelburne Farms Farmhouse Cheddar Cheese
Shelburne, Vermont
802-985-8686
www.shelburnefarms.org
Available nationwide, by mail order, and at their own farm-site store

Family Farms Defenders
Madison, Wisconsin
608-260-0900
Cheese; available in Madison, WI, and nationwide by mail order

North Farm Cooperative
Madison, Wisconsin
800-236-5880 or 608-241-2667
www.northfarm-coop.com
Cheese; available nationwide and by mail order

Salemville Cheese
DCI Cheese Company
Madison, Wisconsin
920-387-5740 or 800-782-0741
Nationwide and by mail order

Beans and Grains

ORGANIC

Arrowhead Mills
Garden City, New York
800-434-4246
www.arrowheadmills.com
Bread mixes, flours, nut butters,
beans, grains, rice; available
nationwide

Cibaria International
Rancho Cucamonga, California
909-941-8142
www.cibaria-intl.com
Canola oil; distributed
nationwide and available via
direct order

Hodgson Mill
Effingham, Illinois
800-347-0105
www.hodgsonmill.com
Bread mixes, cereals, cornmeal,
flaxseed products, soy products;
available nationwide and via
direct order

Nasoya/Vitasoy USA
Ayer, Massachusetts
800-VITASOY (800-848-2769)
www.nasoya.com
Tofu; available nationwide

Nature's Path
British Columbia, Canada
888-808-9505
www.naturespath.com
Cereals, breads, waffles; available
nationwide

New England Natural Bakers
Greenfield, Massachusetts
413-772-2239
www.nenb.com
Cereals, nuts, seeds; available
nationwide

Seeds of Change
Santa Fe, New Mexico
888-762-4240
www.seedsofchange.com
Beans, grains, rice; available
nationwide and via direct order

U.S. Mills
Needham, Massachusetts
781-444-0440
www.usmillsinc.com
Cereal; available nationwide

Wild Oats
Boulder, Colorado
800-494-WILD (800-494-9453)
www.wildoats.com
Bread, grains, nuts, pastas,
soybeans, soymilk, tofu; available
nationwide

Wildwood Natural Foods
Watsonville, California
800-499-TOFU (800-499-8638)
www.wildwoodnaturalfoods.com
Soymilk, soyogurt, tofu, tempeh;
available nationwide

GMO-FREE

Arrowhead Mills
Garden City, New York
800-434-4246
www.arrowheadmills.com
Cereals; available nationwide

Barbara's Bakery
Petaluma, California
707-765-2273
www.barbarasbakery.com
Cereals, cookies, crackers;
available nationwide

Catania Spagna Corporation
Ayer, Massachusetts
978-772-7900 or 800-343-5522
www.cataniausa.com
Canola and soybean oils;
available nationwide

Eden Foods
Clinton, Michigan
888-441-EDEN (888-441-3336)
www.edenfoods.com
Beans, blue cornmeal, miso,
quinoa, rice, sesame oil,
soybeans, soymilk; available
nationwide

Fiddler's Green Farm
Maine
800-729-7935
www.fiddlersgreenfarm.com
Baking mixes, cereals, cornmeal,
stone-ground grains; distributed
nationwide and available via
direct order

French Meadow Bakery
Minneapolis, Minnesota
612-870-4740 and 877-669-3278
www.frenchmeadow.com
Café/store in Minneapolis and
shipped nationwide

Nature's Path
British Columbia, Canada
888-808-9505
www.naturespath.com
Cereals, breads, waffles; available
nationwide

New England Natural Bakers
Greenfield, Massachusetts
413-772-2239
www.nenb.com
Cereals; available nationwide

Shiloh Farms
Sulphur Springs, Arizona
800-362-6832
http://users.nwark.com/~shilohf/
Breads; distributed nationwide
and available via direct order

Wild Oats
Boulder, Colorado
800-494-9453
www.wildoats.com
Down to Earth cereals; available
nationwide

Note: For more information
on GMO-free products, visit
www.truefoodnow.org/gmo_facts/
product_list

Pasta and Flour

ORGANIC PASTA, BREAD, AND FLOUR

Annie's Homegrown
Wakefield, Massachusetts
781-224-9639
www.annies.com
Pastas; available nationwide

Crystal Organics
Malad, Ohio
www.crystalorganics.bigstep.com
Bread/muffin mixes, flours;
available via direct order

Fiddler's Green Farm
Maine
800-729-7935
www.fiddlersgreenfarm.com
Muffin, biscuit, cookie, and cake
mixes; distributed nationwide
and available via direct order

French Meadow Bakery
Minneapolis, Minnesota
612-870-4740 and
877-669-3278
www.frenchmeadow.com
Café/store in Minneapolis;
breads shipped nationwide

Mrs. Leeper's Pasta
Poway, California
858-486-1101
www.mrsleeperspasta.com
Organic soy and semolina pasta;
available nationwide

Pasta USA
Spokane, Washington
800-456-2084
www.pastausa.com
Earth & Life brand pasta;
available nationwide

Pasta Valente
Charlottesville, Virginia
888-575-7670
www.pastavalente.com
Pastas; available via direct order

Silver Hills Bakery
British Columbia, Canada
604-850-5600
www.silverhillsbakery.ca
Sprouted-grain breads, bagels;
available in various locations in
the United States and Canada,
and via direct order

Sobaya
Québec, Canada
www.sobaya.ca
Japanese udon and soba noodles;
available throughout the United
States and Canada

Vital Vittles
Berkeley, California
510-644-2022
www.vitalvittles.com
Organic/kosher breads, rolls,
sweets; available via direct order

*GMO-FREE PASTA,
BREAD, AND WHEAT
FLOUR*

Alvarado Street Bakery
Rohnert Park, California
707-585-3293
www.alvaradostreetbakery.com
Breads, buns, rolls, pizza bread,
tortillas; available nationwide

Eden Foods
Clinton, Michigan
888-441-3336
www.edenfoods.com
Flour, pasta, rice pasta; available
nationwide

Pacific Bakery
Oceanside, California
760-757-6020
www.pacificbakery.com
Breads, bagels; available
nationwide and via direct order

*WHOLE-GRAIN PASTA,
BREAD, AND WHEAT
FLOUR*

Bob's Red Mill
Milwaukie, Oregon
800-349-2173
www.bobsredmill.com
Bread/muffin mixes, bulk grains,
flours; available nationwide and
via direct order

Hodgson Mill
Effingham, Illinois
800-347-0105
www.hodgsonmill.com
Flaxseed pastas, wheat pastas,
flours; available nationwide and
via direct order

Mrs. Leeper's Pasta
Poway, California
858-486-1101
www.mrsleeperspasta.com
Whole-wheat pasta; available
nationwide

Sobaya
Québec, Canada
www.sobaya.ca
Japanese udon and soba noodles;
available throughout the United
States and Canada

Sources and Further Reading

Here are the books, reports, organizations, and Web sites that inspired us to write this book. Specific sources for each chapter appear below, followed by further reading suggestions. To access some of these reports online, find updated Web site links, and see a list of children's books with environmental themes, visit the Generation Green Web site at www.generationgreen.org/cookbookresources or get in touch at freshchoices@generationgreen.org or 800-652-0827.

Sources by Chapter

CHAPTER 1: FROM FARM TO FORK

BENEFITS OF ORGANIC FOOD

Aro, A., et al. 2000. Inverse association between dietary and serum conjugated linoleic acid and risk of breast cancer in postmenopausal women. *Nutrition and Cancer* 38(2): 151–157.

Asami, D. K., et al. 2003. Comparison of the total phenolic and ascorbic acid content of freeze-dried and air-dried marionberry, strawberry, and corn grown using conventional, organic, and sustainable agricultural practices. *Journal of Agricultural and Food Chemistry* 51(5): 1237–1241.

Baker, B. P., et al. 2002. Pesticide residues in conventional integrated pest management grown and organic foods: insights from three data sets. *Food Additives and Contaminants* 19(5): 427–446.

Banni, C. S., et al. 1999. Conjugated linoleic acid-enriched butter fat alters mammary gland morphogenesis and reduces cancer risk in rats. *Journal of Nutrition* 129(12): 2135–2142.

Baxter, G. J., et al. 2001. "Salicylic acid in soups prepared from organically and nonorganically grown vegetables. *European Journal of Nutrition* 40(6): 289–292.

Blankson, H., et al. 2002. Conjugated linoleic acid reduces body fat mass in overweight and obese humans. *Journal of Nutrition* 130: 2943–2948.

Brandt, K., and J. P. Molgaard. 2001. Organic agriculture: does it enhance or reduce the nutritional value of plant foods? *Journal of the Science of Food and Agriculture* 81: 924–931.

Curl, C. L., et al. 2003. Organophosphorus pesticide exposure of urban and suburban preschool children with organic and conventional diets. *Environmental Health Perspectives* 111(3): 377–382.

Dhiman, T. R., et al. 1999. Conjugated linoleic acid content of milk from cows fed different diets. *Journal of Dairy Science* 82: 2146–2156.

French, P., et al. 2000. Fatty acid composition, including conjugated linoleic acid, of intramuscular fat from steers offered grazed grass, grass silage, or concentrate-based diets. *Journal of Animal Science* 78: 2849–2855.

Granstedt, A., and L. Kjellenberg. 1997, March. Long-term field experiment in Sweden: Effects of organic and inorganic fertilizers on soil fertility and crop quality. *Proceedings of International Conference on Agricultural Production and Nutrition.* Tufts University, Boston.

Hamouz, K., et al. 1999. Influence of environmental conditions and way of cultivation on the polyphenol and ascorbic acid content in potato tubers. *Rostlinna Vyroba* 45(7): 293–298.

Houseknecht, K. L., et al. 1998. Dietary conjugated linoleic acid normalizes impaired glucose tolerance in the Zucker diabetic fatty fa/fa rat. *Biochemical and Biophysical Research Communications* 244 (3): 678–682.

Ip, C., et al. 1994. Conjugated linoleic acid. A powerful anticarcinogen from animal fat sources. *Cancer* 74(3): 1050–1054.

Jahreis, G., et al. 1997. Conjugated linoleic acid in milk fat: high variation depending on production system. *Nutrition Research* 17(9): 1479–1484.

Lopez-Bote, C. J., et al. 1998. Effect of free-range feeding on omega-3 fatty acids and alpha-tocopherol content and oxidative stability of eggs. *Animal Feed Science and Technology.* 72: 33–40.

Mayer, A. M. 1997. "Historical changes in the mineral content of fruits and vegetables: a cause for concern?" *British Food Journal* 99: 207–211.

Reganold, J. P., et al. 2001. Sustainability of three apple production systems. *Nature* 410: 926–930.

Scimeca, C. J. A., et al. 1994. Conjugated linoleic acid: a powerful anticarcinogen from animal fat sources. *Cancer* 74(3): 1050–1054.

Searles, S. K., et al. 1999. Vitamin E, vitamin A, and carotene contents of Alberta butter. *Journal of Dairy Science* 53(2): 150–154.

Weibel, F. P., et al. 2000. Are organically grown apples tastier and healthier? A comparative field study using conventional and alternative methods to measure fruit quality. *Acta Horticulturae* 517: 417–427.

Woese, K., et al. 1997. A comparison of organically and conventionally grown foods: results of a review of the relevant literature. *Journal of the Science of Food and Agriculture* 74: 281–293.

Worthington, V. 2001. Nutritional quality of organic versus conventional fruits, vegetables, and grains. *Journal of Alternative and Complementary Therapies* 7(2):161–173.

BUYING LOCALLY

Halweil, Brian. 2002, November. Home grown: the case for local food in a global marketplace. Worldwatch Institute. Available at www.worldwatch.org/pubs/paper/163.

Van En, R., et al. What is community supported agriculture and how does it work? Community Supported Agriculture of North America at University of Massachusetts Extension. Available at www.umass.edu/umext/csa/about.html.

HEALTH EFFECTS OF PESTICIDES

Colborn, T., et al. 1997. *Our Stolen Future*. New York: E. P. Dutton.

Landrigan, P. J. 2001. Pesticides and polychlorinated biphenyls (PCBs): An analysis of the evidence that they impair children's neurobehavioral development. *Molecular Genetics and Metabolism* 73: 11–17.

National Academy of Sciences, National Research Council, Committee on Pesticides in the Diets of Infants and Children. 1993. *Pesticides in the Diets of Infants and Children*. National Academies Press. Available at www.nap.edu/books/0309048753/html.

National Institutes of Health. 2002, December. Report on carcinogens, 10th edition. U.S. Department of Health and Human Services, Public Health Service, National Toxicology Program. Available at ehp.niehs.nih.gov/roc.

Office of Technology Assessment. 1990, April. Neurotoxicity: Identifying and controlling poisons of the nervous system. United States Congress. Available at www.wws.princeton.edu/cgi-bin/byteserv.prl/~ota/disk2/1990/9031/903108.PDF.

Steenland, K., et al. 1994. Chronic neurological sequelae to organophosphate pesticide poisoning. *American Journal of Public Health* 84: 731–736.

U.S. Environmental Protection Agency. 1997, February. Special report on environmental endocrine disruption: An effects assessment and analysis. EPA/630/R-96/012. Available at www.epa.gov/ORD/WebPubs/endocrine.

Wiles, R., et al. 1998. Overexposed: organophosphate insecticides in children's food. Environmental Working Group. Available at www.ewg.org/reports/ops/download.pdf.

ORGANIC MARKETPLACE

Yuseffi, M., and Helga Willer (eds). 2003. The world of organic agriculture: statistics and future prospects. International Federation of Organic Agriculture Movements. Available at www.ifoam.org.

The Natural Marketing Institute. 2002, October. Organic consumer trends report. Available at www.nmisolutions.com/r_organic.html.

Organic Trade Association. 2003, July. "Industry statistics and projected growth." Available at www.ota.com/organic/mt/business.html.

Dimitri, C., and C. Greene. 2002, September. Recent growth patterns in the U.S. organic foods market. U.S. Department of Agriculture Economic Research Service Agriculture Information Bulletin No. AIB777. Available at www.ers.usda.gov/publications/aib777.

WATER QUALITY CONCERNS

Centers for Disease Control and Prevention, National Center for Environmental Health. 2003, January 31. Second national report on human exposure to environmental chemicals. Available at www.cdc.gov/exposurereport.

Environmental Working Group. 2003, July. PCBs in farmed salmon: Factory methods, unnatural results. Available at www.ewg.org/reports/farmedPCBs/es.php.

Wiles, R., et al. 1994. Tap water blues: herbicides in drinking water. Environmental Working Group and Physicians for Social Responsibility. Available at www.ewg.org/pub/home/Reports/Weed_Killer/Weed_Intro.html.

CHAPTER 2: FRUIT

GENERAL

Economic Research Service, U.S. Department of Agriculture. 2003, July. Fruit and tree nuts outlook. Outlook Report No. FTS-305. Available at www.ers.usda.gov/Briefing/FruitAndTreeNuts/Index.htm.

Pollack, S. 2000, September. More land but fewer farms dedicated to fruit production in 1997. Economic Research Service, U.S. Department of Agriculture, Fruit and Tree Nuts Situation and Outlook.

Pollack, S. 2003, August. "Characteristics of U.S. orange consumption." Economic Research Service, U.S. Department of Agriculture, Outlook Report No. FTS-30501. Available at www.ers.usda.gov/publications/fts/aug03/fts30501.

U.S. Department of Agriculture. 2002. Agriculture fact book 2001-2002: Profiling food consumption in America. Available at www.usda.gov/factbook/chapter2.htm#fruit.

Economic Research Service, U.S. Department of Agriculture. 2001, August. Harmony between agriculture and the environment. Available at www.ers.usda.gov/Emphases/Harmony/issues/organic/organic.html.

FRUIT NUTRITION

American Academy of Pediatrics, Committee on Nutrition. The use and misuse of fruit juice in pediatrics. *Pediatrics* 2001 (107): 1210–1213.

Lin, B. H., and Morrison, R. M. 2002, Winter. Higher fruit consumption linked with lower body mass index. Economic Research Service, U.S. Department of Agriculture, *Food Review* (25)3. Available at www.aboutproduce.com.

ORGANIC APPLES

Reganold, J. P., et al. 2001, April. Sustainability of three apple production systems. *Nature* 410: 926–930.

Weibel, F. P., et al. 2000. Are organically grown apples tastier and healthier? A comparative field study using conventional and alternative methods to measure fruit quality. *Acta Horticulturae* 517: 417–427.

PESTICIDE RESIDUES

Baker, B. P., et al. 2002. Pesticide residues in conventional, integrated pest management grown, and organic foods: insights from three data sets. *Food Additives and Contaminants* 19(5): 427–446.

Groth, E., et al. 2000, May. Update: Pesticides in children's foods; an analysis of 1998 PDP data on pesticide residues. Consumers Union. Available at www.ecologic-ipm.com/PDP/Update_Childrens_Foods.pdf.

Wiles, R., et al. 1998. Overexposed: Organophosphate insecticides in children's food. Environmental Working Group. Available at www.ewg.org/reports/ops/download.pdf.

National Food and Agriculture Policy Project. 2001, March. Fruit consumption: Dietary health and policy implications. March 2001. Available at nfapp.east.asu.edu/policy/2001/pb01-03.pdf.

Centers for Disease Control and Prevention. 2001, March. National report on human exposure to environmental chemicals. Available at www.cdc.gov/publications.htm.

CHAPTER 3: VEGETABLES

PESTICIDE RESIDUES

Baker, B. P., et al. 2002. Pesticide residues in conventional integrated pest management (IPM)-grown and organic foods: insights from three data sets. *Food Additives and Contaminants* 19(5): 427–446.

Centers for Disease Control and Prevention. 2001, March. National report on human exposure to environmental chemicals. Available at www.cdc.gov/publications.htm.

Economic Research Service, U.S. Department of Agriculture. 2003. Agricultural chemicals and production technology. Available at www.ers.usda.gov/Briefing/AgChemicals/Questions/pmqa4.htm.

Economic Research Service, U.S. Department of Agriculture. 2002. "U.S. organic farming in 2000-2001." ERS/USDA Publication AIB-780. Available at www.ers.usda.gov/publications/aib780/aib780h.pdf.

Ewe, S., and A. Pustzai. 1999. Effects of diets containing genetically modified potatoes expressing galanthus nivalis lectin on rat small intestine. *The Lancet* 354 (9187): 1353–1354.

Groth, E., et al. 2000, May. Update: Pesticides in children's foods: An analysis of 1998 PDP data on pesticide residues. Consumers Union. Available at www.ecologic-ipm.com/PDP/Update_Childrens_Foods.pdf.

Krebs-Smith, S. M., et al. 1996. Fruit and vegetable intakes of children and adolescents in the United States. *Archives of Pediatrics & Adolescent Medicine* 150: 81–86.

National Academy of Sciences, National Research Council, Committee on Pesticides in the Diets of Infants and Children. 1993. Pesticides in the diets of infants and children. National Academies Press. Available at www.nap.edu/books/0309048753/html.

Wiles, R., et al. 1998. "Overexposed: organophosphate insecticides in children's food." Environmental Working Group. Available at www.ewg.org/reports/ops/download.pdf.

HEALTH EFFECTS OF PESTICIDES

Key, T., et al. 2002. The effect of diet on risk of cancer. *The Lancet* 360 (9336):861.

Landrigan, P. 2001. Children's environmental health: lessons from the past and prospects for the future. *Children's Environmental Health* 48 (5): 1319–1330.

CHAPTER 4: FISH AND SHELLFISH

AQUACULTURE

Boyd, C. E., and J. W. Clay. 1998, June. Shrimp aquaculture and the environment. *Scientific American*. 49–65.

Burros, M. 2003, May 28. Farmed salmon looking less rosy. *New York Times*.

Environmental Working Group. 2003, July. PCBs in farmed salmon: Factory methods, unnatural results. Available at www.ewg.org/reports/ farmedPCBs/es.php.

Fulmer, M. 2002, April 15. A bumper crop. *Los Angeles Times*.

Goldburg, R. J., and T. Triplett. 1997. Coastal shrimp farming in Texas. In *Murky Waters: Environmental Effects of Aquaculture in the United States*. Public Employees for Environmental Responsibility. Available at www.peer.org/murky.html.

Goldburg, R. J., et al. 2001. Marine aquaculture in the United States: Environmental impacts and policy options. Pew Oceans Commission. Available at www.pewoceans.org.

Stephens, F. 2002. Seafood solutions: A chef's guide to ecologically responsible fish procurement. Chefs Collaborative and Environmental Defense. Available at www.chefscollaborative.org.

ENVIRONMENTAL CONTAMINANTS IN FISH

Barlow, J. 2001, June. Heavy consumption of tainted fish curbs adult learning and memory. *U Ideas of General Interest* University of Illinois at Urbana-Champaign. Available at www.newswise.com/articles/ 2001/6/pcbfish.uil.htm.

Colborn, T., et al. 1996. *Our Stolen Future: Are We Threatening Our Own Fertility, Intelligence, and Survival? A Scientific Detective Story*. New York: E. P. Dutton.

U.S. Environmental Protection Agency. 2003, February. America's children and the environment: Measures of contaminants, body burdens, and illnesses. Available at www.epa.gov.

GENERAL FISHERY STATISTICS

National Marine Fisheries Service. 1999. Our living oceans: Report on the status of U.S. living marine resources. U.S. Department of Commerce, NOAA Tech. Memo. NMFS-F/SPO-41. Available at spo.nwr.noaa.gov/olo99.htm.

United Nations Food and Agriculture Organization. 2002. "The state of world fisheries and aquaculture 2002." Available at www.fao.org/docrep/005/y730 0e/y7300e00.htm.

HEALTH BENEFITS OF FISH

Albert, C. M., et al. 2002. "Blood levels of long-chain n-3 fatty acids and the risk of sudden death." *New England Journal of Medicine* 346:1113–1118.

Hu, F. B., et al. 2002. "Fish and omega-3 fatty acid intake and risk of coronary heart disease in women." *Journal of the American Medical Association* (287): 1815–1821.

Hu, F. B., et al. 2003. Fish and long-chain n-3 fatty acid intake and risk of coronary heart disease and total mortality in diabetic women. *Circulation* 107: 1852–1857.

OVERFISHING

Alverson, D. L., et al. 1994. A global assessment of fisheries bycatch and discards. FAO Fisheries Technical Paper, No. 339. Rome, FAO.

Dobrzynski, T., et al. 2002, February 28. Oceans at risk: Wasted catch and the destruction of ocean life. *Oceana*. Available at www.oceansatrisk.com.

Jackson, J. B. C., et al. 2001. Historical overfishing: The recent collapse of coastal ecosystems. *Science* 243: 629–638.

Lee, M., editor. 2000. *Seafood Lover's Almanac*. Islip, NY: National Audubon Society, Living Oceans Program.

Marine Fish Conservation Network. 2001, October 11. Caught in the act: the devastating effect of fisheries mismanagement after five years of the sustainable fisheries act. Available at www.conservefish.org/ press/publications.html.

National Academy of Sciences, Ocean Studies Board. 2002. *Effects of Trawling and Dredging on Seafloor Habitat*. National Academies Press. Available at www.nap.edu/books/ 0309083400/html.

National Marine Fisheries Service. 1998. Managing the nation's bycatch: Programs, activities, and recommendations for the national marine fisheries service. Washington, D.C.: National Oceanic and Atmospheric Administration, U.S. Department of Commerce.

Panetta, L., et al. 2003, June. Pew Oceans Commission final report. Pew Oceans Commission. Available at www.pewoceans.org/ oceans/oceans_report.asp.

Seafood Choices Alliance. 2003, June. The marketplace for sustainable seafood: growing appetites and shrinking seas. Available at www.seafoodchoices.com.

CHAPTER 5: CHICKEN AND TURKEY

POULTRY PRODUCTION STATISTICS

U.S. Department of Agriculture. 2001. Assessment of livestock industry and meat production. Available at www.usda.gov/gipsa/pubs/01assessment/section2.pdf.

POULTRY WASTE MANAGEMENT

Christen, K. 2001. Chickens, manure, and arsenic. *Environmental Science and Technology Online.* Available at pubs.acs.org/subscribe/journals/esthag-w/2001/mar/policy/kc_chicken.html.

Daniels, M., et al. 1998. Soil phosphorus levels: Concerns and recommendations. SERA-17. University of Arkansas Cooperative Extension, Fayetteville, AR. Available at www.soil.ncsu.edu/sera17/publications/ AR_Factsheet/FSA1029_v2.pdf.

Sharpley, A. N., et al. 1999. Agricultural phosphorus and eutrophication. ARS-149. USDA ARS, Washington, D. C., p. 37.

PASTURED POULTRY PRODUCTION

American Pastured Poultry Producers' Association. www.apppa.org.

Fanatico, A. 2002, March. Sustainable poultry: Production overview. Appropriate Technology Transfer for Rural Areas (ATTRA). Available at attra.ncat.org/attra-pub/poultryoverview.html.

Lopez-Bote, C. J., et al. 1998. Effect of free-range feeding on omega-3 fatty acids and alpha-tocopherol content and oxidative stability of eggs. *Animal Feed Science and Technology* 72: 33–40.

ANTIBIOTIC USE IN POULTRY PRODUCTION

Larsson, B. M., et al. 1999. Airway responses in naive subjects to exposure in poultry houses. *American Journal of Industrial Medicine* 35: 142–149.

Leidl, Pat, et al. 2000. Overcoming antimicrobial resistance. Chapter 5. World Health Organization. Available at www.who.int/infectious-disease-report/2000/ch5.htm.

Mellon, M., and S. Fondriest. 2001, January. Hogging it: Estimates of antimicrobial abuse in livestock. Union of Concerned Scientists. Available at www.ucsusa.org.

U.S. Food and Drug Administration, Center for Veterinary Medicine. 2001, January 5. The human health impact of fluoroquinolone-resistant Campylobacter attributed to the consumption of chicken. Washington, D. C. Available at www.fda.gov/cvm/antimicrobial/revisedRA.pdf.

Wallinga, D., et al. Institute for Agriculture and Trade Policy. Sierra Club. 2002, December. Poultry on antibiotics: Hazards to human health, second edition. Available at www.iatp.org/foodandhealth/Library/listContent.cfm.

DIOXINS

U.S. Environmental Protection Agency. 2000. Draft dioxin reassessment. Available at cfpub.epa.gov/ncea/cfm/recordisplay.cfm?deid=55265.

World Health Organization. 1999, July 9. Questions and answers about dioxins and their effect on human health.

POULTRY LABELING TERMINOLOGY

Consumers Union. Eco-labels Web site. Available at www.eco-labels.org.

Food Safety and Inspection Service. 2001, January. U. S. Department of Agriculture, Washington, D.C., 20250-3700. Slightly Revised. Meat and poultry labeling terms. Available at www.fsis.usda.gov/OA/pubs/lablterm.htm.

CHAPTER 6: BEEF AND PORK

ANTIBIOTICS IN MEAT

Chee-Sanford, J. C., et al. 2001. Occurrence and diversity of tetracycline resistance genes in lagoons and groundwater underlying two swine production facilities. *Applied and Environmental Microbiology* 67(4): 1494–1502.

Environmental Protection Agency. 1998, December. *Feedlots Point Source Category Study.* Available at www.epa.gov.

Environmental Protection Agency. 2003, February 12. National pollutant discharge elimination system permit regulation and effluent limitation guidelines and standards for concentrated animal feeding operations (CAFOs) final rule. Available at cfpub.epa.gov/npdes/regresult.cfm?program_id=0&view=all&type=1.

Leidl, P., et al. 2002. Overcoming antimicrobial resistance. Chapter 5. World Health Organization report. Available at www.who.int/infectious-disease-report/2000/ch5.htm.

Leon, W., and C. S. DeWaal. 2002. *Is Our Food Safe?* New York: Three Rivers Press. 56–57.

McDonald L. C., et al. 2001. Quinupristin-dalfopristin-resistant *Enterococcus faecium* on chicken and in human stool specimens. *New England Journal of Medicine* 345: 1155–1160.

Mellon, M., and S. Fondriest. 2001. Hogging it: Estimates of antimicrobial abuse in livestock. Union of Concerned Scientists. Available at www.ucsusa.org.

Sørensen T. L., et al. 2001. Transient intestinal carriage after ingestion of antibiotic-resistant *Enterococcus faecium* from chicken and pork. *New England Journal of Medicine* 345: 1161–1166.

White, D. G., et al. 2001. The isolation of antibiotic-resistant salmonella from retail ground meats. *New England Journal of Medicine* 345: 1147–1154.

DIOXINS

World Health Organization. 1999, July 9. Questions and answers about dioxins and their effect on human health.

Environmental Protection Agency. 2000. Draft dioxin reassessment. Available at cfpub.epa.gov/ncea/cfm/recordisplay.cfm?deid=55265.

National Academy of Sciences, National Research Council, Committee on the Implications of Dioxin in the Food Supply. 2003, July. Dioxins and dioxin-like compounds in the food supply: Strategies to decrease exposure. Available at www.nationalacademies.org.

GRASS-FED BEEF

Aro, A., et al. 2000. Inverse association between dietary and serum conjugated linoleic acid and risk of breast cancer in post-menopausal women. *Nutrition and Cancer* 38(2): 151–157.

Cordain, L., et al. 2002. Fatty acid analysis of wild ruminant tissues: Evolutionary implications for reducing diet-related chronic disease. *European Journal of Clinical Nutrition* 56(3): 181–191. Available at www.nature.com/cgi-taf/DynaPage.taf?file=/ejcn/journal/v56/n3/abs/1601307a.html.

Duckett, S. K., et al. 1993. Effects of time of feed on beef nutrient composition. *Journal of Animal Science* 71(8): 2079–2088.

Fukumoto, G. K., et al. 1995. Chemical composition and shear force requirement of loin eye muscle of young, forage-fed steers. *Research Extension Series* 161: 1–5.

Hart, Richard H. 1998, December 19. Plant biodiversity on short grass steppe after 55 years of zero, light, moderate, or heavy cattle grazing. Tektran, U.S. Department of Agriculture, Agricultural Research Service. Available at www.nal.usda.gov/ttic/tektran/data/000009/12/0000091284.html.

Ip, C., J. A. Scimeca, et al. 1994. Conjugated linoleic acid: A powerful anticarcinogen from animal fat sources. *Cancer* 74 (3 supplement): 1050–1054.

Koizumi, I. Y., et al. 1991. Studies on the fatty acid composition of intramuscular lipids of cattle, pigs, and birds. *Journal of Nutritional Science and Vitaminology (Tokyo)* 37(6): 545–54.

HORMONES IN MEAT AND BREAST CANCER

Gandhi, R., and M. Snedeker. 2000, June. Consumer concerns about hormones in food. Cornell University Program on Breast Cancer and Environmental Risk Factors. Available at envirocancer.cornell.edu/FactSheet/Diet/fs37.hormones.cfm.

Warren, B., and C. Devine. 2000, June. Meat, poultry, and fish and the risk of breast cancer. Cornell University Program on Breast Cancer and Environmental Risk Factors. Available at envirocancer.cornell.edu/Factsheet/diet/fs39.meat.cfm.

IRRADIATION

Centers for Disease Control and Prevention, Division of Bacterial and Mycotic Diseases. Frequently asked questions about food irradiation. Available at www.cdc.gov/ncidod/dbmd/diseaseinfo/foodirradiation.htm.

Consumers Union. 2003, August. The truth about irradiated meat. *Consumer Reports.* 34–37.

Delincee, H. 1998. Genotoxic properties of 2-dodecylcyclobutanone, a compound formed on irradiation of food containing fat. *Radiation Physics and Chemistry* 52: 39–42.

Public Citizen. Top ten reasons to oppose irradiation. Available at www.citizen.org/cmep/foodsafety.

Worth, M. 2002, October. Bad taste: The disturbing truth about the World Health Organization's endorsement of food irradiation. Public Citizen and Global Resource Action Network for the Environment. Available at www.citizen.org/pressroom/release.cfm?ID=1236.

MODERN BEEF AND PORK PRODUCTION

Iowa State University Extension. Livestock confinement dust and gases. Available at the Centers for Disease Control's National Agricultural Safety Database: www.cdc.gov/nasd/docs/d001501-d001600/d001501/d001501.html.

Kliebenstein, J. B., et al. 1983. A survey of swine production health problems and health maintenance expenditures. *Preventive Veterinary Medicine* 1: 357–369.

Leon, W., C. S. Smith, and the Center for Science in the Public Interest. *Is Our Food Safe?* New York: Three Rivers Press, 2002.

Natural Resources Defense Council. America's animal factories: How states fail to prevent pollution from livestock waste. Available at www.nrdc.org/water/pollution/factor/exec.asp.

Pollan, M. 2002, March 31. Power steer. *New York Times Magazine.*

Tokarnia, C. H., et al. 2000. Outbreak of copper poisoning in cattle fed poultry litter. *Veterinary & Human Toxicology* 42(2): 92–95.

PROCESSED MEAT

Van Dam, R., et al. 2002. Dietary patterns and risk for type 2 diabetes mellitus in U.S. men. *Annals of Internal Medicine* 136: 201–209. Available at www.annals.org/issues/v136n3/full/200202050-00008.html.

Norat, T., et al. 2002. Meat consumption and colorectal cancer risk: Dose-response meta-analysis of epidemiological studies. *International Journal of Cancer* 98(2): 241–256.

CHAPTER 7: MILK, CHEESE, AND EGGS

DIOXINS IN DAIRY PRODUCTS

U.S. Environmental Protection Agency, National Center for Environmental Assessment. 2003, January. Questions and answers about dioxin. Available at www.epa.gov/ncea/dioxinqa.htm.

EGGS

American Egg Board. *Egg Fact Sheet*. Available at www.aeb.org/eii/facts/industry-facts-06-2002.htm.

Ibid. *Egg Production Information*. Available at www.aeb.org/eii/production.html.

Ibid. *Basic Egg Facts*. Available at www.aeb.org/facts/facts.html#20.

Soil Association. *Registered Organic Eggs Fact Sheet*. Available at www.soilassociation.org/web/sa/saweb.nsf/848d689047cb46678 0256a6b00298980/80256c840 055c30580256ca600594c96! OpenDocument.

The Soil Association in the United Kingdom has a useful model of standards for certified or "registered" organic eggs, in-cluding regulations on stocking rates, feed composition, beak trimming and antibiotics (both of which are prohibited), and a good definition of "free-range."

Appleby, M. C., and B. O. Hughes. 1995. The Edinburgh modified cage for laying hens. *British Poultry Science* 36: 707–718.

Baxter, M. R. 1994. The welfare problems of laying hens in battery cages. *Veterinary Record* 134: 614–619.

Centers for Disease Control and Prevention, Division of Bacterial and Mycotic Diseases. Disease information on foodborne illness. Available at www.cdc.gov/ncidod/dbmd/diseaseinfo/foodborneinfections_g.htm #riskiestfoods.

European Commission. 1996, October. Report on the welfare of laying hens. Scientific Veterinary Committee, Animal Welfare Section.

Farm Sanctuary. *Factory Egg Production*. Available at www.factoryfarming.com/eggs.htm.

Hu, F. B., et al. 1998. A prospective study of egg consumption and risk of cardiovascular disease in men and women. *Journal of the American Medical Association* 281(15): 1387–1394.

Kritchevsky, S. B., et al. 2000. Egg consumption and coronary heart disease: An epidemiologic overview. *Journal of the American College of Nutrition* 12 (5 supplement): 549S–555S.

Lopez-Bote, C. J., et al. 1998. Effect of free-range feeding on omega-3 fatty acids and alpha-to-copherol content and oxidative stability of eggs. *Animal Feed Science and Technology* 72: 33–40.

Rollin, B. E. 1995. *Farm Animal Welfare: Social, Bioethical, and Research Issues*. Iowa State University Press.

Salmonella Enteritidis Risk Assessment Team. 1998, August 10. Salmonella enteritidis risk assessment: Final report prepared for the Food Safety and Inspection Service, U.S. Department of Agriculture. Available at www.fsis.usda.gov/ophs/risk/index.htm.

U.S. Department of Agriculture, Food Safety and Inspection Service. 2001, January. *Meat and Poultry Labeling Terms*. January 2001. Available at www.fsis.usda.gov/oa/pubs/lablterm.htm.

GRASS-FED COWS

Aro, A., et al. 2000. Inverse association between dietary and serum conjugated linoleic acid and risk of breast cancer in post-menopausal women. *Nutrition and Cancer* 38(2): 151–157.

Dhiman, T. R., et al. 1999. Conjugated linoleic acid content of milk from cows fed different diets. *Journal of Dairy Science* 82(10): 2146–2156.

Ip, C., J. A. Scimeca, et al. 1994. Conjugated linoleic acid: A powerful anticarcinogen from animal fat sources. *Cancer* 74 (3 supplement):1050–1054.

RAW MILK AND RAW MILK CHEESES

Gifford, Dun K. Oldways Preservation & Exchange Trust. *The Cheese Squeeze*. Available at www.eguana.net/organizations .php3?orgid=61&typeID=202& action=printContentItem&item ID=1507&User_Session=c60142 4b6b6a2b979af70ae8d30a7d7c.

Oldways has excellent information on raw milk cheese through its Cheese of Choice Coalition formed in conjunction with the American Cheese Society. Search the Oldways site for more information.

Edward Howell, M.D. 1986. *Enzyme Nutrition*. Lotus Press, March 1986.

U.S. Food and Drug Administration, Center for Food Safety and Applied Nutrition. *The Safe Food Chart: Dairy and Raw Egg Products*. Available at www.cfsan.fda.gov/~dms/fttmilk.html.

rBGH IN MILK

American Medical Association, Council on Scientific Affairs. 1991. Biotechnology and the American agriculture industry. *Journal of the American Medical Association* 265: 1429–1436.

Campbell, P. C., and C. R. Baumrucker. 1985. Characterization of insulin-like growth factor-l, somatomedin-C receptors in bovine mammary gland. *Endocrinology* 116 (Supplement 1, Abstract L 223).

Cancer Prevention Coalition. *Cancer Alert Report*. Available at www.preventcancer.com/alerts/igf.htm.

Center for Science in the Public Interest. *Antibiotic-Resistance Project*. Available at www.cspinet.org/ar.

Chan, et al. 1998. Plasma insulin-like growth factor-I and prostate cancer risk. *Science* 279: 563–566.

Donovan, S. M. 1994. Growth factors in milk as mediators of infant development. *Annual Review of Nutrition* 14: 147–167.

Duckett, S. K., et al. 1993. Effects of time on feed on beef nutrient composition. *Journal of Animal Science* 71(8): 2079–2088.

European Commission. 1999, March. Animal welfare aspects of the use of bovine somatotropin. Scientific Committee on Animal Health and Animal Welfare. Available at europa.eu.int/comm/index_en.htm.

European Commission. 1999, March. Public health aspects of the use of bovine somatotropin. Scientific Committee on Veterinary Measures Relating to Public Health. Available at europa.eu.int/comm/index_en.htm.

Farm Sanctuary. Report on dairy cows. Available at www.factory-farming.com/dairy.htm.

Hansen, M. 1990. Biotechnology & milk: Benefit or threat? An analysis of issues related to bGH/bST use in the dairy industry. Consumer Policy Institute, Consumers Union. Available at www.consumersunion.org/aboutcu/offices/CPI.htm.

Hansen, M., et al. 1997. Potential public health impacts of the use of recombinant bovine somatotropin in dairy production." *Consumers International*. Available at www.consumersunion.org/food/bgh-codex.htm.

Herman-Giddens, M. E., et al. 1997. Secondary sexual characteristics and menses in young girls seen in office practice: A study from the Pediatric Research in Office Settings Network. *Pediatrics* 99: 505–512.

Juskevich, J. C., and C. G. Guyer. 1990. Bovine growth hormone: Human food safety evaluation. *Science* 249: 875–884.

Paul Kingsnorth. 1998. Bovine growth hormones. *The Ecologist* 28 (5).

Mayland, H. F., et al. 2000. Late afternoon cut hay makes more milk. U.S. Department of Agriculture. Agricultural Research Service. Available at www.nal.usda.gov/ttic/tektran/data/000010/39/0000103946.html.

National Institutes of Health. 1991. Technology assessment conference statement on bovine somatotropin. *Journal of the American Medical Association* 265:1423–1425.

Pereira, M., et al. 2002. Dairy consumption, obesity, and the insulin resistance syndrome in young adults: The CARDIA Study. *Journal of the American Medical Association* 287: 2081–2089.

U.S. Department of Agriculture National Agricultural Statistics Service. Milk production 1993–2002. Available at www.usda.gov/nass/aggraphs/milkprod.htm.

U.S. Department of Agriculture. Agricultural Marketing Service. *National Organic Program Standards*. Available at www.ams.usda.gov/nop.

World Health Organization. International Programme on Chemical Safety. 1998. Toxicological evaluation of certain veterinary drug residues in food: report of the fiftieth meeting of the joint FAO/WHO expert committee on food additives. WHO Food Additives Series 41: 125–146.

CHAPTER 8: BEANS, NUTS, AND GRAINS

GMOS

Benbrook, C. 2001, May 3. Troubled times amid commercial success: Glyphosate efficacy is slipping and unstable transgene expression erodes plant defenses and yields. *Ag BioTech InfoNet* Technical Paper Number 4. Available at www.biotech-info.net/troubledtimes.html.

Bernstein, et al. 1999. Immune responses in farm workers after exposure to *Bacillus thuringiensis* pesticides. *Environmental Health Perspectives* 107(7): 575–582.

Environmental Protection Agency. 2001, September 21. Biopesticides registration action document: Bt plant-incorporated protectants: science assessment.

Freese, B. 2003, July. Genetically engineered crop health impacts evaluation: GAPS analysis. Friends of the Earth. Available at www.foe.org.

Pew Initiative on Food and Biotechnology. 2003, August. Genetically modified crops in the United States.

Friends of the Earth. 2001. Antibiotic resistance genes in GM Foods. June 2001. Available at www.foe.co.uk/resource/briefings/antibiotic_resistant_genes.html.

Halloran, J. 2003. Consumers Union hails UN standards on genetically engineered food. Consumers Union Press Release. July 1, 2003. Available at www.consumersunion.org/pub/core_food_safety/000202.html#more.

Johnston, J. 2002, January 10. 2001 global GM crop area grew to 130 mil. acres. Agweb News. Available online at www.agweb.com.

Kilman, S. 2001. FDA warns of misleading labels on genetic modification of foods. *Wall Street Journal*, December 20, 2001.

Losey, J. E., et al. 1999, May 20. Transgenic pollen harms monarch larvae. *Nature* 399(214).

Mooney, P., et al. 2003. Europe's (and the world's) big soy berger: Patently wrong! Action Group on Erosion, Technology and Concentration, May 7, 2003. Available at www.tradeobservatory.org/library/uploadedfiles/Patently_Wrong_Monsanto_species_patent_on_soy_.htm.

National Research Council. 2002. Environmental effects of transgenic plants: The scope and adequacy of regulation. Committee on Environmental Impacts Associated with Commercialization of Transgenic Plants of the National Research Council, National Academy of Sciences. Available at www.nationalacademies.org/publications.

Netherwood, T., et al. 2002, July. Transgenes in genetically modified soya survive passage through the small bowel but are completely degraded in the colon. UK Food Standards Agency.

Persley, G. J. 2003, June. New genetics, food and agriculture: Scientific discoveries, societal dilemmas. *International Council of Science*.

Pollan, M. 1998. Playing God in the garden. *New York Times Sunday Magazine*, October 25, 1998.

Rowell, A. 2003, July 7. The sinister sacking of the world's leading GM expert. *The Daily Mail (UK)*.

The Royal Society (UK). 2002, February. Genetically modified plants for food use and human health: an update. The Royal Society. Available at www.royalsoc.ac.uk.

SAP Bt Plant-Pesticides. 2001, March 12. Bt plant-pesticides risk and benefit assessments: FIFRA Scientific Advisory Panel Report No. 2000–07.

World Health Organization. 2001, January 22. Evaluation of allergenicity of genetically modified foods. Report of a joint FAO/WHO expert consultation of allergenicity of foods derived from biotechnology.

Ye, X., et al. 2000. Engineering the provitamin A (b-carotene) biosynthetic pathway into carotenoid-free rice endosperm. *Science* 287: 303–305.

GOLDEN RICE

Genetic Resources Action International. 2001, February. Grains of delusion: Golden rice seen from the ground. Available at www.grain.org/publications/delusion-en.cfm.

Pollan, M. 2001, March 4. The great yellow hype. *The New York Times*.

World Health Organization. 2000. *Preliminary Report on Recommended Nutrient Intakes*, Joint FAO/WHO Expert Consultation on Human Vitamin and Mineral Requirements, September 30, 1998. Revised July 13, 2000.

HEALTH OF SOY AND OTHER BEANS

Anderson J. W., et al. 1995. Meta-analysis of the effects of soy protein intake on serum lipids. *New England Journal of Medicine* 333: 276–282.

Henkel, J. 2000, May. Soy: Health claims for soy protein and questions about other components. *U.S. Food and Drug Administration Consumer Magazine*. Available at www.fda.gov/fdac/features/2000/300_soy.html.

Jakes, R. W., et al. 2002. Mammographic parenchymal patterns and self-reported soy intake in Singapore Chinese women. *Cancer Epidemiology Biomarkers and Prevention* 11(7): 608–613.

Nagata, C., et al. 1998. Decreased serum total cholesterol concentration is associated with high intake of soy product in Japanese men and women. *Journal of Nutrition* 128: 209–213.

Orme, S., and S. Kegley, 2002. *PAN Pesticide Database*. Pesticide Action Network North America. Available at www.pesticideinfo.org.

U.S. Department of Agriculture Economic Research Service. 1998. Factors affecting dry bean consumption in the United States. Available at www.ers.usda.gov/Briefing/Consumption/readings.htm.

Whigham, K. Soy history. Report of the Iowa State University Department of Agronomy. Available at www.agron.iastate.edu/soybean/history.html.

Wong, W. W. 1998. Cholesterol-lowering effect of soy protein in normocholesterolemic and hypercholesterolemic men. *American Journal of Clinical Nutrition* 68 (suppl.): 1385S–1389S.

HEALTH OF
WHOLE GRAINS

Gerrior, S., and L. Bente. 2001. *Nutrient Content of the U.S. Food Supply, 1909-1997*. Center for Nutrition Policy and Promotion, U.S. Department of Agriculture, Home Economics Research, Report No. 54. Available at www.usda.gov/gipsa/pubs/01assessment/section2.pdf.

Liu, S., et al. 1999, September. Whole-grain consumption and risk of coronary heart disease: Results from the Nurses' Health Study. *American Journal of Clinical Nutrition* 70: 412–419.

McKeown, Nicola, et al. 2002, August. Whole-grain intake is favorably associated with metabolic risk factors for type 2 diabetes and cardiovascular disease in the Framingham Offspring Study. *American Journal of Clinical Nutrition* 76:390–398.

U.S. Department of Agriculture. *Agriculture Fact Book 2001-2002. Profiling Food Consumption in America*. Available at: www.usda.gov/factbook/chapter2.htm.

FAIR-TRADE FOODS

Global Exchange www.globalexchange.org/campaigns/fair trade/coffee

Transfair USA www.transfairusa.org

Van Leo, Rory. 2003, September. "Coming to the Grocery Store Shelf: Fair Trade Food." *Christian Science Monitor*.

CHAPTER 9:
WHEAT FLOUR,
BREAD, AND PASTA

GENETICALLY MODIFIED WHEAT

Gurian-Dherman, D. 2003, January 7. Holes in the biotech safety net: FDA policy does not assure the safety of genetically engineered foods. Center for Science in the Public Interest report. Available at cspinet.org/biotech/reports.html.

Hoban, T., et al. 2001, October. Consumer attitudes on GM wheat. American Bakers Association survey. Available at www.und.edu/misc/ndrural.

Van Acker, R. C., et al. 2003, June. An environmental safety assessment of Roundup Ready wheat: risks for direct seeding systems in western Canada. Canadian Wheat Board report. Available at www.cwb.ca.

Vazquez, C., 2002. Wheat: the next engineered crop? Institute for Agriculture and Trade Policy report. Available at www.iatp.org.

ORGANIC WHEAT

Eskenazi, B., et al. 1999. Exposures of children to organophosphate pesticides and their potential adverse health effects. *Environmental Health Perspectives* 107(S-3): 409–419.

Payne, W. S. 2003, April. Industry and trade summary: Pasta. U.S. International Trade Commission report 3592. Available at ftp://ftp.usitc.gov/pub/reports/studies/PUB3592.PDF.

U.S. Department of Agriculture, Economic Research Service. 2000, August. Forces shaping the U.S. wheat economy. Available at www.ers.usda.gov/publications/agoutlook/aug2000/ao273d.pdf.

U.S. Environmental Protection Agency. 2000, June 8. Chlorpyrifos revised risk assessment and risk mitigation measures. Available at www.epa.gov/pesticides/op/chlorpyrifos/consumerqs.htm.

Vesterby, M. and K. S. Krupa. 2001, September. Major uses of land in the United States, 1997. Economic Research Service Statistical Bulletin No. 973. Available at www.ers.usda.gov/publications/sb973.

WHOLE GRAIN WHEAT FOODS

Jacobs, D. R. 2000. Fiber from whole grains, but not refined grains, is inversely associated with all-cause mortality in older women: the Iowa women's health study. *Journal of the American College of Nutrition* 19 (3 Supplement): 326S–330S.

Meyer, K. A., et.al. 2000. Carbohydrates, dietary fiber and incident type 2 diabetes in older women. *American Journal of Clinical Nutrition* 71:921–930.

Roberts, S. B. 2000. High-glycemic index foods, hunger and obesity: Is there a connection? *Nutrition Reviews* 58(6): 163–169.

Further Reading

CHILDREN'S ENVIRONMENTAL HEALTH

Center for Children's Health and the Environment at Mount Sinai School of Medicine www.childenvironment.org Promoting children's health by conducting environmental health and policy research.

Childproofing Our Communities Campaign www.childproofing.org Aims to protect children from exposures to environmental health hazards in schools and other childcare settings.

Children's Environmental Health Network
www.cehn.org
Aims to protect children from environmental health hazards and promotes a healthy environment.

Children's Health Environmental Coalition
www.checnet.org
Informs parents about and encourages the public to take action against preventable health and development problems caused by children's exposure to toxic substances in homes and in public places.

Office of Children's Health Protection, Environmental Protection Agency
yosemite.epa.gov/ochp/ochpweb.nsf/homepage
Clearinghouse of information about environmental risks to children.

Having Faith by Sandra Steingraber (Perseus Publishing, 2001).

Our Stolen Future by Theo Colburn, Dianne Dumanoski, John Peterson Myers (Plume, 1997).

Raising Healthy Children in a Toxic World by Philip J. Landrigan, Herbert L. Needleman, and Mary Landrigan (Rodale, 2002).

Stein, J., et al. 2002. In harm's way: toxic threats to child development. *Journal of Developmental and Behavioral Pediatrics* 23:S13–S22. Available at www.lwwonline.com/article.asp?J=1161

Our Children's Toxic Legacy: How Science and Law Fail to Protect Us from Pesticides by John Wargo (Yale University Press, 1996).

ENVIRONMENTAL HEALTH ADVOCACY AND POLICY

American Farmland Trust
www.farmland.org
Works to stop the loss of productive farmland and to promote farming practices that lead to a healthy environment.

Environmental Working Group
www.ewg.org and www.foodnews.org
Not-for-profit environmental research organization dedicated to improving public health and protecting the environment by reducing pollution in air, water, and food.

Institute for Agriculture and Trade Policy
www.iatp.org
Promotes resilient family farms, rural communities, and ecosystems around the world through research and education, science and technology, and advocacy.

Consumers Union
www.consumersunion.org
Not-for-profit publisher of *Consumer Reports* with information on food safety and health, including the Healthy Schools, Healthy Kids Project (www.healthykidsproject.org) and the Eco-Labels Project (www.eco-labels.org).

Union of Concerned Scientists
www.ucsusa.org
Works for clean air and energy, and safe and sufficient food. Information about the risks of genetically modified crops, antibiotic use in livestock, and other public health issues.

Center for Science in the Public Interest
www.cspinet.org
Publisher of *Nutrition Action Health Letter*. Advocates for nutrition and health and provides information on food safety, biotechnology, and antibiotic resistance.

Center for Food Safety
www.centerforfoodsafety.org
Works to protect human health and the environment by curbing the proliferation of harmful food production technologies and by promoting organic and sustainable agriculture.

Institute for Agriculture and Trade Policy
www.iatp.org
Guide for meat raised without antibiotics.

Clean and Green by Annie Berthold-Bond (Ceres Press, 1994).

Dinner at the New Gene Café: How Genetic Engineering Is Changing What We Eat, How We Live, and the Global Politics of Food by Bill Lambrecht (St. Martin's Press, 2001).

Hope's Edge by Frances Moore Lappe and Anna Lappe (Tarcher/Putnam, 2002).

Less Toxic Living, Cleaning, and Baby Care: Home Safe Home by Debra Dadd-Redalia and Debra Lynn Dadd (J. P. Tarcher, 1997).

Mothers & Others for a Livable Planet Guide to Natural Baby Care by Mindy Pennybacker and Aisha Ikramuddin (John Wiley & Sons, 1999).

The Botany of Desire by Michael Pollan (Random House, 2001).

The Safe Shopper's Bible by David Steinman and Samuel S. Epstein (Hungry Minds, 1995).

Seeds of Deception by Jeffrey M. Smith (Yes! Books, 2003).

When Smoke Ran like Water by Devra Lee Davis (Basic Books, 2002).

GROWING AND BUYING ORGANIC

Farm Aid
www.farmaid.org
Works to build and strengthen sustainable, family farm-centered food production systems through public education, grants, farm advocacy, and activism. Publisher of *10 Ways to Ensure Healthy Food for You and Your Children.*

Farm to Table
www.farmtotable.org
Sustainable agriculture and cuisine site with food sources.

Organic Trade Association
www.ota.com
Industry and consumer information from the organic industry's trade association.

Organic Consumers Association
www.organicconsumers.org
Campaigns for food safety, organic agriculture, fair trade, and sustainability.

Organic Farming Research Foundation
www.ofrf.org
Why and how to support organic farming research.

Soil Association
www.soilassociation.org
Organic food, farming, and sustainable forestry (U.K.).

U.S. Department of Agriculture National Organic Program
www.ams.usda.gov/nop
Read fact sheets, updates, and the full text of the national organic standards in English or Spanish.

Eat Wild
www.eatwild.com
Clearinghouse for information on pasture-based farming.

Bitter Harvest: A Chef's Perspective on the Hidden Danger of the Foods We Eat and What You Can Do about It by Ann Cooper and Lisa Anne Holmes (Routledge, 2000).

The Newman's Own Organics Guide to a Good Life by Nell Newman and Joseph D'Agnese (Villard, 2003).

The Organic Foods Sourcebook by Elaine Marie Lipson (Contemporary Books, 2001).

The Eco-Foods Guide by Cynthia Barstow (New Society Publishers, 2002).

BUYING AND COOKING LOCALLY PRODUCED FOOD

Local Harvest
www.localharvest.org
Nationwide directory of small family farms, farmers markets, and CSAs.

FoodRoutes Network
www.foodroutes.org
Nationwide directory of local organic farmers, farmers markets, and CSAs.

Growing Power
www.growingpower.org
Nationwide nonprofit organization supporting the development of community food systems.

U.S. Department of Agriculture Farmers Market Directory
www.ams.usda.gov/farmersmarkets/map.htm

U.S. Department of Agriculture CSA Directory
www.nal.usda.gove/afsic/csa
National database of community-supported agriculture operations. Administered by organizations such as the Robyn Van En Center for CSA Resources, the Alternative Farming Systems Information Center (AFSIC), and the Sustainable Agriculture Network (SAN).

The Robyn Van En Center for CSA Resources
www.csacenter.org
Explains what CSAs are and how to start or join one.

Slow Food
www.slowfood.com
International movement with consortia in cities around the world to support the appreciation of sustainably produced, well-prepared, and leisurely enjoyed food.

Oldways Preservation & Exchange Trust
www.oldwayspt.org
Nonprofit educational organization devoted to providing scientific evidence to support the healthfulness of traditional diets and food customs.

Chefs Collaborative
www.chefscollaborative.org
A national network of chefs and food professionals that promotes using high-quality, locally grown, sustainably produced food.

Local Flavors by Deborah Madison (Broadway, 2002).

Coming Home to Eat: The Pleasure and Politics of Local Foods by Gary Paul Nabhan (W. W. Norton, 2001).

POLITICS OF FOOD MARKETING

Fast Food Nation by Eric Schlosser (Houghton Mifflin, 2001).

Fat Land by Greg Critser (Houghton Mifflin, 2003).

Food Politics by Marion Nestle (University of California Press, 2002).

Index

Underscored page references indicate boxed text.

Conversion Chart

These equivalents have been slightly rounded to make measuring easier.

Volume Measurements

U.S.	Imperial	Metric
¼ tsp	–	1 ml
½ tsp	–	2 ml
1 tsp	–	5 ml
1 Tbsp	–	15 ml
2 Tbsp (1 oz)	1 fl oz	30 ml
¼ cup (2 oz)	2 fl oz	60 ml
⅓ cup (3 oz)	3 fl oz	80 ml
½ cup (4 oz)	4 fl oz	120 ml
⅔ cup (5 oz)	5 fl oz	160 ml
¾ cup (6 oz)	6 fl oz	180 ml
1 cup (8 oz)	8 fl oz	240 ml

Weight Measurements

U.S.	Metric
1 oz	30 g
2 oz	60 g
4 oz (¼ lb)	115 g
5 oz (⅓ lb)	145 g
6 oz	170 g
7 oz	200 g
8 oz (½ lb)	230 g
10 oz	285 g
12 oz (¾ lb)	340 g
14 oz	400 g
16 oz (1 lb)	455 g
2.2 lb	1 kg

Length Measurements

U.S.	Metric
¼"	0.6 cm
½"	1.25 cm
1"	2.5 cm
2"	5 cm
4"	11 cm
6"	15 cm
8"	20 cm
10"	25 cm
12" (1')	30 cm

Pan Sizes

U.S.	Metric
8" cake pan	20 × 4 cm sandwich or cake tin
9" cake pan	23 × 3.5 cm sandwich or cake tin
11" × 7" baking pan	28 × 18 cm baking tin
13" × 9" baking pan	32.5 × 23 cm baking tin
15" × 10" baking pan	38 × 25.5 cm baking tin (Swiss roll tin)
1½ qt baking dish	1.5 liter baking dish
2 qt baking dish	2 liter baking dish
2 qt rectangular baking dish	30 × 19 cm baking dish
9" pie plate	22 × 4 or 23 × 4 cm pie plate
7" or 8" springform pan	18 or 20 cm springform or loose-bottom cake tin
9" × 5" loaf pan	23 × 13 cm or 2 lb narrow loaf tin or pâté tin

Temperatures

Fahrenheit	Centigrade	Gas
140°	60°	–
160°	70°	–
180°	80°	–
225°	105°	¼
250°	120°	½
275°	135°	1
300°	150°	2
325°	160°	3
350°	180°	4
375°	190°	5
400°	200°	6
425°	220°	7
450°	230°	8
475°	245°	9
500°	260°	–

Your Job Is to Take Care of Your Family and Loved Ones and to Keep Them Healthy

Our Job Is to Empower You to Do That

Making informed decisions about what to feed your family can do a lot to promote good health. However, many of your choices are limited by government and industry policies. Generation Green keeps parents informed about policies that impact their children's environments, including food. We also provide parents and other concerned citizens with the information they need to make sure that their voice is heard.

To stay informed and learn how to ensure that your voice is heard, sign up to receive the *Fresh Choices Quarterly* newsletter.

Fresh Choices Quarterly **will:**

• keep you up-to-date on government regulations and decisions regarding our food supply,

• tell you about important changes in the marketplace, particularly those that relate to the healthfulness of our food, and

• provide you with new menu ideas and delicious recipes that you can feel good about.

To get free e-mail copies of *Fresh Choices Quarterly*,
e-mail us at freshchoices@generationgreen.org
Or, to get four free issues sent to you by mail,
call us at (800) 652-0827.

For more information and to join, visit us at
www.generationgreen.org